Megalithic Brittany

AUBREY BURL

Megalithic Brittany

A GUIDE TO OVER 350 ANCIENT SITES AND MONUMENTS

with 145 illustrations

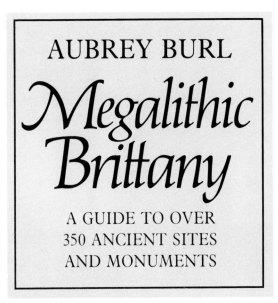

THAMES AND HUDSON

To my cousin, Christopher Farncombe,
for Pershore, Ledbury, Malvern and the hills

Title pages: the stone rows of Kerlescan,
a 19th-century view

Printed and bound in
the German Democratic Republic

Contents

Preface

Years ago, on holiday in the Dordogne valley of France, I would look forward to the last pleasure of each long day, which was to lie in bed reading Glyn Daniel's *Lascaux and Carnac*, later revised and reissued enticingly as *The Hungry Archaeologist in France*. At first I read it for its descriptions of the painted caves in the limestone cliffs of the Dordogne but then, coming to the chapters about the great stones of Brittany, I promised myself to go there also. I did. And was perplexed that there was no general guidebook either in English or in French to tell me how to find those megalithic delights, many of which were in remote parts of the countryside.

This is still true. So it was with pleasure that personal excursions were planned to little-known carved menhirs at the edges of villages, rows of standing stones in the middle of gorse-yellow heaths, tombs of harsh granite slabs in fields of artichokes. There were academic papers to help me and there were colleagues, both French and English, to accompany me on these pilgrimages.

The resulting gazetteer is not comprehensive nor was it ever meant to be. There are hundreds of sites in Brittany that are either in total ruin or almost irretrievably lost in dense and prickly undergrowth. The gazetteer, instead, contains descriptions of the almost 400 places I think worth visiting and it provides as clear instructions about locating them as I can manage. Also included are the museums and a few sites, wrecked and desolate, but of exceptional archaeological importance. Brittany is a megalithic wonderland and I hope that this book will assist others to enjoy its prehistoric marvels.

I must end by thanking all those who have made my visits to Brittany so enjoyable: Professor Richard Atkinson for lending me his personal gazetteer; Evan Hadingham for our tour of the Thoms' astronomical observatories; Dr Ian Kinnes who sent me slides that helped me find elusive megaliths; Dr Jean l'Helgouach for taking me to Dissignac, Les Mousseaux and other passage-graves; to Professor Alexander and Dr Archie Thom for their meticulous plans of the Carnac rows; and to Dr Alex Gibson, Alex Hooper, Judith Lawson and Professor Derek Simpson, all of whom were willing to share cold Muscadet and Gros Plant at the end of our daily searches in the bracken and gorse of Brittany.

How to use this book

A note about the organization of the book is necessary. The sites are listed alphabetically in each of the five départements, rather like English counties, into which Brittany is divided: Côte-du-Nord (abbreviated as CN), Finistère (F), Ille-et-Vilaine (IV), Loire-Atlantique (LA), with Morbihan (M) subdivided to provide a special section for the Carnac region (CA). For easy reference the sites are numbered in order from the first, no. 1a, the menhir of L'Aiguille de Gargantua, CN, to the last, no. 216, the stone rows of Le Vieux-Moulin, CA.

Where several sites are very close together they have been included under one entry to make an itinerary which the reader may care to follow. These itineraries are specified in the Introduction to each département. To avoid confusion, however, such incorporated sites are cross-referenced in the gazetteer. Under **103 Fougères**, for example, there is a descriptive entry, **103b**, for the allée-couverte of La Pierre de Trésor. Elsewhere in the gazetteer for Ille-et-Vilaine there is also a simple entry, **'Pierre de Trésor, La.** *Allée-couverte* (*see* 103b FOUGÈRES)', in the alphabetical sequence.

Not every part of Brittany is thronged with megaliths and for this reason convenient centres for accommodation such as **17 Mur-de-Bretagne** have been included for the benefit of visitors wishing to see a variety of monuments in the vicinity of their hotel or campsite. These megalithic centres are named in the Introductions and details of the sites near them are provided in the gazetteer under the name of the centre.

Maps are essential for the traveller in the hamlets and lanes of Brittany. Despite its countrywide availability the yellow Michelin series, numbers 58, 59, 63 for different areas or 230 for the whole of Brittany, is not very helpful because the scale of 1:200,000 or 2 cm to 1 km is insufficiently detailed. It should be noted, however, that there are instances where this series indicates menhirs and dolmens that are not shown on smaller-scale maps.

A very useful series is the green 1:100,000 sheets of the Institut Géographique National. At a scale of 1 cm to 1 km or roughly half an inch to a mile it is the equivalent of the British Bartholomew series. Although by no means all the megalithic sites are shown, the visitor will be able to locate most of the villages and minor roads referred to in the gazetteer. Numbers 13, 14 cover Finistère; 14, 16, Côte-du-Nord; 16, 17, Ille-et-Vilaine; 15 Carnac and west Morbihan; and 24 east Morbihan and Loire-Atlantique.

The Institut also produces an orange 1:50,000 series with some seventy sheets for Brittany. These maps are sometimes stocked in the Maisons de la Presse of Breton towns. This Carte Topographique series also has a helpful Carte Touristique edition, number 501, for the Gulf of Morbihan from Étel in the west to Vannes in the east and including the whole of the Carnac-Arzon peninsula region.

For those who want detailed, small-scale sheets the Institut also has a blue 1:25,000 series. The catalogue, 'La France en 2000 Cartes', should be referred to as each of these maps covers an area no bigger than 20 × 14 km. There is a special and larger map, *0821 Est*, for the Auray-Quiberon district.

The yellow Michelin maps and the green 1:100,000 can usually be found easily in Brittany, but the smaller scales should be ordered at least six weeks in advance from Edward Stanford Ltd, 12–14 Long Acre, London WC2 E9LP (telephone 01-838-1321).

It is helpful, when searching for the monuments and when checking their orientations, to have a good compass. One of the Silva systems, obtainable from most camping shops, is excellent for this. A torch, preferably with a wide beam, is also recommended for the darker, sometimes decorated tombs. If, when close to a monument, it is defying discovery the enquiry at a shop or farm, 'Où se trouve le dolmen, menhir . . . etc?' will usually elicit helpful directions – as long as one can understand the answer.

Chronology

Readers will find two kinds of date in this book. Because of fluctuations in atmospheric radio-activity, Carbon-14 determinations have produced 'dates' that have quite consistently been found to be too young for earlier prehistoric times. Fortunately it has been possible to correlate these against an accurate tree-ring calendar derived from the long-lived bristlecone pines of California's White Mountains. To avoid confusion between a C-14 assay and its bristlecone pine correction all radiocarbon 'dates' are quoted in full and followed by 'bc'. Correlated dates, giving what is believed to be the true age, are cited with 'BC' after them.

As an example, the allée-couverte of Le Champ-Grosset, CN, provided a charcoal sample whose C-14 date was 1870±200 bc, which in real years was the approximate equivalent of 2340 BC.

For a **time-chart for megalithic Brittany**, turn to page 14.

Introduction

The Prehistory of Megalithic Brittany

Stretching into the Atlantic at the north-west of France the Armorican peninsula is a land of low, grey hills and rocks, with the long gorges of the interior turning and twisting their rivers down to a thousand kilometres of jagged coastline. The inland parts of this peninsula, of which Brittany forms the major region, was called the *Ar-goat*, 'the wooded land', but many of the trees have been felled, the soil has become too poor to support forests and much of the countryside is now open farmland. *Ar-mor*, 'the land by the sea', describes Brittany better. It is the sea that fashioned the prehistoric patterns of life here.

With her tidetorn shores Brittany was almost but never quite an island. She was always open to penetration from the east and it was from this direction that people came to settle on the richer soils near the coasts, first the pioneers, then later groups with different beliefs, searching for land, intermarrying until over long generations intruder and native were indistinguishable. It was a process of change that is fossilized in the hundreds of different megalithic structures that can still be seen in Brittany ('megalith', literally 'a large stone'). In some ways the interaction of landscape and settlement here was like that of Cornwall, equally grey and granitic and austere, only 160 km to the north across the English Channel.

To make a direct comparison between the early prehistory of Britain and Brittany would be misleading and yet the regions had things in common. With the innovation of farming came the innovation of stone-built family tombs. Over the centuries these became more elaborate, the gloomy chambers in Brittany sometimes decorated with carvings of axes and weird representations of a 'guardian' spirit. As trading networks expanded so societies became richer, more powerful, and the tombs were transformed into shrines, perhaps even temples for the living. Local styles of monument developed. Outside influences affected native traditions. There followed a decline and after a period of stagnation the tombs and sanctuaries were abandoned and in their places vast open-air rings of tall pillars were erected, often associated with long lines of standing stones. In Britain there was Avebury and Callanish. In Brittany there were the astonishing Carnac megaliths.

All this happened over many generations, in Brittany earlier than in Britain, between about 5000 and 2000 BC, in the Neolithic or New Stone Age. Before then there were no megaliths. The countryside was covered in a crowded forest of oaks intermixed with elms near the coast. There the sea was lower than it is today, as the present-day half-submerged sites of Er-Lannic, CA (132b), and Kernic, F (70a), testify. (Reference numbers are those of the Gazetteer.)

Even before this man's way of life had altered. As the last of the great Ice Ages receded and the climate improved forests gradually covered the once-stunted tundras of Europe. Herds of mammoth, reindeer and elk that man had hunted drifted northwards to more congenial, cold regions and, in turn, men either followed them or became fowlers, fishers and food-gatherers, wandering along the tree-thick riversides, stalking the red and roe deer in the woodlands. In Brittany traces of the Old Stone Age hunters, so plentiful in the limestone caverns of central and southern France, are rare, a rockshelter near Dol, IV, a cave at Roch Toul, F, being two examples, and even the later fisher-hunter groups of the Mesolithic left little evidence of their existence, the islands of

(Below) Brittany, showing main towns, roads and départements. CN – Côte-du-Nord, F – Finistère, IV – Ille-et-Vilaine, LA – Loire-Atlantique, M – Morbihan. Carnac region (CA) indicated.

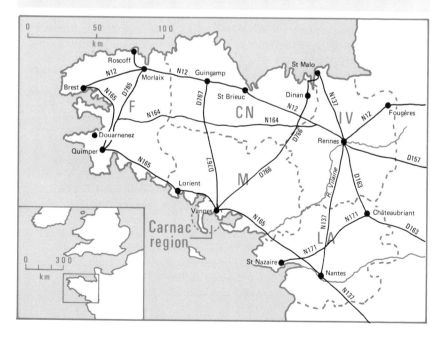

The lines of Kermario, CA (183b), from the SW.

Teviec and Hoëdic off the Quiberon peninsula being the most important sites. Dumps of seashells, crude pebble tools, minute flint flakes, bones of deer and fox and the ashes and charcoal of hearths on the sandy seashore rises that were later transformed into islands by the rising level of the sea – these are almost all that has survived from the long centuries between 10,000 and 5000 BC of this Mesolithic period.

Elsewhere the ability to grow crops had long been known in the Near East. Wild varieties of wheat and barley had been cultivated in Anatolia since 8000 BC and this knowledge of agriculture slowly penetrated westwards, the seed-corn adapting to the moister, cooler, heavier soils of Europe. It has been suggested that this cereal economy spread outwards at a rate of some 18 km each generation, about 70 km in a century, reaching Brittany not long before 4500 BC. The herding of animals seems to have been practised before this.

As early as the 7th millennium BC forms of pastoralism are apparent in the south of France. At Châteauneuf-les-Martigues on the Mediterranean coast of France Mesolithic people belonging to what is known as the Castelnovian culture quite suddenly abandoned the hunting of rabbits and, perhaps encouraged by an increasingly dry climate, took up the breeding of sheep. By the middle of the next millennium sheep and cattle may have been herded in Brittany by families living along the Morbihan coast. These semi-nomadic bands at Hoëdic, Teviec and similar seasonal camps, already had social differences. In their communal graves and stone-lined cists some of the burials had better tools, more neatly worked bones and seashells, and it is possible that the individual ownership or control of herds and flocks conferred prestige upon a person, his status symbolized by the shepherd's crook or the herdsman's yoke.

These were not restless wanderers. Land clearance is known at Dissignac, LA (115), near St Nazaire, as early as 4850 BC, associated with cereal pollen and weeds of cultivation. Centuries later two passage-graves were built here sealing the evidence of agriculture under their huge covering mound. Along the southern coastline, particularly around the Gulf of Morbihan, farming communities established themselves, perhaps several families together for safety, and from the middle of the 5th millennium BC they constructed tombs in a tradition that endured for over a hundred generations from the earliest passage-grave yet known at Kercado, CA (176), dated to about 4650 BC, down to the little allée-couverte of Kerivalan, CN (14), erected as late as 2100 BC.

The very first megaliths may have been no more than solitary menhirs, single standing pillars put up as territorial markers or as ancestor-stones near the settlements of these first farmers. There are still hundreds of isolated stones in Brittany and they are almost impossible to date. It is known, however, that some were decorated with carvings of early Neolithic stone axes or shepherds' crooks such as the art on the menhir at Kermarquer, M (145a), showing how ancient the stone itself must be. Occasionally such menhirs were pulled down and broken to be used as the capstones of Neolithic passage-graves (*see* 132a, 175a,c, 201).

(Above) Kerloas, F (67a), menhir from the N.

(Left) Dol, IV (101), menhir from the S.

Other menhirs, such as the magnificent hammered and smoothed stones of West Léon, a region in Finistère, may have been raised a thousand years later than the earliest pillars. Some were single. Some were set up in groups of two or three. Excavations at their bases have recovered little but fire-reddened stones and charred wood. The coarse sherds and crudely-worked stones found in the Carnac rows, CA (180d, 183b), hint at a Late Neolithic origin for those famous lines.

The first monumental buildings in Brittany were the passage-graves, so-called because of the drystone-walled passage, 11 m or more long and capped with heavy flat slabs, that led to a circular, often corbelled chamber in which the dead were laid. All this was contained in an elaborate cairn held stable by a series of concentric drystone walls that rose in height like a stack of drums over the passage and chamber. The walls were meant to be visible. Even a century ago, after 6,000 years of neglect, it was still possible to see the undamaged side of the gigantic cairn at Barnenez, F (40).

Conspicuous on crests or hills or high places, these first tombs were impressive. In them were the bones of generations of people. Over 300 were found in the Somme tomb of La Chaussée Tirancourt, an allée-couverte, most of them dying in their mid-thirties. In Brittany, unfortunately, the acid soils have almost everywhere destroyed the remains of the dead. Only at Pors Guen, CA (209) and Conguel, CA (168), have skeletons and disarticulated bones been preserved in the sands of the Quiberon peninsula showing how skulls had been set tidily against the walls and other bones heaped up to make room for further burials.

Few grave-goods are found in these tombs other than some flints and sherds of thin-walled, round-bottomed bowls known as Carn ware from its first discovery in the Île Carn passage-grave, F (51). Finely-finished, almost leathery in texture, this coil-built pottery had little decoration except for some applied crescents and simple lugs.

With such scanty and uninformative material and with little knowledge of Early Neolithic settlements in Brittany it would seem impossible to deduce the rites that accompanied the dead, but hints do come from the architecture and the art in their tombs. In nearly all the passage-graves the entrance faced south-

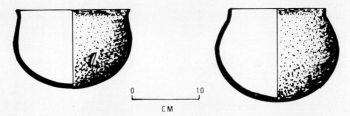

Carn ware, early Neolithic bowls.

13

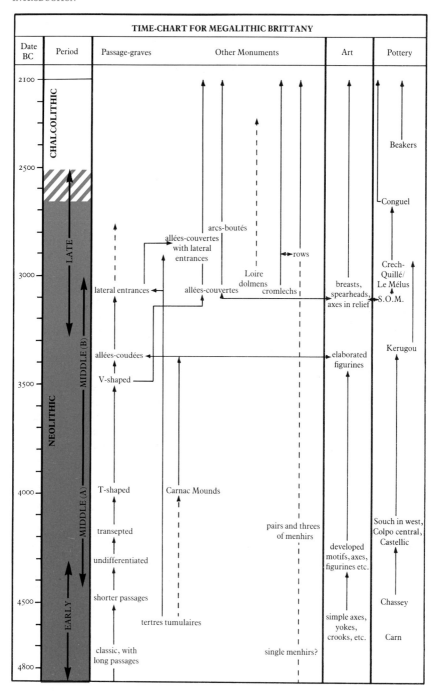

TIME-CHART FOR MEGALITHIC BRITTANY

Date BC	Period	Passage-graves	Other Monuments	Art	Pottery

CHALCOLITHIC

NEOLITHIC

LATE

MIDDLE (B)

MIDDLE (A)

EARLY

Beakers

Conguel

arcs-boutés

allées-couvertes with lateral entrances

rows

lateral entrances

allées-couvertes

Loire dolmens

cromlechs

Crech-Quillé/ Le Mélus

S.O.M.

breasts, spearheads, axes in relief

allées-coudées

V-shaped

elaborated figurines

Kerugou

T-shaped

Carnac Mounds

pairs and threes of menhirs

developed motifs, axes, figurines etc.

Souch in west, Colpo central, Castellic

transepted

undifferentiated

shorter passages

simple axes, yokes, crooks, etc.

Chassey

tertres tumulaires

classic, with long passages

single menhirs?

Carn

2100

2500

3000

3500

4000

4500

4800

Some motifs in early passage-grave art, Brittany. Their modern interpretations are: a *'U';*
b *yoke;* c *'7';* d *crook;* e *axe;* f *hafted axe;* g *'serpent';* h *bow;* i *'figurine'.*

east, somewhere in the arc between 126° and 162° towards a point on the skyline
south of midwinter sunrise and in most cases just south of the moon's most
southerly rising. It could be argued that it was a belief that the moon and death
were somehow connected that led to this orientation, the rhythm of its monthly
cycle being associated with a female deity or spirit. The art also hints at this.

Gradually, as the builders became more certain of their skills, the technique
of drystone walling gave way to orthostatic construction, the walls of the
passage and chamber being lined with upright slabs of granite or schist or
whatever stone was locally available. On some of these rough stones carvings
were made, lightly pecked out on the unprepared surfaces, most often of axes
that were sometimes portrayed by an elementary triangle, more frequently
shown in outline with a haft. Also in this early phase there were yokes and
crooks, symbols of pastoralism, and zigzags and meanders whose significance
has been forgotten, although some of the undulating lines have been interpreted
as serpents. Other motifs of a horizontal line with an upcurved end and with
vertical bars rising from it have been imagined as boats to carry the dead out to
the nearby sea.

Even more dramatic are the ill-named 'shield-idols', which are probably
formalized carvings of a female figurine. These have rectangular frames with a
round top at the centre of which there is often a tiny, knoblike projection. Some
have arcs radiating from the upper part like hair in shock. Sometimes there are
diminutive loops on either side of the body. These austere squares have been
called bucklers, cooking-pots, even octopuses, as well as shield-idols, but when
one compares them with the human-shaped stones standing in the chambers of
other passage-graves (*see* 9, 52) they seem more likely to have been abstract
depictions of a female 'goddess' or guardian watching over the dead. Such
anthropomorphic art, in various forms, is to be discovered all through the
Breton Neolithic.

Architecture was always changing, always being modified. Bottle-shaped
chambers and chambers set asymmetrically to the passage in 'p' or 'q' plans are

also known and, along the west and north coasts, close to the sea, are lines of passage-graves contained under one enormous cairn. Here, at Île Carn, F (51), Île Guennoc, F (52), Barnenez, F (40) and far to the north-east at La Ville-Pichard, CN (38), are the tombs of farming groups spreading out in search of good land. Dates of 3850±300 bc from Île Guennoc, 3820±150 bc from Île Carn, and 3800±150 bc from Barnenez, all around 4600 BC, show how early in the Neolithic these migrations occurred. The incorporation of three, four or five passage-graves in one cairn suggests that several families banded together on their private odyssey. When, later, some of the cairns were enlarged, it was usually the western end that was chosen.

To this Early Neolithic period may also belong some of the tertres tumulaires or tertres allongés, long mounds, which are somewhat similar to British unchambered long barrows. Their rectangular or trapezoidal mounds, usually 40–50 m long but never high, covered a flurry of cists in which, amongst traces of burning, there were flint blades, points, scrapers, transverse flint arrowheads, polished stone axes and sherds of round-based vessels. Some pots from the tertre under the Kermario rows, CA (183c), were similar to Carn ware. It is thought that these unobtrusive mounds with their abundance of artefacts may have been the precursors of the gigantic Carnac Mounds with their wealth of lovely and luxurious artefacts.

By about 4400 BC, at the beginning of the Middle Neolithic, broad tracts of forest had been cleared and parts of the inland which later degenerated into bleak moors through over-farming were being colonized. Mineral sources were exploited. Lacking good flint anywhere in Brittany people prospected for suitable stone, and near Plussulien almost in the centre of the Armorican peninsula they discovered dolerite, a hard, basalt-like rock that could be shaped and sharpened for their axes. This Sélédin axe-factory, CN (31), was in use from about 4000 to 2700 BC (3320±140 bc, 2100±130 bc) and at its height was trading some 5,000 axes yearly, its products reaching to all parts of Brittany and beyond.

Such farspread contacts, whether made by traders travelling long distances on the developing trackways or by goods being bartered or ceremonially exchanged from one community to the next, ever outwards, inevitably resulted in a reverse exposure to influences from outside Brittany. From about 4500 BC signs of the vigorous Chassey culture are apparent.

Named after the type-site, the Camp de Chassey, a fortified hilltop in Burgundy near the modern town of Macon, the makers of distinctive fine pottery had rapidly spread from the south onto distant areas of fertile ground,

(Opposite, above) Dissignac Neolithic passage-graves, LA (115), cairn from the SE.

(Opposite, below) Neolithic axes: fibrolite (left), flint and two of dolerite from the Sélédin axe factory (31).

settling, trading, intermingling with local populations. In the south of Brittany at Er-Lannic, M (132b), and in passage-graves their pots have been found, typically of shouldered, round-bottomed bowls decorated with grooved and dotted geometrical patterns of triangles, lozenges, squares and semi-circles. With them also are flattish dishes and delicate vase-supports like overgrown napkin rings upon which a round-based pot could be balanced. These have the same neat decorations on their sides.

The infiltration of Chassey traits may not always have been a peaceful process. At a rare settlement site, Le Lizo, CA (189a), to the north-east of Carnac-Ville, there were a lot of Chassey vessels on the hut floors and in the multiple ditches that defended this steep-sided village site overlooking the Crach river. The necessity of digging out the ditches and piling up the extensive earthworks probably was the result of a growing competition for land and a developing society with leaders anxious for power and prestige.

By whatever means the Chassey ceramic styles reached Brittany – by trade, by adoption of cult practices, by the quiet immigration of a few farming communities or by land-seizure by larger, aggressive groups – the shapes and patterns of the vessels soon affected native traditions. Mixed with the Chassey sherds at Le Lizo were others known as Castellic ware from a hamlet only a kilometre to the south. The native grooved ware discovered here is similar to the Chassey bowls, with the necks of the pots fluted or lightly incised with semi-circles, often double, around the rim and at the bottom of the neck.

In the west of Brittany, around the Bay of Audierne, the Souch style emerged with Chassey-like cooking pots with vertical lugs for suspension over a fire or from a rafter. Nearer to Carnac, at Colpo 25 km north of the Gulf of Morbihan, potters produced bowls like those of Souch but with the cooking pot attached to a flat domed base, as though a vase-support had been moulded onto a round-bottomed pot, all of it decorated with characteristic Chassey multiple triangles.

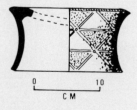
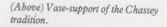

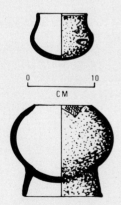

(Above) Vase-support of the Chassey tradition.

(Right) Bowl and footed bowl, Souch ware.

These *vases à pieds creux* with their concave bases have been recovered in passage-graves such as Larcuste, M (149a), and Dissignac, LA (115).

It was a time of flux and adaptation and the architecture of the passage-graves shows this. Now there were chambers subdivided into compartments as at Kerléven, F (66), each perhaps a vault for an individual family in a clan monument. Sometimes small cells were set into the sides and end of the passage. These transepted tombs are to be found mainly in south-eastern Brittany around the Pornic-St Nazaire region of the Loire estuary, where fine examples such as Les Mousseaux, LA (121a), can still be visited. There are others in the vicinity of Carnac like Mané Keriavel, CA (197a).

The Middle Neolithic chambered tombs had shorter passages than their predecessors, more emphasis being placed on the enlarged chamber. The orientations of the entrances were more widely spread, from north-east even to south-west, although the majority were still confined in a relatively narrow arc between 86° and 170°, and there are strong reasons for believing that it was astronomical considerations that determined this.

The capstones of some of these developed passage-graves were gigantic, a need forced on the builders by the greater size of the chamber. A monstrous slab at Mané Rutuel, CA (201), which was probably a re-used menhir, weighed over 50 tons and demanded the efforts of hundreds of people to raise it onto the sideslabs of the tomb. Modern experiments with primitive equipment have shown that a 32-ton concrete slab of the appropriate shape can be moved by some 170 labourers with 30 others shifting rollers along the block's path. At Kerloas, F (67a), the task of dragging the 100 tons of the menhir 2½ km from its source must have involved many scores of families. As for the almost unbelievable 300 tons or more of the Grand Menhir Brisé, CA (175a), tugged centimetre by centimetre from 4 km away, this obsessive undertaking bewilders the modern mind. Even with oxen it would still have required more than 1,000 human beings to elevate such a colossal pillar, and it is quite possible that they failed and the half-lifted monster fell, fracturing into four or five fragments – which is how it lies today. No record has been found of its ever having stood upright.

The art of the Middle Neolithic passage-graves was more organized and detailed. The motifs were the same, with the addition perhaps of cupmarks and radial lines, but they were larger, more deeply cut, the axes more realistic (*see* 175c, 201, 199b). Entire compositions of 'U's and curves and arcs filled stone after stone in the gallery of Gavr'inis, M (132a), in an exuberant tour de force of megalithic devotion.

To this time also may belong the Carnac Mounds; Er-Grah, CA (175b); Kerlud, CA (182a); Mané-er-Hroek, CA (195); Mané Lud, CA (199a); Le Moustoir, CA (205a), Tumulus St-Michel, CA (215a), Tumiac, M (163); monstrous ovoid barrows, towering above the surrounding land in a looming assertion of power. Without entrance or passage like the smaller tertres

Polished jadeite ceremonial axe, perforated for suspension.

tumulaires and without art they were often built against a passage-grave (*see* 215b, 199b), but in them were riches quite unlike the poverty of those tombs. Surrounded by small cists, the central grave was stacked with exotic goods. Here there were pale-green, almost translucent, variscite beads, opaque and slender discs and collars, ornaments of pellucid jasper and smooth green serpentine, axes of rare stone, three-quarters of them crystalline fibrolite, some of them minute and perforated for hanging around the neck like a modern crucifix, others thin and shining, up to 45 cm long and too fragile for anything but ritual use. Over 100 of these ceremonial axes came from Mané-er-Hroek, there were 249 beads at Tumiac, and amongst this sudden lavish wealth there were also bones of animals, of oxen and horses, all of them partly burnt during the funerary rites that had preceded the raising of these manmade hills. The date of the mounds is uncertain. Radiocarbon assays obtained from material excavated years ago are equivocal, but a Chassey vase-support from the closed chamber at Le Moustoir suggests that a Middle Neolithic origin is likely.

The reasons for such abrupt opulence are unclear. It may be that the rise of chieftains controlling the affairs of a territory demanded not only a display of riches but also a burial-place different from that of their forebears, although incorporating such a tomb in the body of the mound. Leaders and chiefdoms in rivalry are indicated elsewhere by defended settlements like that at Machecoul near modern Quimper in Finistère. Dating from about 3800 BC, this earthwork enclosure with its interrupted ditches was occupied by people tending cattle, some sheep and pigs. Masses of sherds in a central cross-ditch were of Kerugou ware, a style developing late in the Middle Neolithic, of round-bottomed bowls with a flattened rim, rounded vases with a straight or gently concave neck ornamented with vertical cordons or little bosses, and of coarse, flat-bottomed domestic vessels. Kerugou pots were native to southern Finistère, but have been found as far away as the angled passage-grave of Goërem, Gâvres, M (133), 24 km west-north-west of Carnac-Ville.

The plan of Goërem, an allée-coudée or bent passage-grave, is only one of a variety of designs that came about in the later centuries of the Middle Neolithic. Among them were V-shaped tombs in which the sole distinction between the passage and the chamber was a gradual rising in height and widening from the entrance up to the tall backstone. Well-preserved examples of this undifferentiated form exist at Mané Kerioned, CA (198), Ty-ar-Boudiquet, F (95a), and Liscuis, CN (15).

No type of tomb, however, better illustrates the increasing importance of the chamber than the allée-coudée. Sometimes slightly bent away from the line of the passage, sometimes at right-angles to it, the chamber is always longer and what art there is is concentrated in it. Early passage-graves such as Île Longue, M (140), had a passage over 10 m long leading to a chamber hardly more than 3 m across, but at Goërem the chamber is twice the length of the passage.

These allées-coudées of southern Brittany, at Goërem, at Luffang, CA (192), Le Rocher, CA (211a), and Les Pierres-Plats, CA (208), are strange monuments. In them the west is emphasized, for it is in this direction that the main part of the chamber lies. Here people carved complex images of the female figurine whose rectangular framework was often stressed by double or treble outlines. At the top of the carving, instead of the earlier tiny projection, there was a little dent, and a vertical line divided the body into equal parts. Circles representing breasts, as many as eight sometimes, were inscribed in these panels, occasionally with spindly hooks of arms. Today, even by the steady light of an electric torch, such carvings are dramatic. To prehistoric eyes, seeing them in

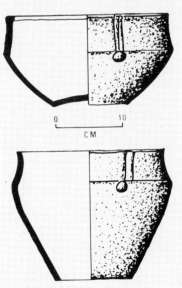

Kerugou ware, Late Middle to Late Neolithic.

'Figurine', Les Pierres-Plats passage-grave, CA (208).

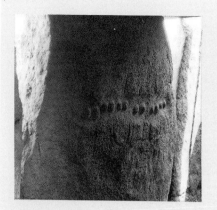

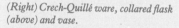

'Breasts', Kergüntuil allée-couverte, CN
(13b).

*(Right) Crech-Quillé ware, collared flask
(above) and vase.*

the writhing flames of a lamp, they may have seemed alive and dreadful, the
embodiment of death itself in the blackness of the chamber. These late sites
have the architecture of a tomb, but the impression is of a ritual centre for the
living in which a cult of ancestors may have been the focus of the rites.

There was an architectural variation to these allées-coudées. At some sites the
long rectangular chamber had a lateral entrance in the south side of the mound
and at its eastern end. Occasionally two low portal stones set at right-angles to
the tumulus stood outside this entrance. Inside, the passage was either short or
non-existent (*see* 180e) and, as the entrances were invariably at the far east, this
custom once again created a long western chamber.

By 3300 BC, at the beginning of the Late Neolithic period, passage-grave
building was in decline. Dolmens, those gaunt tombs with a single chamber and
a cumbrous capstone, may belong to this time and so may the spectacular Loire
dolmens such as Essé, IV (102). These were decades of increasing change and
intermixing of people. From the Paris Basin drifted land-seeking groups of the
Seine-Oise-Marne (SOM) culture with their coarse 'flower-pot' vases or 'Pôts-
des-Fleurs', small collared flasks, long thin stone axes, oblong pendants and
daggers and knives of honey-coloured flint from Le Grand Pressigny near
Poitiers. Their dead had by custom been buried in almost subterranean
megalithic chambers, long and rectangular, whose vestibules were sometimes
carved with the face and breasts of a necklaced 'goddess'.

Except in the event of an implausible mass invasion for which there is no
evidence, it is unlikely that these incomers were responsible for the building of
the long chambered tombs in Brittany known as allées-couvertes or covered

passages. It is probable, however, that SOM beliefs to some extent contributed to this style of megalithic architecture in the north and central regions in the late 4th millennium BC. Native pottery certainly owed much to them. One group, known clumsily as Crech-Quillé/Le Mélus ware from two tombs in the Côte-du-Nord, contained tall, flat-bottomed vases and collared flasks, asymmetrical and of rough texture. It is vessels like these that are frequently found in the 140 or more allées-couvertes of the Côte-du-Nord and Ille-et-Vilaine.

It is a justifiable belief of many French archaeologists that the origins of these north Breton tombs reached back to the V-shaped undifferentiated passage-graves of the Middle Neolithic. With their thick, grey sideslabs exposed, leaning under the weight of their capstones, the allées-couvertes are well-built structures whose entrances faced variously to north-east, east and south-east, the three preferred arcs being 33°–63°, 90°–123° and 143°–163°. The first might have been an approximate orientation on the most northerly moonrise, the second on the equinoctial sunrise and the third might be related to the south-south-easterly alignments of the earliest passage-graves. Two points, however, need to be stressed. That the entrances of most megalithic tombs were directed towards an astronomical event is very likely, but they were only rarely directed

Mougau-Bihan, F (82), *allée-couverte from the SW.*

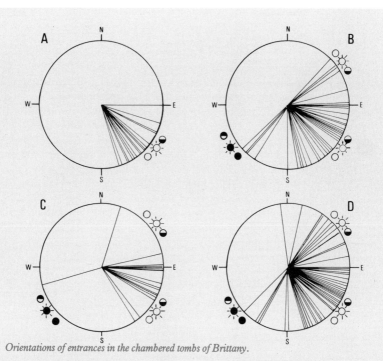

Orientations of entrances in the chambered tombs of Brittany.

A   *Early passage-graves with long passages. Latitude 47°35' (Gulf of Morbihan), c. 4000 BC.*
B   *Later passage-graves with shorter passages. Lat. 47°35', c. 4000 BC.*
C   *Passage-graves with lateral entrances. Latitude 48°45' (northern Brittany), c. 3000 BC.*
D   *Allées-couvertes. Lat. 48°35', c. 3000 BC.*

Symbols to the east of the N–S line are for the risings of the sun and moon. Those to the west are for the settings.
The midsummer sun is to the north of the E–W line, the midwinter sun is to the south.
No symbols are shown for the northern settings of the sun and moon as no tomb entrance faces in those directions.

○   *The moon at its major northern and southern risings.*

☼   *The sun at its midsummer and midwinter risings.*

◐   *The moon at its minor northern and southern risings.*

●   *The moon at its major southern setting.*

☀   *The midwinter setting sun.*

◑   *The moon at its minor southern settings.*

exactly towards the midwinter or midsummer solstices or the extreme northern
or southern risings of the moon. When they were this may have been fortuitous.
The orientations were not apparently linked to a calendar. Nor were they
designed for living observers of solar or lunar events. 'Sunrise' or 'moonrise'
was seemingly sufficient for the builders of megalithic tombs both in Brittany
and Britain, the orientation perhaps decided simply by where the sun or moon
happened to be rising on the skyline when the tomb was being erected.

Some of the allées-couvertes had an additional 'cell' at their western end,
blocked off from the chamber by the end stone and only accessible from outside
the tomb. Here two sidestones continued the line of the chamber, but there was
seldom a capstone and even more rarely a terminal slab, so that this unusual and
unroofed setting was always open. Yet it was here that sometimes carvings of
pairs of breasts in relief were made, four at Tressé, IV (112), others at the
exceptionally cramped cell at Prajou-Menhir, CN (22a), alongside the outlines
of what look like metal daggers. There are lightly engraved necklaces below
many of the breasts in these tombs.

As with the passage-graves, so there are variations in the allées-couvertes. In
a few cases where the mound has been removed it can be seen that the
sidestones were never set upright, but had been inclined inwards so that their
tops touched to form a megalithic 'ridge-tent'. The 'dwarfs' house' at Ty-ar-
C' horriket, F (96a), is a good example of this prehistoric idiosyncracy. There
may, however, originally have been a protective covering of horizontal slabs
resting on the mound or on outer pillars that were taken away when the
tumulus was vandalized in historic times, as at Kerfily, M (143).

These appear to be some of the last megalithic chambers to have been built in
Brittany. The tomb tradition was waning and in its place, especially in the
south, spacious rings of close-set stones were put up, similar but not identical to
the stone circles of the British Isles. In Brittany such enclosures are known as
cromlechs or 'curved stones'.

Around the Gulf of Morbihan there were many cromlechs, a fact which
suggests that they may have been derived from the shapes of the passage-graves
there. Near Carnac-Ville there were complete rings, never circular, at Ménec
(203a, c), probably at Kermario (183), at Kerlescan (180a), and there was
another at St Pierre-Quiberon (204b). To the east, on hills that are now islands
in the Gulf of Morbihan and on the Arzon peninsula, there were others,
different from the Carnac rings because these were horseshoe settings open to
the south-east. They were set up at Kergonan, M (139a), at Grand Rohu, M
(136a), and at other sites now either destroyed or badly mutilated. At Er-
Lannic, M (132b), two tangential rings were erected, one a flattened circle, the
other probably a horseshoe, a juxtaposition that may have been an attempt to
reconcile two separate traditions. A similar combination existed at Kerlescan,
CA (180a, c). There was another horseshoe, isolated, at Champ de la Croix,
Crucuny, CA (167a), to the north of Carnac and 4 km to its west was the

rectangular enclosure of Crucuno, CA (171b), not far from the passage-graves with rectangular chambers of Mané-Groh, CA (196) and Mané Bras, CA (193a).

It has been claimed that the south-east facing horseshoe settings were aligned towards the midwinter sunrise and that the Crucuno rectangle was laid out to indicate the equinoctial and solstitial sunsets. It is of interest, therefore, to note that among the Carnac rings the Ménec 'eggs' had either their long or their short axis directed towards solar events.

Whether at Carnac, Arzon or elsewhere these cromlechs are never less than 50 m across and such spaciousness suggests that they were intended for large assemblies. In the British Isles people in the Late Neolithic had found the interiors of their long chambered tombs too confined for their expanding rituals and they added open-air forecourts to the traditional burial-places. Such architectural enhancement is almost unknown in Brittany, although on the north coast, only 160 km across the English Channel, the probable forecourt at the allée-couverte of Kernic, F (70a), may have resulted from a similar demand for more space. Elsewhere on the Armorican peninsula, especially in the region of the classic southern passage-graves, it was the cromlech, apparently, that was devised to answer this need for more capacious ritual centres.

In this respect a combination of the old and the new may be seen at the Kercado passage-grave, CA (176), where an early chambered tomb was surrounded by a now-incomplete flattened circle of standing stones. In this it has affinities with the Irish Newgrange and the Scottish Clava passage-graves.

If the cromlechs did indeed have their origins in Breton passage-graves then their shape would be similar to the tombs, although uncovered and larger. Beginning with rings or rectangles big enough for just a few families, their size would have increased as society became more cohesive with hundreds of people in a community. It may be significant that the sub-rectangular design of the Kerlescan West Cromlech, CA (180a), with an internal area of over 6000 square m, was almost a duplicate of the 'forecourt' setting at the Manio III tertre, CA (202b), only 300 m to its west, and which enclosed less than 50 square m. The funerary and ritual associations of such tertres are not in doubt, with cists, signs of burning and small standing stones in their mounds, and the Manio 'forecourt' may have been the focus of the rites enacted there as part of the mortuary practices. This interpretation would imply that the vast Carnac cromlechs had a similar function. With this in mind it is interesting that 'Kermario' and 'Kerlescan' mean, respectively, 'place of the dead' and 'place of burning'.

The dating of the cromlechs is debatable, but the association of Er-Lannic's north ring with debris containing Conguel ware points to a time in the Late Neolithic around 3300 BC.

Conguel pottery is one of the last Neolithic ceramic styles in Brittany. Its earliest forms consisted of round-based bowls with a decoration of vertical, horizontal and arc-shaped lines, often in panels, around the neck. In the later

Upper Conguel stage there were more flat-based vessels, sharply angled at their shoulders and with geometrical lines around their tops.

The chronological relationship of the Carnac rows to the cromlechs is not as unclear as has sometimes been claimed, and there is no good reason for believing that lines of standing stones elsewhere in the Armorican peninsula were of a greatly different period. At Carnac, where cromlechs and stone rows are associated it is always the cromlech that stands on the higher, level ground whereas the rows lead uphill towards it, their stones increasing in size as they near the ring. It is likely, therefore, that the stone rows were either contemporary with or later than the enclosure.

From British parallels a processional function is arguable for the rows but, given their marked lack of straightness, any accurate astronomical purpose is improbable. In any of the complexes, moreover, it is very doubtful that the lines were erected as a unity and the fact that there are sometimes too many

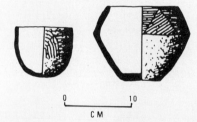

(Right) Conguel ware, Lower (left), and Upper.

(Below) Ménec rows, CA *(203b), from the W.*

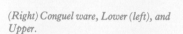

Kerzerho rows, CA (187a), north row from the E.

lines for them all to be connected to the cromlech implies that additions were made to simpler settings. This is apparently confirmed by the several changes of direction and by some shorter groups at right-angles to the main assemblage.

Adding strength to the idea that some rows were expressly intended for rites of death is the recognition that at St Just, IV (110d), the two converging lines consist of tall schist pillars and lower blocks of white quartz just like the lateral lines in the nearby tertre of the Croix-St-Pierre (110i), and at the allée-couverte of Notre-Dame-de-Lorette, CN (18).

Rows without cromlechs are quite widespread in Brittany. There are some in the Côte-du-Nord (5), in Finistère (74, 97a), Ille-et-Vilaine (100, 103a, 104a), and there were once others in Loire-Atlantique (127b). Some of them are fan-shaped and may have been directed towards an astronomical event although, if so, the alignments were crude. These rows, outside the Carnac region best seen at Lagatjar, F (74), Médréac, IV (104a), and St Just, IV (110d), are the last of the Breton megaliths. A vaguely associated date of about 2500 BC (1990±80 bc) from the Alignement du Moulin, IV (110d), indicates that the lines were still being used in the early centuries of the Bronze Age. Beakers were found near the stones. Other beakers have quite consistently been discovered in the recesses of deserted passage-graves and allées-couvertes. But by that time the megalithic tradition was over.

Gazetteer

Côte-du-Nord
Sites 1-38

Finistère
Sites 39-97

Ille-et-Vilaine
Sites 98-112

Loire-Atlantique
Sites 113-129

Morbihan
Sites 130-164

Carnac
Sites 165-216

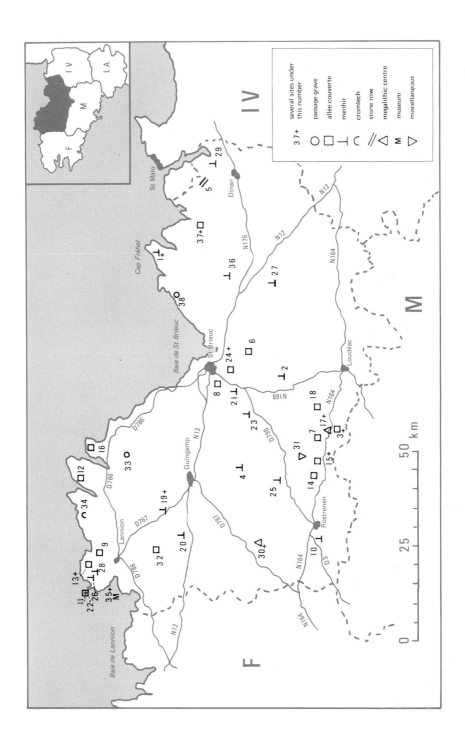

IV

M

F

St Malo

Cap Fréhel

Baie de St Brieuc

Baie de Lannion

St Brieuc

Dinan

Loudéac

Guingamp

Lannion

Rostrenen

N176

N12

N164

N12

N12

N12

N12

N164

N164

N168

D790

D767

D786

D786

D786

D787

D3

29

5

37+

1+

36

27

38

6

24+

8

2

21

23

18

17+

7

31

3+

16

12

33

34

9

19+

4

25

14

15+

20

32

30+

10

35+
M
26
22
11
28
13+

37+ several sites under
this number

○ passage grave
□ allée couverte
⊥ menhir
C cromlech
// stone row
△ megalithic centre
M museum
▷ miscellaneous

0   25   50 km

Côte-du-Nord

Maps: *Yellow Michelin 1:200,000, no. 59*
Green Carte Touristique 1:100,000, nos. 14, 16

It is sometimes assumed that there is little of megalithic importance in this central section of northern Brittany, but this is a mistaken belief. Here there are fine menhirs, stone rows within a few kilometres of St Malo, and chambered tombs, particularly allées-couvertes, in many areas of the département.

Visitors landing at St Malo might well go to the allée-couverte at La Ville-Genouhan (37a), the rows at Pleslin (5) and the decorated stone at St Samson-sur-Rance (29) before turning eastwards to the better-known sites of Dol (101) and Tressé (112) in Ille-et-Vilaine. There are also at least two concentrations of good sites in Côte-du-Nord and there are convenient centres, detailed in the Gazetteer, from which to visit them. One such centre is Trébeurden (35) near the coast, around which there is an enthralling group of monuments, including the Christianized menhir of St Duzec (26) and the great allées-couvertes of Île Grande (11), Kergüntuil (13b), Prajou-Menhir (22a) and Crech-Quillé (9).

Deeper in the countryside is one of the loveliest regions in the whole of Brittany around Mur-de-Bretagne (17), another good centre with the deep, gorse- and heather-thick Daoulas Gorge and the beautiful Poulancre Valley. Here there are equally compelling monuments at Coët-Correc (7) and the elegant sites at Liscuis (15) overlooking a landscape of woods, rivers and wild outcrops of schist and quartzite. These, with the site of the Sélédin axe-factory (31) and several menhirs in the vicinity, make Côte-du-Nord much more than a region to rush through on the way to Carnac. Nor should the visitor ignore the sites around another megalithic centre, St Servais (30), where there is yet another group of standing stones amongst the surrounding villages.

Sites 1-38

1a Aiguille de Gargantua, L', Plévenon.
Menhir
23 km W of St Malo, 38 km NE of St Brieuc, 3 km NE of Plévenon on Cap Fréhel. The stone is on the edge of the heath 300 m SSW of Fort de la Latte on the W of the lane.

Near the fort on the promontory is a standing stone 2.9 m high but only 0.4 × 0.2 m thick. It has been made into a shaft on top of which is a Christian cross.

It is popularly known as the needle of Gargantua, the large-mouthed, greedy giant of Rabelais' 16th-century novel. It is also known as his finger or his walking-stick. Near the stone and half-buried is a flat stone pitted with cavities. Two of the depressions are said to be the imprints of Gargantua's feet alongside a cupmark. Reputedly they were made when the giant jumped from the spot to Henanbihans 12 km away, leaving his stick behind.

Another tradition claims that the menhir was erected over a giant's tomb. His head lay here but his feet were under the village of St Suliac 25 km away.

1b Hardly worth visiting because of its ruinous condition but interesting because of its finds is the 18-m-long allée-couverte of **Le Tertre de l'Église** at Plévenon. Badly excavated, it contained a rare example of human bones in a Breton tomb, six skeletons lying on their backs with heads to the W. With them was a remarkable collection of some forty polished stone axes, a schist pendant, eight beads, a bronze dagger and the sherds of flat-based 'Pôts-des-Fleurs' of the Late Neolithic of the Crech-Quillé/Le Mélus style. The site was covered by a very large mound.

2   Bayo, Ploeuc-sur-Lie. *Menhir*
21 km S of St Brieuc, 19 km N of Loudéac, 3 km SSW of Ploeuc. From Ploeuc take the D27 S towards Uzel. In 2 km road branches SW (R) onto D81 to Uzel. In 500 m take 1st lane to S (L) to Bayo. In 300 m stone is on the E (L) of the roadside.
This menhir is a great domed pillar of granite, 8 m high, in a high, grassy bank. It has an almost square base, about 2 × 1.8 m, from which the NW and SW sides rise vertically. The NE and SE taper inwards up to a small flat top.

3a   Bod-er-Mohed, Cléguerec. *Allée-couverte*
23 km W of Loudéac, 20 km ESE of Rostrenen, 4 km NNE of Cléguerec. From Cléguerec take the lane N past Kerdréan and by the E edge of the Forêt de Quenécan to the hamlet of Bot-er-Mohet.
Here there is an idiosyncratic allée-couverte built of attractive green quartzite slabs. The northern section is entirely wrecked but 19 m to the S are five adjacent cists or cells, each 2–3 m long and set between lateral pillars. Such a segmented form of chamber suggests that the cells were added successively to an originally modest structure. Beaker sherds were found in them.
3b   In the forest of the **Breuil du Chêne**, 4 km N of Cléguerec, there is a 4-m-high menhir.
3c   800 m N of Cléguerec, by the road to Quenécan, there is a big Bronze Age tumulus.

Bois de Kerbénés. *Menhirs (see* 30c ST SERVAIS)

Botrain. *Menhir (see* 17c MUR-DE-BRETAGNE)

4   Caillouan, Plésidy. *Menhir*
30 km WSW of St Brieuc, 15 km S of Guingamp, 6 km SSE of Bourbriac. From Plésidy take the D5 S and in 3 km turn W (R) onto lane towards Magoar. Stone is 300 m along lane in a hollow on the S (L), 100 m into a field.
This is an impressive cylindrical pillar with a quadrangular base measuring about 1.8 × 1.2 m. It has a domed crest and stands about 8 m high. Until a few years ago this was possibly the second tallest standing stone in Brittany after KERLOAS (67a). It was just over 11 m in height but its top was smashed in the 1960s and it no longer ranks in the ten highest menhirs. It is also spelled Cailouan, Caelouan and Kaelonan.

Chaire des Druides. *Rocks (see* 30d ST SERVAIS)

5   Champ des Roches, Les, Pleslin. *Stone rows*
9 km N of Dinan, 12 km SSW of St Malo. From Dinan take the N166 N for 9 km to Pleslin. In centre of village a minor road on the W (L) is signposted 'Champ des Roches'. 200 m beyond last houses and 100 m along a farm track the rows stand in a spinney on the S.
This is a fine and rare example of stone rows in northern Brittany. There are some sixty-five menhirs in five lines, the remains of a once larger complex. The site is sometimes known as the Druids' Cemetery.
    The rows are aligned from NW to SE up a slight slope and are composed of coarse, granite blocks. To the W the ground rises for half a kilometre. The rows run across the lower slope of this undulating landscape. Although many of the stones are fallen the setting is a pleasant one.
    The five lines are somewhat splayed, narrowing towards the SE. At the NW end there is a short line at right-angles to the others. Looking uphill to the SE the four remaining lines consist from left to right of (a) ten or ten stones, most of them fallen, the tallest about 2.4 m high; (b) a shorter line of five or six stones, all fallen and broken; (c) a line, about 80 m long, of nine stones of which two stand; (d) eight standing stones and two or

Les Champ des Roches (5), rows from the NW.

three others prostrate. The biggest is 2 m long. The greatest width of the rows is about 33 m.

The lines are so disordered that it is difficult to make out their former orientation. With an approximate alignment of 65° they may have been set out towards sunrise in early May and August, the times of the Iron Age Celtic festivals of Beltane (May Day) and Lughnasa (the harvest festival).

A folk story reports that fairies were carrying the stones to Mont St Michel but found them too heavy and left them at Pleslin. It is known that around 1860 priests were trying to stop people meeting in the middle of the lines for what was called 'pagan merrymaking'.

6   Champ-Grosset, Le, Quessoy, *Allée-couverte*
11 km SSE of St Brieuc, 28 km N of Loudéac. From Quessoy take the D28 W and in 1 km veer WNW (R) on country lane for 1½ km. Just before crossroads tomb is 50 m S of lane at the W edge of a small fir wood.

This wrecked, ivy-trailed, bramble-thick allée-couverte is interesting, partly because of its lateral entrance like that of the nearby ROCHE-CAMIO (24a), but more for the finds from it during the excavations of 1896 and 1963–5. The chamber is so overgrown and damaged that it is hard to determine its original length. It appears to be aligned E–W but everything today is in a disturbed condition.

There was an open terminal cell at the west and the chamber was roughly paved. In it were some flat-bottomed Kerugou vases, three round-bottomed bowls, three dolerite axes, six flint blades and a schist pendant. Together the architecture and the artefacts reveal the effect of eastern traditions from the Loire Valley reaching into Brittany during the Late Neolithic. A C-14 assay from charcoal gave a date of 1870±200 bc, the equivalent of about 2340 BC.

7 **Coët-Correc**, Mur-de-Bretagne. *Allée-couverte*
37 km SSW of St Brieuc, 19 km W of Loudéac,
3½ km NW of Mur-de-Bretagne. From Mur
take the N167 N. In 1 km turn W (L) onto the
N164 and in 2½ km take the wide, steep road to
the N (R). In ¾ km the farm road to Corn-coat is
on the E (R). Take the footpath opposite (W)
which curves past a little building. The allée-couverte is 300 m to the W in a meadow just at the
N edge of some woods.

This is an average-sized megalithic tomb, but
it is notable for its lateral entrance and its well-made porthole entrance. It was built on the
NW route between the Carnac region to the S
and the N coast of Brittany, where one or two
similar structures can be found. It is aligned
ESE–WNW.

The chamber at Coët-Correc, 11 m long, is
not truly rectangular, but rather straighter and
lower at its western end. It is constructed of
local, easily-worked schists, twenty-five slabs
enclosing a space 1.5 m wide. Six capstones
survive, although some of them have slipped
or broken. Both ends of the tomb are blocked
by heavy stones and the entrance is at the
extreme SE where two slabs, 2 m long and
1.1 m apart, form a portal at right-angles to
the southern wall of the chamber. Where the
portals touch the tomb two of the sideslabs,
standing side by side, have had their inner,
lower corners carefully chipped away to create
a low opening into the chamber. This aperture
is so small, no more than 30 cm wide and
rising hardly 23 cm to its archlike top, that it
would have been exceptionally difficult to
crawl into the tomb.

The site was excavated in 1871 but
produced no finds of importance. It was
discovered that the entire area inside the tomb
had been paved with small, flat stones. There
was no terminal cell at the western end.

(See also 17 MUR-DE-BRETAGNE.)

8 **Couette, La**, Ploufragan. *Allée-couverte*
4 km SW of St Brieuc. In the grounds of the
École Élémentaire Louis Guilloux, 200 m S of
the church in the centre of Ploufragan.
This ruined allée-couverte, aligned E–W, was
excavated in 1854 and was discovered to
contain three compartments. Its jumbled
chamber faces downhill towards a tall menhir
5 m to the E. This stone, known as the Sabot

de Margot, has been split by lightning.

The E of the passage is blocked by a
triangular stone and from it the orthostats of
local diorite decrease in height towards the W,
fourteen on the north side, twelve on the
south, all of them overlain by fallen capstones
with only two in position at the E. Another lies
by the side of the tomb.

The chamber was re-occupied in historical
times by a wealthy Gallo-Roman who paved
the central chamber with bricks, gaining
access to his shelter through a broken
capstone. Under the brick flooring were La
Tène artefacts of the Iron Age.

4 km SE is the allée-couverte of LA ROCHE-CAMIO (24a).

9 **Crech-Quillé**, St Quay-Perros. *Allée-couverte*
32 km NW of Guingamp, 4 km N of Lannion.
From Lannion take the D788 N for 4 km to lane
on the E (R) to Crech-Quillé. Tomb is to E of
D788, 250 m beyond the lane, 150 m into a
gently sloping field.
Excavated in 1963–4, this is an important and
well-preserved allée-couverte whose
architecture, artefacts and art merit
description. The long, almost rectangular
mound, 28 × 8 m, lies almost E–W and is
edged with big kerbstones and drystone
walling. The façade at the W is especially
good. On the S side of the mound there is a
lateral entrance near the eastern end. Here a
short 3-m passage lined with two great slabs
leads past an upright threshold stone to the
chamber, 16.2 m long and 1.8 m wide, its
eastern end being shorter and lower than the
more impressive compartment to the W.
Facing the passage is a gross stone,
anthropomorphically shaped, with carvings of
two breasts in relief with a looped necklace
below them. The head of this stele is indicated
by a shallow depression. A similar stele was
discovered at Trévoux in Finistère, but the
closest analogies to the breasts and necklace of
this 'guardian goddess' slab are in the allées-couvertes of PRAJOU-MENHIR (22a) and
KERGÜNTUIL (13b), 10 km W and 7 km NW
respectively from Crech-Quillé. At Crech-Quillé several of the kerbs also seem to have
been shaped, one at the S being particularly
well smoothed.

The tomb contained many pots of Late

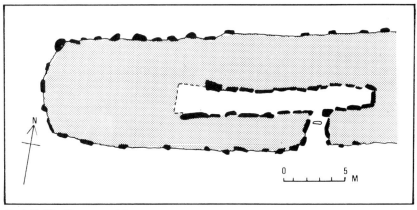

Crech-Quillé allée-couverte (9).

Neolithic Kerugou ware and of 'Pôts-des-Fleurs' of the SOM tradition. Also found were polished axes of flint and dolerite and three black schist pendants. Charcoal from the passage-blocking gave a date of 1790±200 bc, implying that the mound was finally closed around 2200 BC.

A deposit of five whole pots and some pendants in a tiny cist in the passage seemed to be an offering not to the dead but to the 'goddess' facing them only a few metres away.

10   Glomel, Rostrenen. *Menhir*
42 km SSW of Guingamp, 6 km WSW of Rostrenen. From Glomel church take the minor road directly to the E. 1 km from Glomel and 150 m beyond lane to N (L) the menhir is about 80 m NE (L) of the road after a steep rise and only just visible above the steep slope down to the SW and the Coroncq reservoir.
The stone stands against the skyline like a huge granite thumb thrusting out of the bracken and gorse around it. It is one of the tallest of this shape, being a full 8.5 m high. It is thickly elliptical, the circumference of its base being over 11 m. Its broader SW and NE sides measure some 3.5 m against the 1.5 m of the NW and SE edges. From the menhir there are splendid views to the S and SW and it is interesting that its broad SW face looks towards the hills around Minez-Du, 5 km away at the northern end of the Montagnes-Noires, about which there are many legends.

11   Île Grande, Trébeurden. *Allée-couverte*
11 km NW of Lannion. From Prajou-Menhir (22a) continue NW along the Rue de l'Île Grande for ¾ km to junction of several roads. Turn E (R) onto Rue de Roi Arthur. In 150 m turn N (L) onto Rue de Dolmen. Tomb is 250 m immediately on W (L) of road.
The mound of this fine allée-couverte is still just visible. The megalithic chamber is 9 × 1.5 m in plan but less than 1 m high. Two long capstones of local granite cover it. Outside the main uprights can be seen the remains of lower lateral stones which once supported the covering mound.

The allée-couverte of PRAJOU-MENHIR (22a) is 1 km to the SSE.

Kerbénés. *Menhir* (*see* 30a ST SERVAIS)

12   Kerbors (Men-ar-Romped), Tréguier.
Allée-couverte
31 km N of Guingamp, 24 km NE of Lannion, 7½ km NNE of Tréguier. From Kerbors take the minor road NW of the church and go N for 1.6 km to l'Île à Poule. On the NE side of the estuary walk NE (R) along track for 300 m. Tomb is on N side of a little field.
Standing as it does on the coast overlooking the estuary of the River Jaudy this allée-couverte commands splendid views across the sea. 7.5 m long it faces ENE, its thick granite sideslabs supporting three even thicker capstones. There is a transverse slab at the

entrance and, inside, the chamber is paved beyond the sillstone of the vestibule. Finds from the excavation were almost exclusively Chalcolithic, there being in particular some fine maritime beakers and a long bracer or archer's wristguard. The tomb is sometimes known as Men-ar-Romped.

Kergeuzennec. *Menhir* (see 19c PÉDERNEC)

13a Kergüntuil, Trégastel. *Dolmen*
39 km NW of Guingamp, 10 km NNW of Lannion. From Lannion take the D788 N and in 2 km turn W (L) onto D11. In 8 km at crossroads to Trégastel on E (R) turn W. Follow lane for 1¼ km to Kergüntuil farm. Turn N (R). Dolmen is 150 m on E (R) of lane.
The tomb is aligned ESE–WNW and has a rectangular chamber surmounted by a huge capstone, 5 × 2.5 m and 50 cm thick. Of the chamber only three orthostats survive, with modern drystone walling helping to support the capstone. There is a wide gap at the N.
13b Allée-couverte. *From the dolmen walk S along the lane to the footpath alongside the farm. Tomb is 200 m to E in the hedgerow.* This splendid allée-couverte, 9 m long and 1.5 m wide, has lost the sidestones of its lateral entrance which was probably at the far SE corner. This area is now obstructed by the hedge, but access was possibly over a low slab. The rectangular chamber is aligned ENE–WSW with seven granite stones on the S side and six on the N, with one apparently missing at the NW where the gap now permits access from the footpath. If this were the original entrance then it was quite different from all other allées-couvertes with lateral entrances.

Four great capstones cover this well-preserved monument in which the chamber is rather higher at the W. On two slabs to the NE of this modern entrance eight breasts in four pairs have been fashioned in low relief in a horizontal line. Each pair has a lightly engraved collar or necklace below it (see 9, 22a, 112). Such art is rare in allées-couvertes and is confined to northern Brittany, its inspiration possibly deriving from the SOM culture of the Paris Basin.

Two Late Neolithic collared flasks were discovered in the tomb and sherds of round- and flat-bottomed ware of the local Crech-Quillé/Le Mélus style. Grand Pressigny flint

knives indicate SOM influence as the art itself suggests.

14 Kerivalan, Plélauff. *Allée-couverte*
10 km E of Rostrenen, 44 km SW of St Brieuc. From Plélauff take the road E through Kerflech for 2½ km to the D5. Turn N (L) and in 1¾ km turn W (L) to Kerivalan hamlet in 400 m.
This badly damaged allée-couverte was excavated in 1974 and produced the latest dates yet known from a Breton chambered tomb. Oriented E–W the paved chamber was 9 m long and 2 m wide. The capstones had gone. There was no end cell but at the SE corner a tiny vestibule had a lateral entrance. Access to the chamber from it was through a semi-circular aperture cut out of the bottoms of two transverse slabs. The opening had been closed with two small schist blocks. Sherds of Crech-Quillé/Le Mélus 'flower-pots', beakers, a Grand Pressigny dagger and four dolerite axes were found. Charcoal provided assays of 1730±110 bc and 1690±110 bc, averaging about 2100 BC at the very end of the megalithic grave tradition.

Kerpinson. *Menhir* (see 30b ST SERVAIS)

Keryvon. *Chambered tomb* (see 22b PRAJOU-MENHIR)

15 Liscuis, Laniscat. *Allées-couvertes*
28 km WNW of Loudéac, 15 km E of Rostrenen. From Gouarec take the D76 N and E for 3 km and turn SE (R) opposite lane N to Restirou. Follow the country road SE for 1½ km and turn W (R). In 200 m a wooded track to S is barred to cars. Signposted 'Sentier Piétonnier, interdit à tous véhicules'. Follow the hollow way 400 m to crest of hill where well-defined paths cross. At signpost turn W (R). The first allée-couverte is 100 m along footpath.
This important and spectacular complex of three allées-couvertes on a hillside overlooking long views across the Gorge du Daoulas has been known since 1884. The tombs are only 6 km SW of the SÉLÉDIN axe-factory (31), whose dolerite products were being

(Above) Kergüntuil allée-couverte (13b), from the WNW and (below) interior from the SW showing carvings of 'breasts'.

manufactured between 4000 and 2700 BC. All three lie on the Liscuis heath and were excavated between 1973 and 1975.

15a Liscuis II. This is a classical allée-couverte in a conspicuous mound, 15 × 8 m, with a core of large schist blocks. Within it a sinuous arrangement of thin slabs twists from a vestibule at the NNE through a rectangular chamber to a terminal cell at the SSW. The vestibule, 2.5 m long, faces NE. Access to the chamber was through a cramped, triangular space at the bottom edge of a transverse slab. The chamber had one capstone in place and was paved with overlapping schist slabs laid side by side on a bedding of tiny sandstone blocks. Beyond the chamber is the open terminal cell which, being aligned to the SSW, gives the monument a strangely serpentine shape.

Sherds of 'Pôts-des-Fleurs' vessels, akin to Kerugou ware, a fibrolite axe-pendant and four dolerite axes from an early phase at Sélédin were found during the excavations. Two C-14 assays of 2500±110 bc and 2220±110 bc, the latter for the time when the end-cell was remodelled, suggest activities in the allée-couverte around 3300–2900 BC, late in the Neolithic.

15b Liscuis I. *Follow the footpath WNW for 200 m to the crest of the hill.* This elegant allée-couverte in a prominent situation may be the earliest of the three tombs here. It is slightly V-shaped, perhaps indicating an intermediate position between the V-shaped passage-grave of the Middle Neolithic and the rectangular allée-couverte at the end of that period.

Its symmetrical thin slabs stand in an oval mound, 11.5 × 8 m, with a good stretch of kerbing still standing on the N side. One kerb has 'shoulders', apparently deliberately shaped as an anthropomorph.

A vestibule at the SSW, 1 m high but only 80 cm wide, leads to the chamber through a tiny triangular space in a transverse slab. The chamber itself is rectangular, 9.5 × 1.8 × 1.8 m high and still covered with three big capstones. It was paved. Beyond it is a well-preserved terminal cell 1.7 m wide and 1.5 m long.

Coarse Kerugou sherds were discovered in this neatly-built tomb, but these appear to have been brought in when the allée-couverte was already old, for a C-14 assay from charcoal in the chamber produced a date of 3190±110 bc which implies an early construction around 3950 BC at a time when the dolerite outcrops were first being exploited at the nearby SÉLÉDIN axe-factory (31).

15c Liscuis III. *500 m SE and downhill from Liscuis I & II.* At the ESE of the oval mound, 15.5 × 10 m, is a delicately straight façade, 6.5 m long, of six upright schist slabs, a setting unparalleled elsewhere in Brittany. At its centre an entrance only 30 cm wide gives access to a triangular vestibule widening to 1.2 m where a small aperture cut in the bottom

Liscuis I (15b), terminal cell of the allée-couverte from the ENE.

of a transverse slab leads to the chamber. This, 7.5 × 1.7 m wide, has one surviving capstone. Two dates of 2250±110 bc and 1730±110 bc indicate that this allée-couvature was in use around 2900 to 2150 BC.

The importance of the Liscuis region in prehistoric times can be judged from the fact that a circle 16 km in radius from Gouarec would encompass nearly thirty menhirs, the SÉLÉDIN axe-factory (31), allées-couvertes at the Bois de Gouarec 1¾ km SSE, at Gouarec 3½ km WSW, at Rohanno 9 km NE where there are also standing stones (17d), at BOD-ER-MOHED (3a) 7 km to the SW, KERIVOËLAN (14) 4 km W of Liscuis, and COËT-CORREC (7) 9 km to the E. Many more sites will have been destroyed on the low-lying agricultural land between Plouguérnevel and St Nicholas-du-Pélem. (*See* 17 MUR-DE-BRETAGNE.)

16 Mélus, Le, Ploubazlanec. *Allée-couverte 30 km ENE of Lannion, 28 km N of Guingamp. From Paimpoul take the D789 N for 1 km, turn NW (L) onto D15. In 3 km turn W (L) for 200 m to T-junction. Turn N (R). Allée-couverte is 200 m on W of road.*
Excavated in 1933 this lateral-entranced allée-couverte is interesting for the simplification of its entrance. Here the usual portal slabs at right-angles to the chamber have been replaced by two small stones on either side of the lintelled entrance. Inside is a rectangular chamber, 13.5 × 1.4 m, oriented E–W. Seven capstones remain on the sideslabs, some of which lean inwards. During the excavations coarse, flat-based collared flasks were found, many footed bowls of Kerugou style, a large 'Pôt-de-Fleur', four dolerite axes, a flint axe, flints including a Grand Pressigny knife and a grinder, all indicating eastern SOM influence at the end of the Neolithic. The pottery, with its localized traits, became known as Crech-Quillé/Le Mélus ware.

Men-ar-Romped. *Allée-couverte (see* 12 KERBORS)

17 Mur-de-Bretagne. *Megalithic centre 39 km SSW of St Brieuc and 25 km E of Rostrenen.*
This little town in the middle of one of the loveliest regions of Brittany is also the convenient place for a visit to many menhirs,

allées-couvertes and other prehistoric monuments. Map 1:50,000 orange Carte Touristique, no. 0818.
17a Modern cromlech. *From Mur take the D767 N towards Corlay. At the top of the hill on the outskirts of Mur is the Chapelle Ste Suzanne.* On the chestnut-surrounded lawn outside it is a circle of small standing stones erected in 1958.
17b La Trinité. *Menhir. Follow the same road N as 17a for 4 km then turn W (L) opposite the sign to the Vallée de la Poulancre. 300 m down the lane in the angle between minor roads is a fine menhir of schist about 3 m long. It fell* about 1958 and is now difficult to locate in the brambles.
17c *Return to the D767 and continue N. 6 km N of Mur come to the hamlet of* **St Mayeux.** *On* the Roch al Lein are three menhirs.
17d *Also on the D767, 2 km farther N, at the village of* **La Rohanno,** *are two more standing* stones at the foot of the steep hill and on the W (L) of the road. One is called the Menhir du Minhas (of the Cat) and is 3 m high. The other is at the edge of the wood and is surrounded by gorse. Nearby is the allée-couverte of Rohanno.
17e Le Botrain. *Menhir. From Mur-de-Bretagne take the N164 E and in 1½ km veer NE (R) onto the D35. In 1½ km turn SE (R) towards the farm of Le Botrain in 300 m. The menhir is 100 m SE of the farm. This* rectangular stone, commanding fine views, tapers to a pointed top 3.5 m above the ground. It leans slightly. There used to be a second standing stone nearby, but it fell in the last century and was buried.
Also in the vicinity of Mur-de-Bretagne is the site of the SÉLÉDIN axe-factory (31) at Plussulien, the splendid allée-couverte of COËT-CORREC (7) 3½ km NW of Mur, and the three magnificent allée-couvertes of LISCUIS (15) 13 km to the W.

Museum, Trégastel-Plage (*see* 35 TRÉBEURDEN)

18 Notre-Dame-de-Lorette, Le Quillio. *Allée-couverte 13 km WNW of Loudéac, 33 km E of Rostrenen. From Le Quillio take the D35 SW and after 1 km turn NW (R) towards Le Rohello. In 1 km turn SW (L) up to hilltop and heath. Stones are by the*

chapel of Notre-Dame-de-Lorette.
At first sight this looks like two parallel lines of standing stones near the N wall of a chapel built in 1854. It is, in reality, the remnant of a denuded allée-couverte oriented E–W and measuring 20 × 7 m. The stones lean outwards. The S line, nearer the chapel, has eighteen tall schist pillars in it. The N line has twelve lower stones of quartz. The mound that once covered them has gone.

At either end of this rectangle are slabs at right-angles to the lines. Three metres to the W and on the major axis is a 2-m-high menhir. Elsewhere in Brittany in tertres tumulaires the western end of the internal rectangular structure is broken and the gap is occupied by a similar menhir. This feature, noticed in at least three tertres without a chamber, reveals the close association between such monuments and allées-couvertes with lateral entrances. These are often found near an earlier tertre, good examples existing at LE FOUR-SARRAZIN, IV (110j) and KERLESCAN, CA (180e).

Although Le Four-Sarrazin is a full 90 km SE of Notre-Dame-de-Lorette it can hardly be coincidence that it lies near the TERTRE DE CROIX-ST-PIERRE, IV (110h–i). Like Notre-Dame this long mound also contained parallel lines of quartz and schist stones and, significantly, when considering the purpose of stone rows in Brittany it is noteworthy that close to the Tertre de Croix-St-Pierre at the ALIGNEMENTS DU MOULIN, IV (110d) the two rows of freestanding stones were also composed of quartz and schist.

Excavation at Notre-Dame discovered artefacts only at the eastern end in the probable area of burials. There were five pieces of quartz including two blades, three triangular arrowheads, and some undistinguished sherds.

Parc ar Men Sul. *Menhir (see* 30e ST SERVAIS)

19a   Pédernec, Bégard. *Menhir*
12 km WNW of Guingamp and 18 km SE of Lannion. From Bégard take the D15 S. In 2½ km, just past a road on the E (L) to Guénézan, there is a farm track on the E signposted 'Menhir de Crech-goul'. Do not take it. Instead, take the next farm track 100 m farther on. This is not suitable for cars. Menhir is 600 m

walk in field to the N of a wood.
The Pédernec stone, which is actually 2½ km NW of that village, is a fine domed 'thumb' of granite, 8.5 m high, with an elliptical base measuring 3 × 1.5 m. It is the biggest of these domed menhirs, GLOMEL (10) being slightly taller but not as broad.

19b   Cromlech. In 1837 it was reported that there was a large enclosure to one side of the menhir and, just north of the stone, a cromlech of twelve slabs in a U-shaped setting with seven more across the diameter of the semi-circle. Today there are no signs of this complex, only a few large, flat stones lying on the ground in the field where the menhir stands.

19c   Kergeuzennec *menhir. From Bégard, 4 km NW of Pédernec, take the D15 NE towards Brélidy. After 2 km, beyond hamlet of l'Enseigne, turn S (R). In 1½ km menhir is visible on E (L).* This towering pillar is one of the tallest standing stones in Brittany. It is 10 m high, very thick, and measures almost 3 m around its base. It tapers to a pointed top. It is a fine white stone like that at PERGAL (20).

20   Pergal, Louargat. *Menhirs*
15 km W of Guingamp, 20 km SSE of Lannion. This site is hard to find. From Louargat take the D31 N towards St Eloi. In 1¾ km, 100 m before a lane to the E (R) signposted 'Pergal' and 'Kerespez' there is an unobtrusive footpath in the woods on the E (R) where the road descends into a hollow. This path leads through marshy woodland for 200 m to stones in an open meadow. Described as a 'charming and very pretty little dale'. It is.
The main Pergal menhir is one of the tallest standing stones in Brittany, perhaps third after KERLOAS, F (67a), and CAILLOUAN (4).

Standing at the SW end of a short row of three menhirs, one fallen, it rises 10 m above the ground, an impressively white pillar with a triangular base whose W side is 2 m wide. It has been erected at right-angles to the row on an axis of about 96°–276°.

2 m to its NE a prostrate stone, 6 m long and 1 m wide, lies in the grass, NE–SW, just off the line of the row. 11 m NNE of the tall menhir is a lower stone, 2 m in height. It has been suggested that this short alignment, like others in Brittany, may have been intended to

act as an egress marker from the valley, pointing towards the River Léguer.

A heavy, very round stone found near here, weighing 10 kilos (22 lbs), was used in a contest between peasants who threw it from one to the other, participants being disqualified if they dropped it or allowed it to touch the ground. The winner was thought to be guaranteed a good harvest that year.

3 km to the SE is the great tumulus of Pen an Stang.

21 Plaine-Haute, Quintin. *Menhir*

8 km SSW of St Brieuc, 25 km ESE of Guingamp. From Quintin take the D790 NE towards St Brieuc. 4 km N of the junction with the N168 take W (L) lane to La Saudraie. After 900 m, at the foot of a steep hill, take the lane to the E (R). Menhir is visible from it to the S. This is a heavy block of granite, 5.5 m tall, standing on a NE–SW axis, its broader faces, 3 m wide, to the NW and SE. It is about 1 m thick. All around it the land rises except to the N, where it falls at first only to rise again in the distance.

22a Prajou-Menhir, Trébeurden. *Allée-couverte*

10 km NW of Lannion, 3 km NW of Trébeurden. From Trébeurden centre take the Rue de Kerariou N for 2 km to D788. Turn E (R) for 1 km and at the D21 turn NW (L) onto Rue de l'Île Grande. Allée-couverte is 500 m on W (L) of road, 600 m down footpath. Signposted 'Allée-couverte, Prat-ar Min-Hir'. This splendidly restored tomb, now surrounded by bushes and bracken, was excavated in 1965. It is aligned ESE–WNW, and is higher at the E where an entrance only 80 cm wide leads into a short triangular vestibule which in turn leads into the rectangular chamber, 9.5 × 2.4 m wide and 1.5 m high. It is lined with slabs of local granite and capped with seven heavy slabs. The W end is blocked by a thick transverse stone beyond which there is a terminal cell, unusual both because it is triangular, narrowing to a 60-cm-wide gap at its W, and also because it is covered with a capstone.

It is possible to squeeze between this and a sideslab at the S to inspect the art for which this site is famous. In the end cell four stones are decorated. The W face of the blocking slab

Prajou-Menhir (22a), 'breasts' inside a cartouche in the terminal cell.

has two square 'figurines' juxtaposed against an inverted 'Cypriot' copper dagger which, lacking the characteristically hooked tang of such weapons from Cyprus, is just as likely to have been a native Breton spearhead. Another 'dagger' is half visible on the right of the rectangles which have miniature cupmarks dotted along their interiors. Similar 'daggers' can be seen at the allée-couverte of MOUGAU-BIHAN, F (82), 47 km to the SSW.

At Prajou-Menhir the sideslab to the left of the blocking slab has another 'dagger' and to its left there is a pair of breasts with a necklace below them. The slab to its left has another figurine which measures 42 cm along its sides. It has a strange bent 'arm' on its upper concave side. To the S the first sideslab has two pairs of breasts in relief inside a small cartouche. In both pairs the two to the left are smaller. Similar breasts can be seen not only at KERGÜNTUIL (13a), only 4 km NE of Prajou-Menhir, but also at TRESSÉ, IV (112), no less than 110 km to the ESE.

In the excavations some collared flasks related to SOM pots and some local Crech-Quillé/Le Mélus sherds were found with flints, polished stones and pebbles, all material which belongs to the Late Neolithic period.

22b Keryvon. *Returning to the mainland at the junction with the D788 turn NE (L). Tomb is 1 km on the W (L) of the road.* Here there are the sidestones and capstones of an unimpressive chambered tomb.

ÎLE GRANDE allée-couverte (11) is 1 km NNW of Prajou-Menhir.

Quintin (23), menhir from the E.

23   Quintin. *Menhir*

18 km SW of St Brieuc, 28 km NNW of Loudéac. Menhir is near the D790 on the SE outskirts of Quintin on the S side of the valley by a small lake. A road at the NE corner of the lake leads 400 m to the stone on the S side of the road. A short footpath leads to it.

This is a beautifully tall and slender pillar like an elegant granite shuttle perched on its pointed end with a single skein of extruded quartz twisted loosely around it. The stone is a full 7 m high, almost rectangular at its base, thickening around its middle and rising to a pointed tip. At its broadest it measures about 2 m wide on the NW and SE, 1 m on its narrower sides. Its orientation would appear to be towards the SE.

24a   Roche-Camio, La, Plédran. *Allée-couverte*

31 km N of Loudéac, 6 km S of St Brieuc. From Plédran take the D27 N for 1½ km and turn W (L) to La Roche-Camio hamlet. Take N (R) farm road to Cadio farm. Tomb is 200 m S of farm at the head of a slope.

Standing on a low rise with oaks growing around it this allée-couverte is composed of striking slabs of black shale. The encircling mound is still apparent and, inside it, the rectangular chamber, 15.5 m long and 1.3 m wide, is aligned ESE–WNW. It is blocked at the W end but at the E is a terminal cell, open to the E and to the sky, 2.7 m long and 2 m wide. Seven capstones remain in position over the main chamber.

10 m from the W end and on the S side is a short lateral passage, 3 m long, made of two sideslabs that provide a low and narrow entrance to the tomb.

24b   2½ km to the ENE is another allée-couverte at Romain. (*See also* 6, 8.)

Rohanno, Le. *Menhirs* (*see* 17d MUR-DE-BRETAGNE)

25   Rossit, St Nicholas-de-Pélem. *Menhir*

25 km S of Guingamp, 35 km SW of St Brieuc. From St Nicholas take the D5 N and in 1 km, about 500 m before Bothoa, take a lane to the E (R). Just after a little bridge follow a footpath uphill to the SE (R). Menhir is in a small wood two-thirds up a slope to the NW.

Sometimes known as the Menhir of Locqueltas this is a massive stone, rounded at its base where it is about 2 m thick, and with flat E and W faces that taper to a curved top. The menhir is 4.5 m high. It is rumoured that it is the petrified remains of a careless cowherd who was turned to stone, a fate suffered also by his beasts who lie around him.

26   St Duzec, Penvern. *Menhir*

9 km NW of Lannion, 3 km NNE of Trébeurden. From Penvern take the D21 E towards Pleumeur-Bodou. In 500 m turn N (L). Stone is 500 m along forest road on its W (L). There is a lay-by.

This Christianized menhir is one of the marvels of prehistoric Brittany. It stands some 8.1 m high and on its S face are some magnificent carvings. They were executed in

St Duzec (26), Christianized menhir from the S.

1674 when a chapel was built 500 m away near Penvern hamlet.

The stone was erected on a slope which rises behind it but which falls away to the S. The broad, flat face of the menhir looks towards this direction. It is of smooth granite, slightly bowed in shape and of 'playing-card' type with its long axis ENE–WSW. It is now enclosed in a low, walled rectangle.

The menhir is surmounted by a cross with an image of the crucifixion on it. The upper part of the stone has several carvings in low relief. At the top there is a cock representing the denial of St Peter. The Virgin Mary is immediately below between a sun with twelve rays to her left and the moon on her right. Both have human faces. Underneath there are several instruments of the Passion, the veil of St Véronique and, below them, a large cross bearing the crucified Christ.

St Mayeux. *Menhirs* (*see* 17c MUR-DE-BRETAGNE)

27 St Mirel, Plenée-Jugon. ***Menhirs***
28 km SE of St Brieuc, 31 km WSW of Dinan. From Plenée-Jugon take the D792 SW for 4½ km to St Mirel. A tree-lined walk on S (L) of road leads to a chapel on the hill.
In the hamlet close to the chapel dedicated to St Mirel are two menhirs with the chapel between them, it having been built there to Christianize the site. At the junction of the avenue with another path there is a meadow at the bottom of which there is a standing stone. It is 3.5 m high, almost square, its sides measuring 2 × 1.5 m and rising to a pointed top. 50 m to its S and about 200 m W of the chapel is a natural stone, 1.5 m high and roughly 3 × 1.5 m in plan. Its top appears to have been artificially hollowed to hold water.

In a field near the top of the hill and to the N of the chapel are five or six weirdly shaped rocks, and 200 m to their SE is the second menhir. It is 4 m high and rectangular, 2 × 2 m, with a flat top.

28 St Samson, Penvern. ***Menhir***
8 km NNW of Lannion, 3 km NNW Pleumeur-Bodou. From Penvern take the N786, the Corniche Côte du Granit, northwards. After 1½ km take E (R) lane through Keralies. Stone is 2½ km farther on on S (R) of lane alongside a chapel. Reached by a footpath 100 m from the attractive, wooded lane.
This unimpressive little stone, no more than 2 m high, stands on the W side of a chapel built between 1575 and 1631 and dedicated to St Samson. The menhir was reputed to cure illnesses if rubbed against. Alternatively, a piece of the stone could be dropped into a potion and drunk. The worn-down side of the stone testifies to the popularity of this practice.

29 St Samson-sur-Rance, La Tremblais. ***Menhir***
18 km S of St Malo, 5 km NNE of Dinan. From Dinan take the D766 N for 4 km, turn E (R) onto the D57 through St Samson. 1½ km beyond the

village, stone is on N side of the lane by a track almost opposite the turn to La Quinardais. The stone is clearly visible at the W edge of a little wood.

This is a fine granite menhir, over 6 m long and leaning considerably towards the E. Its rectangular base is about 2 m square and from it the pillar narrows gently to a rounded top. Like DOL, IV (101), 25 km to the E, the stone has been smoothed with mauls, perhaps to give it some protection from the effects of weathering.

It is remarkable for the engravings on it. Not noticed until 1972 they can only be made out, with some difficulty, on a sunny morning between about 1100 and 1200. On the upper western face there is a series of horizontal bands, five or more, consisting of lightly-pecked juxtaposed rectangular figures, some with internal cupmarks. In this they resemble the art on the allée-couverte of PRAJOU-MENHIR (22a).

At one time young people would slide down the stone in the expectation that if they did not fall off they would marry within the year. The thin vein of quartz running diagonally across the face of the menhir was believed to be the whip or the chain of the Devil.

St Samson-sur-Rance (29), decorated menhir from the W.

30   St Servais, Callac. *Megalithic centre 18 km NE of Carhaix-Plougeur, 25 km SSW of Guingamp.*

St Servais was a saint whose cult was once so powerful that women would walk barefoot from up to 60 km away to worship in his church on the day of his Pardon. This custom has long been abandoned and today the tiny village is most attractive for the number of megalithic remains around it. For these a useful map is the 1:50,000 orange Carte Touristique, no. 0717. St Servais itself lacks hotels. There is the Auberge du Moulin at Callac 3½ km NW and there are hotels in Carhaix-Plougeur 18 km SW.

30a   Kerbénés. *From St Servais church take the minor road S towards St Nicodéme. 1 km S of the church Kerbénés farm is on the E (L) of the road. Menhir is 200 m W of the farm.* This is a tall stone, 6.5 m high, its sides measuring 2 × 1.6 × 1.5 × 1 m. Its narrower W and E edges taper to a point but the broader N and S sides are vertical and terminate in a flat top.

30b   Kerpinson. On this farm, ½ km closer to St Servais, there is a smaller stone, 2.5 m high and 1.2 × 0.5 m in plan.

30c   Bois de Kerbénés. In the forest to the east of St Servais there are several menhirs, difficult to find amongst the trees. One stands at the summit of the wooded hill 1·km SE of the village.

30d   Chaire des Druides. *From Mael-Pestivien, a hamlet 6½ km E of St Servais, take the minor road ESE for 1 km and turn S (R) for 200 m to the farm of Kerohou.* The farm lies at the NW foot of a steep-sided knoll about 15 m high and some 150 m across. It is covered in trees and scattered with scores of rocks. Two of these, at the northern edge of the summit, are known as the Druids' Chair and it is said that a cavity has been carved into them to receive burials. They lie together on an E–W alignment, 0.8 m high.

30e   Parc ar Men Sul. At Kerroch, 1½ km N of Servais there is a menhir in the Parc ar Men Sul or 'Field of the Sun'. It is said to dance at midnight on Christmas Day and St Jean's Day, the days of the midwinter and midsummer solstices.

31   Sélédin, Plussulien. *Axe-factory 36 km SW of St Brieuc, 19 km ENE of Rostrenen.*

The most important site in Brittany for the production of stone axes existed on the N flank of the Laniscat-Merléac hills 3 km S of Plussulien. It covered nearly 100 ha on the summit and SW slope of Roch Pol hill 1 km N of Sélédin. From this area of fine dolerite came some 40 per cent of all the axes in Brittany. The products were traded into Normandy and as far away as 400 km from their source. The exploitation of the stone, at first of rock taken from natural outcrops, started around 4000 BC. Later the dolerite was mined from pits and, finally, a technique for quarrying by the use of fire was developed. As many as 5,000 axes yearly may have been manufactured at Sélédin which was ultimately abandoned around 2700 BC when the use of metal was becoming widespread.

32　Sept-Saints, La Chapelle, Plouret. *Allée-couverte*

21 km WNW of Guingamp, 11 km SSE of Lannion, 4½ km NE of Plouaret. From Plouaret take the D11 N. In 1 km turn E (R) and drive 4 winding km to the quiet village of Sept-Saints. The church is on the E of the road. It covers the remains of an allée-couverte.

Without doubt this is one of the megalithic curiosities of Brittany. From the front of the church a few steps on the right where the S transept stands lead down to an open entrance and the great stones of a chambered tomb.

The church was erected between 1702 and 1714, perhaps on the site of an earlier Christian building. It is in the form of a simple Latin cross with the tomb hidden beneath its right arm, Christianized not only by its incorporation into the church but also by the addition of seven crudely-carved statuettes placed on a niche at its eastern end. The former size of this truncated allée-couverte is not known. Today it is about 4.9 m long, 2 m high and 1.5 m wide, roofed by two capstones of which the easternmost is a massive granite slab. The alignment is approximately E–W.

The tomb is barred a third of the way along by a wooden grill. Through it one can make out the seven figures which, it is said, were found in the earth floor of the tomb when it was first explored centuries ago. The names inscribed on their bases are Constantin, Jean, Denis, Marc, Serafein, Maximilien and Martineau.

One tradition states that the effigies were representations of the Seven Sleepers of Ephesus, a group of Christians whom, in AD 252, the Roman emperor Decius ordered to be walled up in a cave for refusing to worship idols. Two hundred years later their tomb was unblocked and they were found sleeping and in perfect health. A Breton legend claims that they were later buried at Sept-Saints.

The significance of the number 7 is unclear. There was an ancient belief, possibly pre-Celtic, that its use bestowed the power to foresee the future as many Irish myths about the hero Cochabar demonstrate. The origin of the seven Sept-Saints figurines, however, is unknown and the reason for their presence in this sanctified prehistoric tomb is equally forgotten.

Outside Brittany other megalithic chambers integrated in or beneath chapels are known in Guernsey at St Michel and La Hogue Bie, in Spain at Santa Cruz de la Victoria, Oviedo, and in Portugal at Alcobertas and Pavia.

There is a Breton legend that the allée-couverte at Sept-Saints dates from the beginning of the world.

Tertre de l'Église, Le. *Allée-couverte* (*see* 1b AIGUILLE DE GARGANTUA)

33　Tossen-ar-Run, Paimpoul. *Passage-grave*

30 km NW of St Brieuc, 20 km NE of Guingamp. 7½ km S of Paimpoul. From Paimpoul take the D7 S. Tumulus is in NW angle of the crossroads W to Quemper-Guennec.

Only the round barrow, 42 m in diameter and 5 m high, is visible. It covered a circular cairn 25 m across and 3 m high which in turn concealed a little passage-grave. A 4-m-long passage, facing SE, led to an exactly circular chamber, 3.5 m wide, drystone-walled and with a corbelled roof 2.7 m high. It may have been capped with a flat stone. An extended burial, on its back, lay at the E. Near it was a split pebble, grooved for shaping arrowshafts, flints, some small fragments of Middle Neolithic ware and some coarse sherds of SOM type.

34　Tossen-Keler, Penvenan. *Cromlech?*

30 km NNW of Guingamp, 15 km NE of Lannion.

Although nothing can be seen today recent excavations at Tossen-Keler near Penvenan uncovered an intriguing monument. Surrounding a 10-m-high and 50-m-long tertre which concealed two ritual hearths, one of which was dated to 2550 ± 260 BC (*c.* 3300 BC), there were fifty-eight small and irregular blocks, mostly of granite. They were arranged in a horseshoe open exactly to the E, the long axis measuring 29 m. Three of the blocks bore carvings, one of a hafted axe in relief like those at the allées-couvertes of MOUGAU-BIHAN, F (82), and KERALLAN, M (159e), and another had an anthropomorphic 'figurine' on it. The third stone, a long and straight little pillar, had a pattern of chevrons. It is possible that Tossen-Keler was a three-phase monument, the tertre and foyers being Late Neolithic additions to a freestanding cromlech like the enormous 'horseshoes' of Morbihan. The carved stones were probably re-used slabs from a nearby dismantled allée-couverte. Two of them were inverted and the third, with its chevrons, was standing at right-angles to its expected position which suggested that the stones had been moved.

35 Trébeurden, Lannion. *Megalithic centre*

38 km WNW of Guingamp and 8½ km WNW of Lannion, on the Côte de Granit Rose.
This pleasant seaside resort, with a Syndicat d'Initiatif from which local maps can be obtained, is conveniently placed for a day's visit to many interesting sites in the order listed below. Helpful maps are the 1:50,000 orange Carte Touristique, nos. 0714, 0715.

3½ km to the N of Trébeurden is Île Grande with the allées-couvertes of PRAJOU-MENHIR (22a), and ÎLE GRANDE (11). From there one should go to the Christianized menhirs of ST DUZEC (26) 3½ km to the NE and ST SAMSON (28). The fine allée-couverte and nearby dolmen of KERGÜNTUIL (13) are 6½ km NNE of Trébeurden.

Other sites in the vicinity are the Iron Age stele with Le Tène curvilinear patterns carved on it at Ste Anne, Trégastel-Plage, 7½ km NNE. Beyond it, on the Île Renote, is a ruined allée-couverte. On Coz-Pors beach, Trégastel-Plage, a cave has been converted into a museum with some prehistoric objects on display. There is also an aquarium. It is open throughout the summer, 0900–2100 in July and August, and 1400–1830 in June and September. From 15 March to 31 May it is open at weekends and holidays. Admission, 8 Fr.

Finally, one should go to the fine allée-couverte of CRECH-QUILLÉ (9) 9 km E of Trébeurden.

36 Trégomar, Lamballe. *Menhir*

27 km W of Dinan, 25 km ESE of St Brieuc.
From Lamballe take the D28 E to La Poterie and then the D52a ESE to Trégomar 6 km from Lamballe. Before the church turn N (L) and immediately E (R) to Le Clos Perrine 500 m away. Turn N (L) and in 500 m at a T-junction turn E (R). The menhir is 400 m along the lane on the E (R), its top visible in a field.
Known as La Roche de Guihalon and at a wood of the same name, this is a fine dark stone. On the way to it the visitor will pass two fallen stones 50 m from the edge of the wood where, just above a cluster of brambles, the top of a 2.5-m-high menhir can be seen. 30 m farther on there is another 2-m-high stone. Following a footpath SE around the brambles one will come to the large menhir, leaning slightly to its W, a thin granite slab, 5 m tall and measuring about 2 × 1 m at its base.

There is a tradition that this was a stone being carried on the head of the fairy Margot. Angry when she dropped a lot of smaller stones by accident from her apron she threw the big pillar onto the heath of Gast where it now stands. The story is similar to many in Ireland and Wales in which an elderly hag also dropped stones from her apron. Falling to earth they formed massive cairns like those at the passage-grave cemetery of Loughcrew in Co. Meath, the chambered tomb of Barclodiad y Gawres (the apron of the giantess) on Anglesey, and many others.

Trinité, La. *Menhir (see* 17b MUR-DE-BRETAGNE)

37a Ville-Genouhan, La, Trégon. *Allée-couverte*

18 km SW of St Malo, 17 km NW of Dinan.
From Plancoët take the D768 N for 6 km to the junction with the D786. Turn W (L) towards

Matignon. Tomb is 1 km on S (L) of road, 200 m into a field.

This 9-m-long chambered tomb is in fair condition with nine stones on its NE side, many collapsed, and eight on the SW. The chamber is aligned SE–NW. A gap at the SW may indicate the original entrance. There are five large and coarse capstones tumbled over the sideslabs. A second row of orthostats, possibly to add extra revetment, have been added to one side of the chamber but not to the other.

37b   La Hautière. *1¼ km to the SE, to the E of the D768.* Here, in the cultivated fields, there is the ruin of another allée-couverte. Another, in even worse condition, with its stones in heaps, lies nearer the farm.

38   Ville-Pichard, La, Pléneuf-Val-André.
Passage-graves
36 km WNW of Dinan, 19 km NE of St Brieuc. On the coast to the N of Pléneuf at La Ville-Pichard.

Once thought to be the ruins of Gallo-Roman houses, these are the dilapidated remains of three classic passage-graves that were encapsulated in a great long mound like those of BARNENEZ, F (40), nearly 100 km to the W. Now in poor condition the three tombs had short passages, 2.5 to 4.4 m long and very straight, leading to circular chambers 3 m in diameter. All, unusually, were aligned to the SW. They are the most easterly of such early tombs on the N coast.

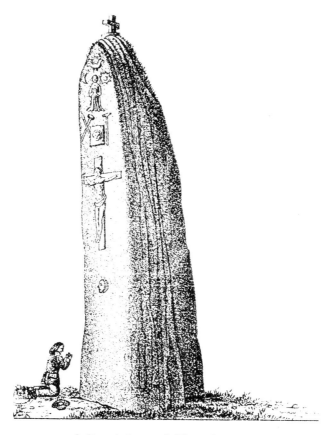

St Duzec (26), an early lithograph.

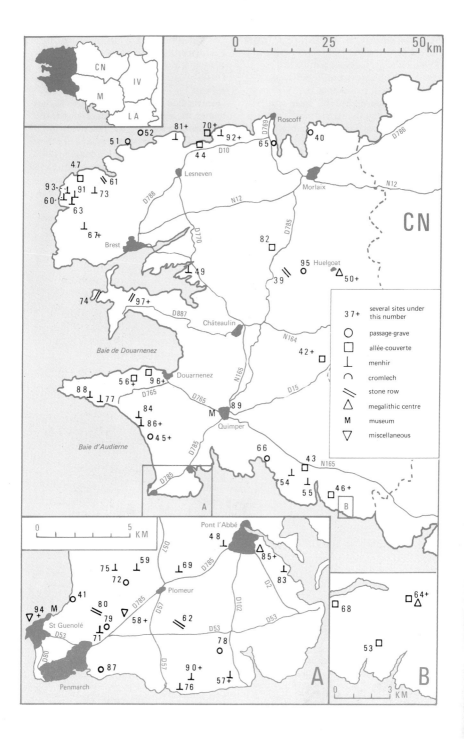

0 · 25 · 50 km

CN
IV
M
LA

Roscoff
81+ · 70+
51 ○ 52 · 92+
65 ○ · 40
44 · D10
D769
D786

47
61
93 · 91 · 73
60
63
Lesneven
67+
Brest
49
Morlaix
N12
D788
N12
D710
D785
82
95 Huelgoat
39 · 50+

several sites under
37+ this number
○ passage-grave
□ allée-couverte
⊥ menhir
⌒ cromlech
∕∕ stone row
△ megalithic centre
M museum
▽ miscellaneous

74 · 97+
D887
Châteaulin
N164
42+
Baie de Douarnenez
N165
Douarnenez
56+ · 96+
88 · 77
D765
D765
84
86+
45+
M · 89
Quimper
D15
Baie d'Audierne
D785
66
43
N165
54
55
46+
A
B

CN

Pont l'Abbé
48
85+
0 · 5 KM
D57
75 · 59
72
69
D785
83
D2
41
94+ M
St Guenolé
80
79
58+
D785
D57
Plomeur
62
D102
D53
D53
68
D53
71
D53
87
78
90+
57+
76
Penmarch
A
53
0 · 3 KM
B

Finistère

Maps: *Yellow Michelin 1:200,000, no. 58*
       Green Carte Touristique 1:100,000, nos. 13, 14

Literally 'Land's End', Finistère has similarities to the British Land's End with its profusion of standing stones and its peculiarly parochial versions of chambered tombs.

Shaped menhirs, smoothed, almost polished by the hammering with stone mauls before the pillar's erection, are a feature of West Léon at the north-west of the département where Kerloas (67a) is the tallest stone still standing in Brittany. There are many menhirs in the south also, where the granite has tended to split into a broad, domed, shieldlike shape reminiscent of the anthropomorphic figurines of the southern passage-graves.

Lines of stones are not common in Finistère. There was once a notable concentration of shortish rows on the Crozon peninsula, with its precipitous, multi-coloured cliffs, but these have mostly been pulled down and only at Lagatjar (74) in the extreme west do the stones survive impressively against the low, flat landscape. In the south even the 500 stones recorded at La Madeleine (80), near Lestriguiou, in the 19th century have now nearly all gone and it can be no more than an act of megalithic piety to visit their former site.

With chambered tombs it is different. Around the coast from Kerléven (66) at the south to Île Carn (51) and Île Guennoc (52) at the west to Barnenez (40) at the north there are fine passage-graves, often grouped together under one mighty cairn. In south Finistère on the Penmarch peninsula there is a medley of regional forms, transepted, rectangular-chambered, angled. These are best seen at the evocative Lesconil-Plobannalec (78) and at the oddly-reconstructed Run-Aour (94b).

Yet it is the allée-couverte that is the common form of tomb in Finistère, Mougau-Bihan (82) with its carvings being perhaps the finest example. Enthusiasts should go also to Ty-ar-C'horriket (96a) to see the strange arc-bouté monument with its inward-leaning sideslabs, and to Kernic (70a) – having ascertained that the tide is low – to realize how much the sea-level has risen since prehistoric times.

Finistère is rich in megaliths and no one centre is well placed for seeing all of them. The Penmarch peninsula at the south-west corner, however, contains a satisfying variety of menhirs, chambered tombs and the pleasant little museum at St Guénolé where the exhibits are not only in the two rooms but also outside in an outdoor display of menhirs, tombs and neatly-channelled Iron Age stelae. A convenient base for a tour of the sites would be Pont l'Abbé (85) with its castle and local history museum.

In the hilly countryside of central Brittany the picturesque town and scenery of Huelgoat (50) is another focus of megalithic activity.

Sites 39-97

39   An Eured Ven, St Michel Brasparts.
Stone rows
27 km SSW of Morlaix, 20 km NNE of
Châteaulin. From Brasparts take the D785 N for
5 km to Chapelle St Michel Brasparts. Rows are
on the moors to the E of Mont-St-Michel.
At the Montagne du Casque is a complicated
setting of standing stones in rows of differing
orientations that are difficult to separate. One
line of twenty stones is oriented E–W. The
complex is called An Eured Ven, the 'Stone
Wedding', because it is supposed to be the
members of a wedding party petrified because
they refused to allow a priest to go on his way.

7 km to the ENE is the passage-grave of TY-
AR-BOUDIQUET (95a), and 6 km NNW is the
allée-couverte of MOUGAU-BIHAN (82).

40   Barnenez, Plouézoch. *Passage-graves*
10 km NNW of Morlaix. From Morlaix take the
D76 N for 8 km to Plouézoch and 3 km N of the
village leave the main road, taking a minor road
to the N (L) to St Goulven and Kernéléhan and
the islet of Barnenez. Cairn is at end of small W
(L) fork at entrance to the hamlet. Fenced. Open
26 March to 30 September, 0900–1200, 1400–
1800. Closed Tuesdays and Wednesdays.
Admission 3 Fr, students 1.50 Fr, groups of
25+, 2 Fr per person. Even if cairn is closed it
can still be very adequately viewed through the
wire meshing that encloses it.
This cairn, one of the most monumental in
Brittany, is a huge pile and is like a stepped
pyramid. Its architecture is impressive, its
archaeology is informative, and although
rather disappointing to visit because most of
its internal passage-graves are closed off it
should still be seen.

The site is at the summit of a small
promontory with wide views in all directions.
The sea is close to the N but in the 5th
millennium BC, when Barnenez was erected,
the landscape was different. To the S is the
Kernéléhan Valley, to the E is a deep bay
which was dry 7,000 years ago, and to the W
and SW flows the River Morlaix, little more
than a wide stream in prehistoric times.

On this conspicuous hillock eleven passage-
graves stood in line under an enormous cairn.

About 100 m to their N there was once a
second cairn, perhaps 30 × 20 × 3 m high, but
this was demolished in 1954 by a road
contractor. Little is known about the mound
except that it contained at least one drystone-
walled chamber with a massive granite
capstone.

The surviving cairn was damaged at its NW
corner by a bulldozer in the same year and the
damage can still be seen. Rescue excavations
from 1955 onwards produced evidence of
different styles of architecture amongst the
underlying chambers and it became clear that
the cairn had been built in two phases, the
earlier to the E on level ground, an extension
being added on the W where the slope
compelled the builders to erect several inner
retaining walls which are still splendidly
preserved.

Primary cairn Aligned NE–SW and
trapezoidal in plan, 35 m long, 20 m wide at
the W and narrowing to 13 m to the E, 8 m
high, this great cairn was revetted by two
drystone walls, 2 m apart, all of it constructed
of local dolerite stones. Within it were five
small passage-graves, their entrances facing
downhill to the SE and the river. These may
have been the tombs of individual families.
They varied in plan, most of the chambers
having been corbelled, the central having a
gigantic capstone for a roof. Levelled beds of
stones had been laid down for flooring. Ultimately
several of the passages were blocked. Flanking
their entrances and surrounding the cairn was
a low, sub-rectangular drystone wall. Today
all the passages in this cairn and four of the six
in the western extension are now inaccessible.
Only passage C and D, the third and fourth
from the W, can be entered.

The passage-graves (lettered according to the
excavator's plan)

J. At the extreme NE of the cairn, facing
162°, there is a passage 5.7 m long, bending
slightly to the N and leading to a tiny circular
chamber with a corbelled roof. The underside
of the first passage capstone has a carved sub-
rectangular 'figurine' on it with wavy lines at
its top right-hand corner. This is probably a
representation of the female 'guardian-spirit'
who watched over the dead.

I. The passage of this tomb is 7.5 m long. It
faces 162° and leads to a circular, corbelled
chamber.

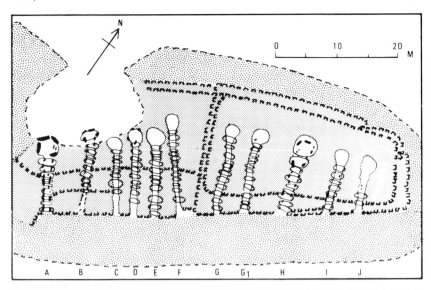

Barnenez passage-graves (40). Plan (top of page): the lettered tombs are discussed in the text. (Above) Walls of east cairn from the SW. (Right) Ruined chamber of Tomb C from the NW.

H. Facing 165° this is different from the passage-graves on either side of it. Its architecture is elaborate. A passage lined entirely with granite stones, upon which drystone walling supports a roof of heavy capstones, leads to a corbelled antechamber beyond which is a sub-rectangular chamber with a great flat capstone.

On the W entrance pillar of the passage a bow has been carved pointing along the passage as though to protect the dead. One of the two pillars in the antechamber has three axes outlined on it and there are other images, now too faint to identify. On the W slab between this and the main chamber there are two deeply-cut and superimposed triangles which are formalized versions of stone axes. On the next stone is a long line and an arc. On its other face is an isosceles triangle, probably another axe with its cutting edge upwards. There is also a crook. In the main chamber a stone at the W has four symmetrical lines of zigzags pecked into it and the end stone carries undulating lines, an inverted triangle and a yoke.

From this central 'tomb' some classic round-based sherds of Carn ware were recovered, the only artefacts to be found in the primary cairn which may have been cleared out when the later cairn was added to it. Their presence here may be significant. The variation in architecture and the carvings suggest that passage-grave H was not a simple tomb like the others but, instead, may have been a sanctuary or shrine or mortuary centre for funerary rites over the dead before the bodies were taken to the adjoining sepulchres.

G1. Facing 155° the long passage decreases in width about halfway along. It leads to a sub-circular, corbelled chamber. On the left of the chamber entrance is a freestanding, thin, rectangular slab of granite, perhaps the equivalent of the anthropomorphic stelae discovered in the similar passage-graves on ÎLE GUENNOC (52), and a physical counterpart to the 'figurine' carved in tomb J at Barnenez.

G. Looking towards 155° like G1 this passage-grave, although similar to G1, I and J, was interesting because of the finds from it. The passage had been filled with rubble and amongst it were human tibiae, the only bones to be recovered from the primary cairn. The blocking consisted of a thick layer of earth and charcoal which gave a C-14 assay of 3800 ± 150 bc or about 4600 BC. Above this layer was a rough spread of small stones.

The passage leads to a diminutive chamber no more than 2 m across and only 2.5 m high to the top of its beehive corbelling. Much of it is built of granite, as is the narrower inner section of the passage, and it is possible that the outer doleritic stretch was an extension to an earlier and very small tomb.

Secondary cairn When the primary cairn was already two or three centuries old it was enlarged. Six new passage-graves with long, straight passages were erected, their entrances fairly well in line with their predecessors. The builders were forced to put them up on the SW edge of the downward slope and to prevent collapse several internal walls for the cairn were constructed, stepped and graduated in height, the tallest 6 m high. The cairn itself had a core of local dolerite, but its surface was a capping of regular granite stones in contrast to the first cairn. From a distance the difference in colour is very apparent.

The nearest source for the granite would have been about a kilometre to the NW on what is now the Île Sterec but what was once a low hill at the far end of the Barnenez range. Altogether in the two cairns there were some 5½ tons of dolerite and 3½ tons of granite. The dolerite need have been carried no more than 500 m, but much of the granite would have been shifted uphill from nearly 2 km away. The excavator calculated that even with 200 people working 10 hours daily the first cairn would have taken 3 months or more to complete. The second cairn, with its much larger proportion of granite, would have taken far longer. Both these neatly-walled cairns were eventually submerged under a vast, sub-circular mound 87 m long and 26 m wide.

The secondary passage-graves

F. Facing 140° this is the sixth entrance from the W. It has the longest passage of all, 14 m in length, leading to an ovoid, corbelled chamber a mere 2 m across but 3.5 m high, shrinking rapidly to a constricted 50 cm at its head. Charcoal provided two C-14 determinations of 3600 ± 140 bc and 3150 ± 140 bc that approximated to 4500 BC and 3925 BC.

E. Facing 148° the 11-m-long passage leads to a 3-m-wide sub-circular, corbelled chamber in which there were some Neolithic sherds. The tomb had been re-entered in medieval times.

D. The entrance faces 148°. It is possible to walk along this 11-m-long passage to a subcircular chamber. Bronze and Iron Age material in the passage were later intrusions. In the chamber there were not only burnt human bones but also sherds of scalloped, round-based Neolithic vessels. In the lower levels of the chamber's filling there was a fine barbed-and-tanged flint arrowhead and some beaker sherds showing that there had been use, or re-use, of the chamber in Late Neolithic times.

C. This also is open. The entrance faces 146°. The passage, 10 m long, leads to a chamber which, because it was half-wrecked by the bulldozer, is now partly open to the sky. There were many finds here. There was a fine, tanged, copper dagger of Beaker type, the metal containing over 2 per cent of arsenic to give it hardness. The weapon had been hammered into shape. There were sherds of early beakers and twelve transverse flint arrowheads, all testifying to the tomb's continuing function in the Late Neolithic.

This was confirmed by the discovery of Middle Neolithic Chassey footed bowls, beaker sherds and even Iron Age pottery scattered on the ground up to 2 m from the façade between passages C and D. It is evident that the well-built wall was still standing virtually undisturbed after 4,000 years.

B. This is different from the other chambers because it is megalithic. The passage, facing 154°, is 11 m long and leads to a rectangular chamber somewhat skewed to the W. Its walls are composed of big granite slabs enclosing a space about 2 m square. Human bones and Neolithic sherds lay in the passage.

A. Like passage-grave J at the E, whose contents were presumably known and respected by the builders of the later structures, there is a decorated stone at the entrance to the chamber of this extreme western passage-grave. The 9-m-long and straight passage, facing 146°, leads to a subrectangular chamber 3 m square. A C-14 assay gave a date of 3500 ± 150 bc or about 4400 BC.

The first stone on the right of the chamber had seven wavy lines or 'U's carved on it as well as hafted axes and a bow. There was some suggestion that a wooden door may have stood at this entrance where there was also a strangely perforated stone, a rectangular opening about 12 cm square that had been hacked and smoothed through it. This may have been a 'soul-hole' for the spirits of the dead. Many Neolithic sherds, including Souch ware, came from this tomb.

Despite the frustration of being unable to enter so many of the passage-graves, Barnenez must be one of the main attractions of megalithic Brittany. The construction of its walls, splendidly achieved in the early centuries of the Neolithic, is a wonderful testament to the skill of its builders. The variations in plan and materials reflect the improvisation that was allowed even in structures as closely arranged as these. There was no imposed blueprint in prehistory and Barnenez is witness to this.

The mystery of its art and the purpose of its eleven passages and chambers remain a challenge to our questions. There is a legend that this was once the home of fairies and that the N and S cairns were linked by an underground passage which led out to sea. Around 1850 peasants dug into the mound hoping to discover treasure. Instead they found human bones, the voiceless relics of the people who built and finally occupied this temple and home of the dead.

41 Beg an Dorchenn, Plomeur. *Passage-grave 26 km SW of Quimper, 10 km WSW of Pont l'Abbé. From Plomeur take the D785 SW and in 500 m turn W (R). It is 4½ km to the coast at the Pointe du Coussin, sometimes called the Pointe de la Torche. At the end of the lane W of Coguel-Runaour hamlet a short walk westwards leads to the rocky knoll on which the tomb was built.* The passage-grave faces ESE inland. To its W are rocks, the sea and, only a few metres away, a towering outcrop. In this attractive setting there is the denuded outline of a passage-grave with a short passage and sub-octagonal chamber that was later converted into transepted cells by a 5-m extension to the passage. With the sidestones completely exposed today the plan is very clear. The passage changes its direction halfway along where the extension links with the original entrance. There are now no capstones on this additional stretch. The first passage-grave had faced almost exactly E. Three capstones remain partly covering its 3-m-long passage. The chamber had been modified by the introduction of extra stones to make compartments to N and S. A metre beyond the last sidestones is a fallen, triangular endslab.

Human bones have been found here. There was also Middle and Late Neolithic material including Chassey sherds, Grand Pressigny flints, four schist and one fibrolite pendant and, nearby, a Souch bowl.

The site had been previously occupied. Charcoal from a Mesolithic layer gave a date of 4020 ± 80 bc (c. 4900 BC). A subsequent Neolithic hearth provided an assay of 3190 ± 110 bc or about 3975 BC. The first passage-grave here must have been later than this.

42a   Castel-Ruffel, St Goazec. *Allée-couverte*

25 km S of Huelgoat and 27 km ESE of Châteaulin. From Rondouallac, 6 km SE of St Goazec, take the D41 N. The tomb is 2 km on the N (R) of the road near a mine.

This is a good example of an allée-couverte arc-bouté like TY-AR-C'HORRIKET (96a) in which the sideslabs of the chamber, instead of supporting capstones, lean inwards to form a ridge-roofed structure. There is another at

Castel-Ruffel (42a), allée-couverte arc-bouté showing leaning sideslabs.

COAT-MENEZ-GUEN (43) 28 km to the S of Castel-Ruffel near the little village of Melgven.

Castel-Ruffel was erected near the summit of Coat-Plein-Coat, 290 m high, in the Montagnes Noires. The stones are fine, thin slabs of quartz but today several are missing.

It is said that the tomb was once the home of a giant and his daughter. Finding that she had been seduced by his servant, the giant furiously threw three stones at them as they fled westwards. He missed and the stones landed on St Jean heath 4 km away (42b).

42b   Tri-Men. *Row. On St Jean heath, 3 km S of St Goazec. To the N of the D41 and just before its junction with the D6 to the S.* Here there is a line of three big stones, two of them fallen, said to be slabs from CASTEL-RUFFEL allée-couverte (42a) thrown by a giant at his eloping daughter.

Cloître, Le. *Menhir (see* 50b HUELGOAT)

43   Coat-Menez-Guen (Coat-Luzuen), Melgven. *Allée-couverte*

32 km E of Pont l'Abbé, 26 km ESE of Quimper. From Pont-Aven take the D24 NW for 3 km. At the fork at Cleu-Nizon keep to the main road to the ENE for 1¾ km. Tomb is on the N side of the road.

This well-preserved allée-couverte with its inward-leaning sideslabs stands rather unusually at the lower end of the Odet Valley and is characteristic of the south Finistère allées-couvertes, with its thick flat slabs and ponderous construction.

Here twelve stones of local migmatite, a metamorphic rock that splits naturally into regularly laminated flags, stand six on each side of a long rectangular chamber facing the SSE. The oval mound, 35 × 22 m, that enclosed this chamber is in good condition. It is composed of a rubbly mixture of pebbles and quartz.

The chamber is 14 m long. The sideslabs on the E are erect, each about 5 m square, but those on the W lean in considerably. On this surprising structure rest three massive capstones, the largest 5.5 × 3 m and weighing over 20 tons. They are supported on the W not by the inclined stones but by the surrounding barrow.

Entry to this arc-bouté was by a transverse

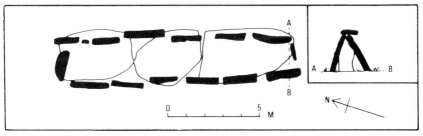

Coat-Menez-Guen allée-couverte arc-bouté (43).

slab from which a shallow crescent had been removed low down on its W side. Only four other allées-couvertes are known to have such 'half-porthole' entrances, two of them at LISCUIS, CN (15). Arc-bouté allées-couvertes, however, do exist fairly close to Coat-Menez-Guen, notably at TY-AR-C'HORRIKET (96a) 50 km WNW.

Coat-Menez-Guen was excavated in 1875 and beaker sherds were found suggesting a date in the Late Neolithic period. Legend has it that two of the stones bear the marks of fairies' fingers.

There are other but disrupted allées-couvertes near Melgven at St Antoine, 1½ km S; Cadol, 4 km NNW; and Kerambrunou, 4 km to the SSE.

44   Cosquer, Goulven. *Allée-couverte*
34 km WNW of Morlaix, 6 km NNE of Lesneven. From Goulven take the D125 S and in ¾ km turn E (L) to Viz ar Roch in 1 km. Turn S (R) for 1 km. Allée-couverte is on E (L) of lane.
Standing on a pronounced slope this allée-couverte still has part of its mound surviving with some kerbs visible. Small stones outside the main sideslabs may have been intended to give extra support.

45a   Crugou, Plovan. *Passage-grave*
21 km WSW of Quimper, 13 km NW of Pont l'Abbé. 1¾ km NNW of Plovan-sur-Mer. From Plovan take road N past Kergurun. In 1¾ km at crossroads the tomb is on S of lane to E (R).
Here there are the remains of a V-shaped passage-grave like that at TY-AR-BOUDIQUET (95a). It stood in a round mound, 45 m in diameter. The entrance, 2 m wide, facing SSE, led into an 11.5-m-long passage which curved to the NNE and widened to 2.7 m at its

northern end. It was capped with six heavy stones, increasing in size towards the chamber.

Excavations in 1875 recovered Kerugou sherds of the Late Neolithic and the sherds of at least six beakers.

45b   Renongar. The disturbed stones of another passage-grave, also with Kerugou ware, are to be seen near the SE corner of the same crossroads. According to Forde the tumulus once covered 'a vast system of dolmens and parallel galleries giving access to open chambers'. Today it is a ruin.

Gaignog, Île. *Passage-graves (see 52 ÎLE GUENNOC)*

46a   Goulet-Riec, Riec-sur-Belon. *Allées-couvertes*
38 km E of Pont l'Abbé, 35 km SE of Quimper. From Riec-sur-Belon take the SW road through the straggling village. In 2¾ km pass by Kertallic and in 200 m turn W (R). In 250 m turn S (L). After 500 m take the SW (R) fork. The allée-couverte is ¾ km on the W (R) of the road near the lane to Kergoalec.
The importance of this overgrown chambered tomb is that it is another example of an arc-bouté like TY-AR-C'HORRIKET (96a), with the sideslabs propped against each other to make a ridgelike structure.

46b   La Porte Neuve. *2 km SSE of Riec-sur-Belon.* There are traces of a surrounding mound at this allée-couverte which faces ESE and has a lateral entrance and a terminal cell at its western end.

47   Guilliguy, Ploudalmézeau. *Allée-couverte*
24 km NW of Brest, 27 km W of Lesneven. From

Ploudalmézeau take the D168 W for 3½ km to Bar al Lan near Portsall. Tomb is at the end of the creek.

This is a tumbled allée-couverte with extra stones, all low, acting as an outer revetment to the main sideslabs. The chamber is divided. A Christian cross dominates this pagan burial place which is also known as Men Milliget, 'the Cursed Stone'

48 Guirec, Le, Pont l'Abbé. *Menhir*
17 km SW of Quimper. From Pont l'Abbé take the D785 SW and 1 km, after crossing the D2 on the outskirts of Pont l'Abbé, turn NW (R). In 500 m, at the end of the minor road, the menhir stands at the edge of a small wood.
This is a fine 5-m-tall granite slab. At its base Neolithic sherds, a quern, flint piercers and charcoal were discovered.

49 Hameau de Rungleo, Daoulas. *Menhir*
45 km SW of Morlaix, 18 km ESE of Brest. From Daoulas take the D770 S for 4 km and turn W (R) at Kerbiaouen. Straight on for 2 km to Rungleo. Opposite farm is footpath to N signposted 'Croix des Douze Apôtres'. 100 m walk to junction of several tracks.

Hameau de Rungleo (49), Christianized menhir from the NNE.

This is one of the two most lavishly Christianized menhirs in Brittany, the other being at ST DUZEC, CN (26). The stone is 2.2 m high. On its N face masons have carved four panels in niches 4 cm deep. At the top is Christ. Three lower compartments contain the apostles in groups of four. The stone has been shaped on all its surfaces and is surmounted by a cross.

The date of the carvings is unknown and they have been ascribed variously to the Roman period and to the 13th and 15th centuries. There is some similarity to a cross of the latter century in the square of Plechâtel, Ille-et-Vilaine, which has figures of three apostles on each of its four sides. There is also a close likeness between the Rungleo menhir and another at Moone, a village in Co. Kildare, Ireland. This fine and very slender high cross stands on a pedestal and on its shaft are deeply cut animals and scriptural scenes. Below them, on the pyramidal base, is a panel containing the crucified Christ between two soldiers. Below are the twelve apostles in three vertical panels. The stone at Moone was raised in the 9th century alongside a 6th-century chapel.

50 Huelgoat. *Megalithic centre*
31 km NE of Châteaulin, 25 km SSE of Morlaix.
There are menhirs and a ruined allée-couverte in this attractive region of Finistère with its forests of beech and oak, its rivers and streams and tumbles of granite and sandstone boulders. The name of Huelgoat signifies 'the high wood'.

Just to the NE of the town is the Camp d'Arthus, an enormous hillfort of *murus gallicus* type mentioned by Caesar in his description of the siege of Avaricum (modern Bourges). Its bivallate enclosure sprawls in the middle of the forest on a spur of the hilly countryside.

For locating the various sites around Huelgoat the orange Carte Touristique, 1:50,000 map, no. 0617, is very useful.

50a Kerrampelven. *Menhirs. From Huelgoat take the road N towards Berrien and in 2 km turn W (L) to the hamlet of Keranpelven as it is sometimes spelled. The first menhir is 300 m down lane on W.* This is a great standing stone, rectangular in shape with a tapering top. It is about 1 m square in plan but stands 5 m tall. 100 m down the lane, but on the other side, is the second, less impressive, stone.

50b At **St Guinec** is one of the largest menhirs in Brittany. *From Huelgoat take the D764 W towards Brest. After 1½ km take minor road on S (L) and follow it SW for 2 km to major road junction. The menhir is in the N angle of the junction.* Sometimes known as *Le Cloître* it is 8.5 m high and very regular in shape like a thin triangle. It is very weathered. Its broad faces, to the SW and NE, are about 2 m wide and its narrow SE and NW sides measure less than 1 m.

50c A kilometre from St Herbot, a hamlet 6 km SW of Huelgoat, a devastated allée-couverte at **Bé-Keor** is said to be the resting-place of a giant.

The V-shaped passage-grave of TY-AR-BOUDIQUET (95a) is 7 km to the W of Huelgoat at Brennilis.

51   Île Carn, Ploudalmézeau. *Passage-graves*
28 km W of Lesneven and 26 km NW of Brest. From Ploudalmézeau take the D168 W and in 1½ km turn NW (R) to Kerros. The islet is 500 m N of Kerros and is accessible only at low tide. This is one of the most spectacular and informative of all the Breton megalithic tombs. It was excavated between 1954 and 1972.

On a hillock overlooking an eastern, forested landscape of oaks, elms, limes and hazels Neolithic people around 4200 BC erected a little passage-grave. Its short, ESE-facing passage led to a beautifully constructed, corbelled chamber, 3 m high, of drystone walling. The chamber was somewhat offset to the left of the passage giving the monument a q-shaped plan. In it were fine sherds of round-bottomed Neolithic bowls to which the name of this site has been given. Charcoal produced assays of 3390 ± 250 bc (*c.* 4200 BC) and 3280 ± 75 bc (*c.* 4100 BC).

5 m to the S of this tomb a second was built, similar to the first and in plan like a wriggling tadpole. The chamber here also was intact, preserved by the blocking when the tomb was abandoned. This was the first French megalithic tomb to yield a radiocarbon date, a determination of 3440 ± 150 bc (*c.* 4300 BC). This caused consternation in 1959 because at

that time it seemed unacceptably early. It is rather ironical that the architectural evidence suggested that this structure was actually secondary to the other passage-grave.

8 m N of the first tomb was a third with a curious double-chamber like lobster claws, a short passage leading to two sub-rectangular chambers separated from each other by a massive pile of masonry. The S cell was the larger. It was clear that the N chamber had been used well into the Late Neolithic, for in it was a collared flask of the Crech-Quillé/Le Mélus tradition and some variscite beads. This phase was dated to 2890 ± 150 bc, about 3650 BC.

Ultimately the three tombs were blocked and enclosed in a monstrous trapezoidal cairn with a fine, metre-high wall around it. It was damaged when employed as a fortification during the Second World War.

At Île Carn it is possible to envisage an early encroachment of Neolithic people along the western coasts of Brittany, settling, erecting their family tombs which, eventually, were encapsulated under one great cairn like those at BARNENEZ (40), and ÎLE GUENNOC (52), the latter only 5 km to the NE.

52   Île Guennoc, Ploudalmézeau. *Passage-graves*
26 km NW of Brest, 23 km W of Lesneven. 6½ km N of Ploudalmézeau but not accessible except by special arrangement. Enquire at the Syndicat d'Initiatif, Ploudalmézeau. These three great cairns are included in the Gazetteer because of their importance. This little island, once a low hill joined to the mainland, has yielded evidence of occupation from Palaeolithic to medieval times, and in the 5th millennium BC early Neolithic settlers constructed a series of small passage-graves along the central ridge of the hill. It was a home of the dead, the sea to its W, and to the E a countryside of deep forest with patches of cultivated land.

The crest of the hill was buckled, running N to S along its southern half and then angling away to the NW. In every case the passage-graves were built to face across this spine, those at the S looking E, those at the N oriented to the NE. They were enclosed in great rectangular or trapezoidal cairns, each, like BARNENEZ (40) and ÎLE CARN (51),

containing three or four little chambered
tombs that were perhaps the burial places of
families grouped together under these huge
piles of stones.

Three passage-graves under Cairn I at the S
were built of drystone walling. Some flints and
fine early Neolithic sherds came from their
circular chambers. Cairn II, in contrast,
covered tombs with rectangular chambers,
their shapes conditioned by the use of big
slabs for their megalithic walls. The plans
resembled squared 'q's. A crook was carved
on a stone in chamber C.

Cairn III at the north of the island is more
revealing of the funerary rites that were
enacted here. The site was excavated between
1960 and 1972. Under a ponderous trapezoidal
cairn, 28 m long, 18 m wide at its SE but only
8 m wide at the NW where it was damaged in
prehistoric times, there were four drystone-
walled tombs, all facing NE. Carbon-14 assays
suggest they were in use between 4600 and
3900 BC.

The most northerly tomb was half-wrecked.
To its SE Tomb A had a 4-m passage leading
to a sub-circular, corbelled chamber about
2.8 m in diameter. Tomb B, 5 m to the SE,
had a shorter passage and a circular chamber
in which there were traces of human bone. No
sherds were discovered, only a meagre
assemblage that included a dolerite axe, two
grinders and seven crude beads of grey schist.
To its SE, Tomb C was 'q'-shaped with four
capstones over its 5.4-m-long passage.

These four tombs were protected by the
cairn. Centuries later a fifth passage-grave was
added to the SE on the same orientation. Flint
flakes and a piercer were found in it.
Immediately to its SW a sixth tomb, F, was
built, facing SW with the end of its chamber
lying head to head with that of D. Charcoal
produced a date of 2550 ± 120 bc or about
3300 BC, a thousand years later than another,
from Tomb C, of 3850 ± 300 bc (4630 BC).
From Tomb C came another assay of
3125 ± 140 bc (c. 3910 BC). Both Tombs D
and E were concealed beneath an extension to
the cairn.

The few simple grave-goods in these
passage-graves do not suggest any great wealth
amongst these early inhabitants of north-west
Brittany, but some stones in the tombs do tell
us something about their beliefs.

Anthropomorphic stelae with rough heads and
shoulders hacked out of slabs of local granite
had been set upright just to the left of the
entrances to the chambers of Tombs, A, B and
C. These freestanding blocks may have been
symbols of a guardian spirit to watch over the
dead. A similar but undecorated stone in
chamber G1 of BARNENEZ (40) may have had
a comparable function.

Irvit. *Menhir (see* 92b ST EDEN)

53 Kerandrèze, Moëlan-sur-Mer. *Allée-couverte*
*40 km ESE of Quimper, 43 km E of Pont
l'Abbé. From Moëlan take the D216 SW. Allée-
couverte is visible in the fields after 3 km, on the E
(L) just past the lane to Kernou-Argoat.*

This 15.3-m-long tomb, 1.8 m wide and
aligned E–W, stands in the middle of
cultivated fields on level ground. There is a
short vestibule at the W end and from it a low
sillstone demarcates the entrance to the
chamber which was paved with thin, flat slabs
on a bedding of yellow earth.

Excavation in 1883 recovered many
artefacts from this well-preserved monument
including a round-based bowl, some Crech-
Quillé/Le Mélus ware, beaker sherds, five
polished-stone and one flint axe, three
pendants, two flint arrowheads, blades
including one of Grand Pressigny flint, a
copper knife and an archer's wristguard.

54 Kerangallan, Tregunc. *Menhir*
*25 km SE of Quimper, 28 km E of Pont l'Abbé,
and ¾ km N of Tregunc town centre after the last
houses on the NE (R) of the road to Melgven. In
a little hollow.*

This is a finely-smoothed, almost polished
menhir, rather like a needle, its base
measuring 3 × 3 m. The stone is 7.4 m high. It
has been Christianized by the addition of a
small cross. It is now half-hidden in trees and
bushes. Near it, and without a cross, is a
second menhir, 5.4 m in height.

55 Kerangosquer, Pont-Aven. *Menhir*
*30 km ESE of Quimper, 35 km E of Pont
l'Abbé. From Pont-Aven take the D783 W and
in 2 km turn S (L) on the minor road to Névez.
After 1 km take 2nd lane on E (L) at Poulpry.*

Menhir is 200 m on the N (L) in a field after a wood.
This is an imposing 7-m-high menhir of granite. It is known as La Pierre du Coq and it is claimed that at Easter and Christmas a cock which guards a great treasure will fly away. Should it land on one's shoulder it signifies an invitation to take the gold.

56a   Kerbannalec, Beuzec-cap-Sizun. *Allée-couverte*
26 km WNW of Quimper, 9¹⁄₂ km W of Douarnenez. From Beuzec-cap-Sizun take the D7 E for 4 km, passing the lane N to Lescogan. In 500 m take the next lane N(L) to Kerbannalec farm. Tomb is 300 m N of the farm.
This allée-couverte, 13 m long, is aligned SSE–NNW. There are the remains of kerbing along the W side. At the entrance the chamber is 1.9 m wide, but it broadens to 2.2 m near the middle only to contract to 1.9 m at the NNW end. In this it resembles KERMEUR-BIHAN (68). The entrance is somewhat triangular with a transverse slab reducing the space to a mere 50 cm. In front of it there is a short vestibule.

Excavations amongst these granite stones in 1880 recovered three round-bottomed bowls, two 'Pôts-des-Fleurs' of SOM affinities, some beaker sherds, a dolerite polished axe, flints, all Late Neolithic, the bowls being of the local Rosmeur-Collé tradition, peculiar to south Finistère but related to the Kerugou styles.
56b   At **Lescogan,** ³⁄₄ km NW, a rock by the chapel of St Conogan is said to be the magic boat in which the Irish saint sailed from the British Isles.

57a   Kerdalaé, Lesconil. *Menhir*
23¹⁄₂ km SSW of Quimper, 7¹⁄₂ km S of Pont l'Abbé. From Lesconil take the D102 N for 600 m. Menhir is in fields 250 m W (L) of main road at Kerdalaé-Lesconil.
This is yet another of the shield-shaped slabs that are frequently to be found in south-western Brittany. Leaning a little, it is a thin block but over 4 m high and 6 m wide at its base. Excavations at its foot recovered a pot filled with cremated bone.
57b   On the shore at **Lesconil** is another menhir, 2.5 m high, which is partly submerged at high tide. Similar finds to those at Kerdalaé were made at its foot.

Kerdanet. *Allée-couverte* (*see* 96b TY-AR-C'HORRIKET)

58a   Kerdanno, Penmarch. *Dolmen*
24 km SSW of Quimper, 7 km SW of Pont l'Abbé. From Penmarch take the D785 NE. The dolmen is on the W (L) of the road on a bank 3¹⁄₂ km from Penmarch.
Half-hidden in gorse and against a hedge all that is left of this chambered tomb is the square chamber, its two sideslabs and backstone, each about 1.5 m high and capped with a wide, thin slab 2.5 m long. In its present state it very much looks like the Coves to be seen in some British stone circles such as Avebury. It faces ESE and stands on a slight rise in the level countryside.
58b   In the fields behind it and not easily seen is a great slab of a menhir like a squat shield in shape. Only 1 m thick, this granite block is about 4 m high but over 5 m wide at its base.

59   Kerégard-Vraz, Plomeur. *Menhir*
23 km SW of Quimper, 6 km WSW of Pont l'Abbé. From Plomeur take the D57 N and in ³⁄₄ km turn W (L). In 1³⁄₄ km Kerégard-Vraz hamlet will be on the N (R).

Kerégard-Vraz (59), Christianized menhir from the NE.

Kerreneur menhir (60), a 19th-century lithograph.

This is a thin, rounded cylinder of granite quite unlike the majority of the south Finistère slabs. It stands near the chapel on the N side of the road, 2 m high, with a small cross on its top.

60 Kerreneur (Kerhouézel), Porspoder. **Menhir**
24 km NW of Brest, 31 km WSW of Lesneven. From Porspoder take the lane E towards Larret. After 1 km turn N (L) to Kerdalvaz. Menhir is 100 m on the N of the lane just inside a field.

Like ST GONVARCH (93), this is a tall, shaped granite menhir. It is some 6.5 m high but very slender, and it has been smoothed with stone mauls as is customary with these West Léon standing stones. In plan it measures 2 × 1 m with its major axis arranged NE–SW.

Another menhir on the Île Melon near Porspoder was 7 m high and weighed over 80 tons. It was destroyed during the Second World War.

61 Ker Eol, Ploudalmézeau. **Rows**
19 km NW of Brest, 22 km WSW of Lesneven. From Ploudalmézeau take the D26 E for 3 km.
On the S side of the road there is a line of small, upright stones aligned ESE–WNW. Three others stand at right-angles to the row at its W end and on the other side of the road.

62 Kerfland, Plomeur. **Row**
23 km SSW of Quimper, 6 km SSW of Pont l'Abbé. From Plomeur take the D57 S for 2½ km to Pendreff. Turn E (L) at the crossroads and in ¾ km take the NE lane past Kerfland farm. Row is in field to the N of the lane.
Here there are three tall menhirs, spaced 4 m apart, aligned NNE–SSW. Their respective heights are 4.3, 4.4 and 3.3 m. 200 m to the S is a fallen stone, 3.5 m long. Excavations at the base of the stones have produced sherds, charcoal and a quernstone.

63 Kergadiou, Porspoder. **Menhir**
22 km WNW of Brest, 3½ km SE of Porspoder. From Brélés, 8 km SSW of Ploudalmézeau, take the D28 N signposted, 'Ploudalmézeau'. In 1¼ km menhir will be visible on the skyline to the NW in a field close to a farm track.

Kergadiou (63), paired menhirs from the SW.

Moëlan-sur-Mer (64b), menhir by the church.

There are two menhirs close together at Kergadiou, one standing 8.8 m high, the other 10.5 m long but almost fallen. They are 80 m apart on a NNE–SSW axis and are of local granite.

Typically, in this area of West Léon, both have been shaped and smoothed with mauls, the standing stone at the SSW being one of the most perfect with its elegant, playing-card rectangular shape. From a distance, in its regular outline, it resembles a symmetrical obelisk. It weighs about forty tons.

The second stone has been smoothed only on its upper surface which is so flat that it may have been intended to receive carvings. The under face is irregular and it is possible that this menhir, now only 15° from the horizontal, may have toppled from the impact of the constant hammering and beating of the mauls. Its weight is some sixty tons.

The pair were erected in a conspicuous position on an elevated plateau and were it not for intervening trees one could see the enormous menhir of KERLOAS (67a), 8 km away to the SSE.

Near these stones at Kergadiou Neolithic flint scatters have been found as well as Bronze and Iron Age objects, none of which gives any indication of the date of the erection of the menhirs.

64a Kergoustance, Moëlan-sur-Mer. *Allée-couverte*
49 km E of Pont l'Abbé, 45 km SE of Quimper. 500 m W of Moëlan town centre. From Moëlan take the D24 W and in 500 m turn N (R) towards Kergoustance. Tomb is 150 m along road on W (L).
This is a ruined allée-couverte with its seven capstones in disarray. It is 14.5 m long, aligned NE–SW with a terminal cell at a slight angle at the SW end. This open cell measures about 2 × 2 m.

64b In Moëlan-sur-Mer there is a menhir standing at the NE corner of the church inside the church wall.

3 km SW of Moëlan is KERANDRÈZE allée-couverte (53). KERMEUR-BIHAN allée-couverte (68) is 5½ km W of the town.

65 Kerivin, St Pol-de-Léon. *Passage-grave*
28 km ENE of Lesneven, 13 km NW of Morlaix. From St Pol-de-Léon take the D769 S and in 2 km fork SE (L) onto the D58. In ¾ km

take 2nd lane on the E (L) signposted
'Kerangouez'. Tomb is down a track on the R at
the first sharp bend.

This is a well-preserved T-shaped passage-grave around which the remains of the mound and a few kerbstones can still be seen. The passage, 4.6 m long but badly damaged, leads from the SE to a 5-m-long chamber arranged almost at right-angles to it. Access is by means of a tiny lateral aperture 70 cm wide but only 40 cm high. Beyond it is the asymmetrically-placed chamber which is shorter and lower at the NE. On its SE wall, facing the entrance, is a granite slab with two quite large protruberances on its edge. It has been speculated that this stone was intended as a representation of a female guardian spirit watching over the dead like the decorated stele at CRECH-QUILLÉ, CN (9), 40 km to the ENE. (*See also* 52 ÎLE GUENNOC.)

66 Kerléven, La Forêt-Fouesnant.
Passage-graves
15 km SE of Quimper, 20 km ENE of Pont l'Abbé, 3 km SE of La Forêt-Fouesnant at Kerantec, 1½ km E of Kerléven. In camping site on low promontory between Kerléven beach and estuary of Anse St Laurent, 30 m from sea.

Damaged by an extension to the camping site in 1960 and with its chamber now unroofed, this intriguing monument was excavated and restored between 1961 and 1965. The trapezoidal cairn, now 21 × 11 m and arranged WNW–ESE, was badly mutilated at its north where a triangle of material of at least 80 sq.m had been removed. With it had gone virtually all of a primary passage-grave with a 4-m-long passage facing SSW and leading to a probably rectangular chamber.

To its SSE had been added two later passage-graves on the same orientation, their walls attractively constructed of alternating dressed pillars and masonry. Tomb B, at the centre, had a 3.4 m passage giving access to a rectangular chamber, 3.8 × 4.3 m, with a small cell added at its NW corner. A freestanding stone had been placed just inside its entrance. (*See* 52 ÎLE GUENNOC.)

The easternmost tomb, C, had a similar rectangular chamber which had been subdivided by septal slabs and transverse stones with a rectangular compartment in its SE corner. When these tombs were

abandoned the passages were blocked with big stones.

Amongst the material found during the excavations there were many sherds of Chassey ware, including a small vase-support like those from ER-LANNIC, M (132b), a broken dolerite axe and some later Kerugou ware. C-14 assays from Chamber B of 2875 ± 125 bc and from Chamber C of 1850 ± 120 bc indicate a minimum span of life for this complicated and strangely-designed monument from about 3650 to 2300 BC.

67a Kerloas (Kervéatoux), Plouarzel.
Menhir
16 km W of Brest, 30 km SW of Lesneven. From Plouarzel take the D5 E. In 2 km, 100 m beyond crossroads, take S (R) minor road. Menhir is 1½ km on S (R) side, clearly visible on skyline 200 m through field. If approaching from St Renan take D67 SSW. 1 km beyond the D6 to the W take the country road to the W (R) signposted, 'Menhir'. 3 km to parking-space on S (L) of road.

At Kerloas, 'the place of sadness', there is a stupendous menhir, the tallest prehistoric stone now standing not only in Brittany but in the whole of western Europe. Playing-card in shape with a profile like a cutlass blade it was originally fully 10 m high with its long axis lying ENE–WSW. As with the majority of the Breton standing stones, and quite unlike many in the British Isles, it is probable that the significant orientation was at right-angles to its broad faces and not along its breadth. Like many menhirs in West Léon this granite pillar has been assiduously smoothed before erection.

It was put up on a long, level ridge at 123 m above sea-level near the major summit of the Léon plateau although, surprisingly, it is not at the highest point in the vicinity.

In direct measurements the Kerloas stone is 9.5 m from base to top, but it is surrounded by a mound of broken rock and rubble hacked out of the pit in which it was to stand. In total length it must be some 12 m. At one time it was even longer, but about 200 years ago, during a thunderstorm, its top was fractured and for years the fallen fragment was used as a cattle-trough on the adjoining farm.

The menhir is roughly rectangular in plan,

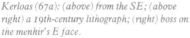

Kerloas (67a): (above) from the SE; (above right) a 19th-century lithograph; (right) boss on the menhir's E face.

the width of its four sides being 1.8 m at the NNW; 0.4 m, ENE; 3 m, SSE; and 1 m, WSW. Examination has shown that it had been detached from natural rock, the NNW side being the surface broken off, the SSE being the weathered exterior. The cumbersome slab, which must weigh about 100 tons, had to be brought from the Âber-Ildut, at least 2½ km to the W, and dragged up a slope from the River St Renan 25 m below its present situation. Whether hauled by oxen or by men using a sledge, it would have demanded the strength of several hundred people to heave it upright.

Its date is unknown. Investigation of the packing-stones in its stonehole uncovered a deposit of Bronze Age sherds 2 m away from its base, but these were possibly placed there when the menhir was already centuries old.

About a metre above the ground on both the narrow WSW and ESE sides there are artificial bosses, about 15 cm across, hammered out of the granite in low relief when the stone was being dressed. These may be the only survivors of a more complex sculpting or they may be the counterparts of the 'breasts' known in some of the allées-couvertes of north Brittany such as KERGÜNTUIL, CN (13b) and in passage-grave stelae like those at ÎLE GUENNOC (52).

At one time newly-wed couples would go to the stone at night, strip and, one on each side of the stone, rub themselves against the bosses in the hope of having sons. By the end of the 19th century the custom became more decorous and on the second night of their marriage the man and woman would embrace the stone from either side. If they could touch hands they also would be assured of sons.

The purpose of such splendid pillars is debatable. They could have been landmarks to proclaim a group's territory and it is interesting that were it not for modern trees it would be possible from Kerloas to see the impressive menhirs at KERGADIOU (63), 8 km to the NNW. Astronomically all that can be said of Kerloas is that it does not seem to mark any important celestial event in any direction although, of course, it could have been used as a foresight from observing positions some distance away.

67b In the town of Plouarzel nearby there is a fine rectangular menhir, 1.6 m high, in the cemetery by the church.

Kermenhir. *Menhir (see* 96c TY-AR-C'HORRIKET)

68   Kermeur-Bihan, Moëlan-sur-Mer. *Allée-couverte*
40 km E of Pont l'Abbé, 37 km SE of Quimper. From Moëlan take the D116 W for 4½ km, turn N (R) and in ¾ km turn W (L) to Kermeur hamlet in 1½ km. Tomb is at edge of woods 500 m W of hamlet near the banks of the River Belon.
This allée-couverte, erected on a pronounced slope, is 9.5 m long and aligned SE–NW. It is unusual inasmuch as it widens from 1.2 m at its entrance to 3 m at its centre, only to narrow to 1.2 m again at its far end. It is covered by four great capstones. The chamber is paved. Unusually, it is blocked at both ends like a long cist. A second line of low sideslabs acted as an extra revetment for the chamber.

Excavations in 1883 recovered three Crech-Quillé/Le Mélus bowls, a 'Pôt-de-Fleur', a vessel like others from the Channel Isles, eight polished stone axes, four of dolerite and one of quartz, flint flakes and two pendants.

69   Kernévez, St Jean Trolimon. *Menhir*
19 km SSW of Quimper, 4 km WSW of Pont l'Abbé. From Plomeur take the D57 N. In 500 m turn NE (R) onto minor road. After 1½ km menhir is in field just E (R) of the road at the N end of a wood.
This is a lovely, jagged stone of brilliant white. It is a full 3 m in height, 2 m wide at its broader WNW and ESE faces, 1 m across its uneven SSW face and upright NNE side. It tapers to an uneven top. Its long axis is almost N–S. It was erected on level ground which falls gently to the NE. It is said that, for no obvious reason, it was thrown down in 1910, but that the farmer almost immediately re-erected it for fear of the stone's vengeance.

Not far away at Kerviltré an octagonal stele was discovered in an Iron Age cemetery together with skeletons and urns. The 1.3 m high, deeply-channelled stone is now in the grounds of the museum at ST GUÉNOLÉ (94a).

Kernévez (69), menhir from the SW.

70a Kernic, Plouescat. *Allée-couverte*
29 km WNW of Morlaix, 12 km NE of
Lesneven. 3 km W of Plouescat. From Plouescat
follow the D30 all the way W via Porz Guen to
Lann an Italy. Turn W (R) for 500 m to Palud
Bihan. Walk along track immediately S of the
tennis courts, keeping a collapsed tor to the L.
Tomb is 200 m on the sea shore.

Nothing could show more dramatically the
change in sea level since prehistoric times than
this seaweed-wrapped tomb of speckled
granite resting on the N shore of the Anse de
Kernic, regularly submerged 3.5 m below the
sea at high tide. A huge outcrop looms 100 m
to its W.

The allée-couverte faces SW down the
beach and, originally, to the river of a shallow
valley below it. Its mound has long since been
washed away, but on its W is a fine run of low
kerbstones curving round to link with a
terminal cell at the higher NE. The kerbs on
the E are toppled, but it can be guessed that
the enclosed mound may once have been as
large as 22 × 6 m and perhaps 1.5 m high.

Unusually for Brittany there may have been
a rectangular forecourt at the SW where two
stones still stand by the entrance, the relics of
a three-sided, open-air enclosure 7.2 m long
and 5 m wide with the entrance in the middle
of the NE side. Two other big stones stand at
the sides of this entrance which leads to a
chamber 9.7 × 1.6 m wide, the western
sideslabs leaning slightly inwards. At the far
end the closing slab is a huge block 1.5 m
wide, 1.6 m high and 75 cm thick, weighing
over four tons. Beyond it is a sub-triangular
end-cell 3 m long and 1.5 m wide, narrowing
so sharply to the NNE that access would have
been impossible at ground-level (*see* 22a
PRAJOU-MENHIR). It is possible that this
terminal cell, like many others, never
possessed a capstone.

No excavations are recorded here, but
occasional finds include some coarse, flat
bottomed SOM ware, beaker sherds, fibrolite
pendants and flint arrowheads and blades.

70b   Other tide-affected menhirs in the
region include an allée-couverte on the beach
at **Lerret** near Kerlouan, 6½ km WSW of
Brigognan-Plage.

70c   Near Lilia, 4½ km WNW of
Plouguerneau, the **Men Ozach** menhir is
similarly situated below the high tide mark.

Kernic (70a), allée-couverte from the N at low tide.

Kerrampelven. *Menhirs* (*see* 50a HUELGOAT)

71 Kerscaven, Penmarch. *Menhir*

25 km SSW of Quimper, 9 km SW of Pont l'Abbé. From Penmarch take the D785 NE for 1½ km. Menhir is on private land in a field opposite the E (R) turn of the D53 to Plobannalec. It is 250 m NW of Perinaguen.
This is one of the most impressive menhirs of south Finistère. Sometimes known as the Menhir de la Vierge, it is a tall granite slab, its sides runneled by rain and green with lichen, 6 m high with a strangely lopsided top like an elf's cap. Its base was explored in 1876 and sherds, a quernstone, some flint flakes, charcoal and black earth were discovered.

Another menhir stands near it on lower ground away from the road and concealed in the trees and undergrowth.

72 Kerugou, Plomeur. *Passage-grave*

23 km SW of Quimper, 7 km WSW of Pont l'Abbé. From Plomeur take the D785 SW and in ¾ km turn W (R) and ¾ km farther on turn N (R) towards Kerugou. Tomb is 1 km on W (L) just after crossing of a minor E–W lane.
Two great granite capstones almost crush the small sideslabs on which they rest. The remnants of a short passage lead off to the ESE. The uncovered passage is about 6 m long. At its W end are two transepted chambers to N and S, each about 2 m square. The tomb once lay under a circular mound about 30 m in diameter and nearly 3 m high. Excavations in 1877 found fragments of flat paving on a bed of small pebbles rammed into a 15–20 cm thick layer of yellow earth. Dolerite and fibrolite axes were recovered, fibrolite pendants and flint flakes, but the site is most important for the distinctive Late Neolithic pottery in it, originating towards the end of the Middle Neolithic. It included undecorated round-bottomed bowls, decorated carinated vessels and other flat-based pots which, together, comprise the assemblage known as Kerugou ware.

Kervadel. *Stele* (*see* 89 QUIMPER museum)

73 Kervignen, Ploudalmézeau. *Menhir*

23 km WSW of Lesneven, 20 km NW of Brest. From Ploudalmézeau take the D26 SE towards Plouguin. After 1½ km take the 2nd lane S (R) through Kerscaven and in 1½ km turn SW (R) past Kervignen. In ¾ km turn S (L). 250 m, the stone is in field to E (L).
This is a tall and straight granite menhir about 150 m from the lane in the middle of a wide field. It is partly hidden in a clump of gorse. It stands erect, 4 m high with a tapering top. It is playing-card in shape and is set on a NE–SW axis.

Kervillogant. *Passage-grave* (*see* 90c RUEN, LE)

74 Lagatjar, Camaret-sur-Mer. *Rows*

39 km WNW of Châteaulin, 17 km SW of Brest, 9 km WNW of Crozon at the western end of the Crozon peninsula. From Crozon follow the D8 W, by-passing Camaret to the N (R). At junction with D8a turn NE (R). Rows are immediately to the W.
The lines of standing stones here are the most remarkable of the Crozon megalithic sites. At the beginning of the century many of the stones were prostrate, overturned by an earthquake it was said, but in 1928 they were

Kerugou (72), passage-grave from the E.

re-erected and are now a protected site.

As at the destroyed rows of LEURÉ (97b) and RAGUÉNÉS (97c) they have the distinctive feature of lines set at right-angles to others. At Lagatjar there is a long row, arranged on a NE–SW axis, and from it two shorter rows on its W side extend to the NW. They are about 40 m apart, so that the arrangement resembles an enormous but unfinished megalithic rectangle. To the SE of the longest line there is a short row of three stones, separate from the others and aligned ENE–WSW. Today there are some 100 stones at Lagatjar, but it is likely that there were once perhaps three or four times that number, the others having been taken for the walls, roads and buildings of the town close by.

The rows at Lagatjar were erected on a noticeable slope down from the WSW to the ENE and from NNW down to the SSE. The land rises to the NNW and WSW and these are the directions, respectively, of the two short rows and the separate three-stone row. Also to the W, but out of sight, is the coastline of the Anse de Pen-hat.

The longest row at Lagatjar has forty-two low stones in it, the largest occupying the area between the ends of the two rows to the NW. The line is fairly straight and has an approximate orientation of 30°–210°.

30 m from its NE end a line of thirteen jagged white pillars extends to the NW, curving gradually towards the NNW. The tallest of these stones, the eighth from the SE end, stands over 3 m high. The row is some 40 m long and has a rough orientation of 135°–315°.

40 m to its SW a second line of tall stones also leads from the long row. This is longer

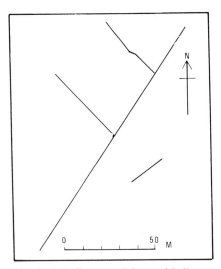

Lagatjar (74), diagrammatic layout of the lines.

than its partner to the NE, over 50 m in extent and with seventeen pillars, not as impressive as in the other line, set in a slightly curving arc towards the NW. The orientation is similar to that of its counterpart. What stones are missing from these settings and how accurately they were replaced cannot now be determined.

30 m to the ESE of where this row is joined to the longest line there is a group of three big and heavy pillars in a row 20 m long, each of the stones being over 2.5 m high with the tallest at the WSW. The orientation of this detached alignment is about 55°–235°.

The purpose of such a complex can only be a matter for speculation. It can be observed,

Lagatjar (74), rows from the ESE.

however, that the longest row is visually the least important and may have had no other function than that of linking the bigger and more upstanding pair of rows leading to the NW from it. At this latitude of 48°16′, and with a nearby, low but rising skyline, both the north-western rows would have provided a declination of about 28°30′ suggesting that they may have been aligned on the most northerly setting of the moon. The bleak whiteness of their stones may therefore have had a symbolic significance.

If there had been a lunar association in those rows then it is of interest that the line of three great stones with the biggest at the WSW appears to have been in line with the midwinter sunset. It is possible, therefore, that at Lagatjar there are the ruins of a megalithic complex once used for rites involving both the sun and the moon.

75   Lanvénael, Plomeur. *Menhir*
23 km SW of Quimper, 7 km WSW of Pont l'Abbé. From Plomeur take the D57 N and in ¾ km turn W (L) for 2 km to Beuzec. At Beuzec take the NW lane towards Lanvénael. After 200 m a farm lane leads S (L). Menhir is in field 350 m from the Beuzec–Lanvénael lane.

This is an imposing menhir, 4.7 m high, interesting because of the finds discovered at its base. Buried there in a pile of ashes was a broken diorite axe, coarse beaker sherds, flints, quern fragments and horses' bones. It is doubtful whether these Late Neolithic/Early Bronze Age artefacts were contemporary with the erection of the stone. They were probably later deposits akin to those found by standing stones in the British Isles.

The Lanvénael pillar in a cultivated field is an irregular ovoid in plan with its long axis NNE–SSW, its sides measuring 2.5 m × 75 cm. It stands in level countryside.

At the village of Beuzec another menhir, now destroyed, also had sherds of a large and roughly-made beaker at its foot.

500 m S of Beuzec is KERUGOU passage-grave (72).

76   Léchiagat, Léhan. *Menhir*
25 km SSW of Quimper, 8½ km SSW of Pont l'Abbé. From Treffiagat take the D153 S and in 1 km go straight on when main road turns to W (R). In ¾ km reach coast road and turn W (R).

In 100 m menhir is on N (R) in very marshy ground.

This broad granite slab stands in marshy terrain. It was discovered when the lake of Lehan was drained towards the end of the 19th century. Standing on a NW–SE axis it is about 5 m high and 5 m wide and is roughly shield-shaped. Its E side is vertical but its W edge is markedly concave and rises to a tapering summit. Two flint arrowheads were found near it.

Lerret. *Allée-couverte (see* 70b KERNIC)

77   Lervilly, Audierne. *Menhir*
34 km W of Quimper, 29 km WNW of Pont l'Abbé. From Audierne take the D784 W and in 1½ km turn S (L) past Esquibien to Lervilly 3 km to the S.

Near the hamlet of Kervilly is the chapel of Ste Evette. There is a painting of this saint in the nearby church. By the chapel itself is a tall menhir which has been Christianized by the addition of a carved cross whose arms terminate in cupmarks.

78   Lesconil-Plobannalec, Treffiagat. *Passage-graves*
24 km SSW of Quimper, 6 km SSW of Pont l'Abbé. From Pont l'Abbé take the D102 S. In 5 km pass over D53 and in 500 m turn W (R). In 1½ km, just beyond Tronval, turn N (R) for 300 m to junction of tracks at SE corner of a pine spinney. Tombs are 100 m NW through gorse in clearing in the wood.

On a sunlit day this is one of the loveliest sites in Brittany, the stones almost translucently golden against the greens and darknesses of the trees around them. It is a remarkable complex. Here there are the footings of three transepted passage-graves whose collapsed, drystone walls were removed during the excavations of 1883, leaving only the basal stones behind.

The first tomb has an 11-m-long passage, ESE–WNW, leading to two side-chambers

(Top left) Lanvénael (75), menhir frm the NE.

(Top right) Léchiagat (76), menhir from the S.

(Right) Lesconil-Plobannalec (78), menhir and passage-grave from the SSW.

each of which has a second cell to its W. A short passage, consisting of two sideslabs and a capstone, faces SW towards an isolated menhir. Sherds of Carn ware suggest that this tomb may have been a contemporary of BARNENEZ II, (40), built around 4400–4300 BC. The oval chamber, 5 × 3 m, was probably corbelled.

19 m to its SW is a triangular menhir, 2.3 m high and 1.7 m wide at its base. There is a natural gutter at the centre of its NE face. 34 m to the NW are the remains of the westernmost passage-grave, 8 × 8 m overall, its passage gone but with side-chambers each about 3 × 3 m. Beyond them is a large chamber with a convex W wall. 6 m to the E of this tomb is the third passage-grave, 15.5 m long. It is T-shaped with two extra side-cells halfway along its passage. It is 4 m to the W of the first site.

To the N of this fine group is the lowered mound of a tertre tumulaire. There were once also some ten little barrows each with one or more cists, and from them came a variety of Neolithic and Bronze Age material including a 'Pôt-de-Fleur' vase, spindle whorls, polished axes, two bronze axes and a chisel, a copper dagger and eight amber beads 'unfortunately destroyed at the time of discovery'.

Some of these artefacts belong to the Tréboul tradition of the Bronze Age, as late as 1700 BC, implying that Lesconil-Plobannalec may have been a burial and ritual centre for almost 3,000 years. Altogether the sites stretched over some 300 m, much of it now planted with trees.

79 Lestriguiou, Plomeur. *Passage-grave*
25 km SW of Quimper, 8 km SW of Pont l'Abbé. From Plomeur take the D785 SW for 2½ km, turn WSW on lane to Lestriguiou and in 250 m turn SE (L). Tomb is on bank, amongst bushes, 50 m down lane to S.

The damaged remains of this tomb stand on level ground with a narrow passage of granite slabs facing almost exactly E. There was a lateral entrance of two slabs at the eastern end on the S side. These, at right-angles to the main body of the tomb, led to a passage 4 m long with four stones on each side rising in height to a mutilated chamber now measuring about 2 × 1.5 m. Four orthostats survive supporting a heavy capstone. The western

part has been destroyed. A sillstone separated the passage from the chamber.

Excavations in 1876 recovered three round-bottomed, carinated Kerugou bowls of the Late Neolithic, a flat-bottomed carinated vase of the same tradition, a large flint blade, two dolerite axes, pendants and an archer's stone wristguard.

Leuré. *Rows (see 97b* TY AR C'HURÉ)

80 Madeleine, La, Lestriguiou. *Stone rows*
25 km SSW of Quimper, 8 km SW of Pont l'Abbé. From Penmarc'h take the D785 NE and 1 km beyond the junction with the D53 on the E take the lane to the W (L) towards Lestriguiou. In 250 m take the 2nd lane on the W (L) at the entrance to the hamlet. The stones are 250–300 m farther on on the N (R) of the lane in the fields.

Here there was once a large complex of four parallel lines of standing stones stretching over a kilometre of the countryside. They have systematically been robbed. In the middle of the 19th century there were still 500 or 600 stones surviving, but by 1885 only about 200 were left and today there are merely a few isolated and tumbled boulders to show where these rows once stood. In the 1920s Daryl Forde described this wreckage of an alignment and a cromlech 'less than a kilometre long and consist[ing] of four lines of stones. The circle at the eastern end is very mutilated. The stones left standing are small.' Sixty years later there is even less to see.

81a Men-Marz, Brigognan-Plage. *Menhir*
39 km WNW of Morlaix, 11 km N of Lesneven. 1 km NNW of Brigognan-Plage on the Terre de Pont. From Brigognan follow road signposted 'Phare-Menhir' towards Kerverven for ¾ km. Menhir is on S (L) of road just against the chapel.

This is a gigantic, sharply tapering stone, 8 m high, 3.5 m wide at its base and about 1 m thick. 2 m to the NE is a huge, fallen stone, the Men-Marz or 'Miracle Stone'. The standing stone is of playing-card shape and is on an E–W axis. The rocks from which it was detached are close by. A small cross has been placed on top of the menhir.

It was called the Miracle Stone because St Pol de Leon is reputed to have come here to arrest the constant erosion of the land by the encroaching sea. He forbade the water to come any further than this spot and to mark the place his sister put up the stone.

81b There are other standing stones in the neighbourhood, one at **Kervezvel** 300 m S of Men-Marz, another at **Kervizouarn** 4½ km to the SW.

81c At Diévet, 500 m NNE of Plounéour-Trez, is a ruined allée-couverte built of local granite stones.

82 Mougau-Bihan, Commana. *Allée-couverte*

32 km SE of Lesneven, 22 km SSW of Morlaix. From Plounéour-Menez on the D785 15 km S of Morlaix take the D785 S for 3½ km. Turn W (R) for 5 km to Commana crossroads.Turn S (L). Tomb is 1 km on W (R) of lane just beyond hamlet and partly concealed by a hedge.

Standing on the western slopes of the Montagne d'Arrée this magnificent allée-couverte was put up on level ground from which the land fell to the S and then rose towards the 'Hell Marsh', now an area of reed and bogs. It is a spectacular setting and the tomb itself is spectacular because of its heavily impressive architecture and its delicate art. Its name means, 'Little House'.

Eighteen granite slabs form a rectangular chamber aligned SSE–NNW, 11 × 1.5 m wide and rising in height from 1 m at the NNW to 1.8 m where the end-stone forms the back of a terminal cell near the lane at the S. Five capstones cover this megalithic structure. The end-cell is rectangular, 1.4 m wide and 2.3 m long. It is uncovered and undecorated. The lateral entrance to the tomb is at the NNE.

Inside the chamber the end-stone has a fine carving of a hafted axe which is almost a

(Above) Men-Marz (81a), Christianized menhir from the SW.

(Below) Mougau-Bihan (82), interior of allée-couverte with dagger-carving on end-slab, and plan.

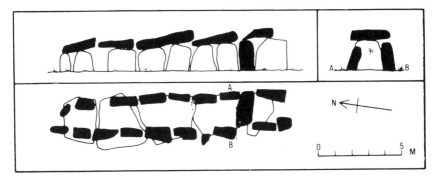

replica of that at the TOSSEN-KELER cromlech, CN (34). Alongside this stone the next slab has carvings of two spearheads or daggers on it. They have been termed 'Cypriot', probably mistakenly (*see* 22a PRAJOU-MENHIR).

From the entrance the second stone on the S has carvings of two pairs of breasts, one above the other, those at the top being smaller, with a third 'Cypriot' dagger carved, blade up, to their right. Such art links Mougau-Bihan with three other allées-couvertes at TRESSÉ, IV (112), PRAJOU-MENHIR, CN (22a), and KERGÜNTUIL, CN (13b). Mougau-Bihan is the most westerly of this small group.

Museums (*see* 89 QUIMPER, 94a ST GUÉNOLÉ)

83 Pen Loic, Pont l'Abbé. *Menhir*
17 km SSW of Quimper, 2³/4 km SE of Pont l'Abbé. On the D2, 2 km SE of the bridge on Pont l'Abbé, take the 2nd lane on the E (L). Go past Kerdual. 500 m from the main road the lane

Plozévet (84), menhir by the church.

turns S (R). Take the first lane E (L) to Pennglaouic. From the hamlet a footpath by the wood leads N 100 m to the menhir at the side of the Anse de Pouldron.*

Standing as it does on the seashore this grey, tapering pillar, 3 m high, is half-submerged at high tide, demonstrating the changes in sea level since prehistoric times. The granite stone has a circular base but sub-rectangular sides.

84 Plozévet. *Menhir*
23 km W of Quimper, 13 km SSW of Douarnenez. Menhir is in the churchyard.
In the main square of this little town is the 13th-century church with its Romanesque nave-arcades. In the churchyard there is a sacred fountain and a menhir at the E corner. It is a thin, grey pillar, striated by the weather. It stands 2.3 m high and has been incorporated into a memorial to the dead of the First World War.

85 Pont l'Abbé. *Megalithic centre*
17 km SSW of Quimper.
This busy holiday town has a museum of local Bigouden material including costumes and models of boats inside the round castle tower. Around the town, on the Penmarch peninsula, is a profusion of megaliths, not always impressive or well-preserved but often worth visiting. The density is best seen on the map of the département. Menhirs include LE GUIREC (48), KERDALAÉ (57a), KERÉGARD-VRAZ (59), KERNÉVEZ (69), LANVÉNAEL (75), LÉCHIAGAT (76), LERVILLY (77), and PEN LOIC (83). There are stone rows, or the remains of them, at KERFLAND (62) and LA MADELEINE (80). Chambered tombs exist at the splendidly-situated BEG-AN-DORCHENN (41), KERDANNO (58a), KERUGOU (72), LE RUN (90b), the reconstructed RUN-AOUR (94b), LESTRIGUIOU (79), POULGUEN (87), and the evocative LESCONIL-PLOBANNALEC (78). To animate these empty stones there are the objects in the museum at ST GUÉNOLÉ (94a).

A pleasing short tour to reveal the variety in these sites, starting from Pont l'Abbé, might include, in order, LESCONIL-PLOBANNALEC (78), LÉCHIAGAT (76), ST GUÉNOLÉ museum (94a), BEG-AN-DORCHENN (41), KERUGOU (72), and LE GUIREC (48). The blue Carte Topographique 1:25,000 map, no. 0520

Ouest, is invaluable. There are also two orange 1:50,000 maps, nos. 0420 and 0520.

Port Neuve, La. *Allée-couverte* (*see* 46b
GOULET-RIEC)

86a   Pouldreuzic, Plozévet. *Menhir*
24 km W of Quimper, 15 km SSW of
Douarnenez. From Plozévet take the D2 E
towards Pouldreuzic but in 500 m turn S (R)
through Lostallen and past Lezavrec. Menhir is
on coast 300 m SE of Kerrest hamlet.
This tall, brown pillar stands by the coast
between the hamlets of Kerrest and
Kerbouron. It has rectangular sides, the
western face being somewhat inclined. It is
2.5 m high and is known as Les Droites de
l'Homme.
86b   Another menhir, 2.6 m high, at
Penquer stands at the edge of a small stream
flowing into a shallow ravine.

87   Poulguen, Penmarch. *Passage-grave*
26 km SSW of Quimper, 9 km SW of Pont
l'Abbé, ¾ km W of Poulguen on the farm track
to Stêr Poulguen.
Visually a visit to this grossly ruined
monument is a disappointment, but the site is
important because it was one of only three T-
shaped passage-graves, a variant form of allée-
coudée, the others being KERIVIN (65) and
KERUGOU (72). The chambers, at right-angles
to the passage, lay under a great circular
barrow, 40 m in diameter and 8 m high.
     Excavations in 1862, 1902, 1927 and 1948
found that the 8-m-long passage, facing ENE,
led to chambers, one to the NNW and to a
much shorter one at the SSW. Both were built
of local granite. At the end of the passage a S
sidestone had cupmarks on it. In the NNW
chamber, subdivided by two transverse slabs,
there was a cartouche with a 'figurine' in it,
carved on a W stone.
     A layer of fine black soil almost filled the
chambers and between it and a lower layer was
a mass of charcoal, human bones and ashes.
From this deposit came a Late Neolithic 'Pôt-
de-Fleur', three polished axes, flints and a
13.5-cm-long Grand Pressigny blade. From
charcoal obtained during the 1902
investigations a C-14 assay produced a
corrected date of about 2000 BC for activities
in this strange megalithic tomb.

88   Primelin, Audierne. *Menhirs*
38 km W of Quimper, 23 km WSW of
Douarnenez, 5 km W of Audierne. From
Primelin take the road E for 1½ km to Chapelle
de St Théodore in Tugen hamlet.
This chapel was built against an enormous
dolmen, now vanished, whose capstone was
like a canopy with space enough beneath it for
a person to sleep. The walls were of heavy
sideslabs. A legend records that a holy man
meditated here for many years, lying on his
back, hands on his chest, without food or
drink, never speaking, He seemed as granitic
as the tomb. Moss and lichen grew on his
clothes and only his open eyes showed he was
alive. One day they closed. His corpse was
taken to Primelin church where he was buried
in the choir.
     The chapel is dedicated to this saint, Tujen,
supposedly the St Eugene or Eoghan, a Bishop
of Derry in Ireland who died in AD 618. The
chapel, a replacement for an older building,
was erected between 1515 and 1530 and its
altar, 2.3 m long and 80 cm wide, was carved
out of a menhir. It stands on two Gallo-Roman
columns. The saint's statue stands against the
altar with a carving of a dog biting another,
evidence that this saint was the protector
against mad dogs.

89   Quimper. Musée Départemental
Breton. *Museum*
On Rue Gradlon, Quimper, S of the cathedral
close in the old bishops' palace. Open 1 July to 15
September, 1000–1200, 1400–1800. Otherwise
1000–1200, 1400–1700. Not Tuesdays from 16
September to 30 June and holidays. Admission
1 Fr.
This museum has a small but interesting
collection of Finistèrian archaeology and
history. In the courtyard there is a fine Iron
Age stele from Ros-an-Trémen, 3 km WSW of
Plomeur. Its top has been damaged but is still
3 m high and is decorated with multiple
grooves.
     In the museum there is also the fantastic
stele from Kervadel near Plobannalec. It is
sometimes wrongly called the Menhir de
Kernuz from the name of the manor in which
it was once kept. It was discovered in 1878.
On it are carvings of seven Gallo-Roman
deities. There is a group of a man, woman and
child, and near them a warrior with horned

helmet, leaning on his shield. By him can be seen the figures of Hercules and Mercury who is holding a small person by the hand.

Raguénés. *Rows* (*see* 97c TY AR C'HURÉ)

Renongar. *Passage-grave* (*see* 45b CRUGOU)

Rostudel. *Dolmen* (*see* 97d TY AR C'HURÉ)

90a   Ruen, Le, Treffiagat. *Menhir*
25 km SSW of Quimper, 8 km S of Pont l'Abbé. From Treffiagat take the D153 S and in 300 m take the SE (L) fork at Kergroez. In 1¼ km at the crossroads turn E (L) and in 300 m turn to S (R). Menhir is S of the bend in a lane by the farm.
This is a remarkable, jagged pillar of granite, 5.5 m high with its broad S face towards the sea. It is a tapering rectangular column, standing on an E–W axis at the edge of a terrace with the land falling towards the S. Near it were found sherds, flint flakes and piercers and straight-edged flint arrowheads.

Le Ruen (90a), menhir from the ESE.

90b   100 m away are the remains of the **Le Run** V-shaped passage-grave with an 11.5-m-long passage which widens from 1 m at its ESE entrance to 1.8 m at its WNW end. 8 m from the entrance there is a sillstone marking the beginning of the chamber which is otherwise undifferentiated, and in the chamber there is another subdividing it into two compartments in tandem. The best example of such V-shaped tombs is TY-AR-BOUDIQUET (95a).

Excavations at Le Run unearthed sherds of two round-based bowls with light lines incised around their necks. There was also a flat-bottomed Kerugou vessel, pendants, flint arrowheads and dolerite axes, all of the Late Neolithic/Early Bronze Age transition.

90c   1 km NE of Treffiagat is the ruined passage-grave of **Kervillogant** from which a fine assemblage of Chassey ware was obtained.

Run, Le. *Passage-grave* (*see* 90b LE RUEN)

Run-Aour. *Passage-grave* (*see* 94b ST GUÉNOLÉ)

91   St Denec, Porspoder. *Menhirs*
23 km NW of Brest, 31 km WSW of Lesneven. From Porspoder take the SE lane at the extreme S of the village. In 500 m take the SSE (R) fork and in 100 m turn E (L). In 1 km come to farm of St Denec on the N (L) of the lane.
In the field just to the W of the farm and on the other side of the lane there are two standing stones 10 m apart on a NE–SW axis. Each is about 2 m high and sub-rectangular. They have not been shaped. The St Denec group is remarkable for the art noticed on a fallen stone belonging to the line which at one time consisted of the two standing and two fallen granite pillars. On the upper face of one prostrate stone were carvings of two hafted axes. Despite the unsuitable nature of the coarse granite they had been fashioned in low relief. In style they looked like two shepherd's crooks with crossbars added to them. The stones are on private ground and the fields are firmly barred and gated.

92a   St Eden, Plouescat. *Menhir*
28 km WNW of Morlaix, 17 km NE of Lesneven. From Plouescat take the D30 W and in 1 km turn N (R) through Pen ar Prat. Menhir

is on Kergoura farm just before St Eden village. This is a superb standing stone, shaped, and a full 7 m high. Its sides are perforated by two holes. It is said to guard treasure which can only be recovered on Christmas Night and Palm Sunday. Some cupmarked stones nearby are called Kerreg an Tan or 'Rocks of Fire', and Skudellon er Zabbat, 'Sunday bowls'. In Merovingian times peasants lit fires by these stones in some forgotten ritual.

92b At **Irvit** hamlet, 2½ km E of St Eden and on a road to the E of the D330, is a menhir which is supposed to strike twelve at noon and midnight but only 'pour les oreilles attentives'.

92c Close to St Eden but now gone was a cromlech with a central stone which was still standing in 1912 and which had been used to hang criminals in chains.

92d By the seashore at St Eden is a strange rock with twenty-five natural basins of several sizes on it. It is called **La Roche de St Eden**. One basin always has water in it and to drink it was an excellent cure for illnesses.

93 St Gonvarch, Porspoder. *Menhir*
30 km WSW of Lesneven, 23 km NW of Brest. From Porspoder take the D27 N. After 1 km turn E (R) onto the D68. After 2½ km turn N (L) past St Gonvarch church. Menhir is 300 m farther on on NW (L) of lane.
This fine menhir, 200 m from the road in an open field, is 6 m high and has been shaped with stone mauls. This is a characteristic of the granite pillars of West Léon. It is a neat,

rectangular menhir and it stands in a slight depression in otherwise level countryside.

94a St Guénolé. Musée Préhistorique Finistèrien. *Museum*
28 km SW of Quimper, 11 km SW of Pont l'Abbé. From St Guénolé take the D53 E. In 1 km turn N (L) past Kervilou and Kervédal and in 100 m take NW (L) fork. Museum is 500 m on S (L) of road. Open from 1 June to 30 September, 1000–1200, 1400–1800. Closed Tuesdays. If closed, apply to curator on premises. Admission 4 Fr.
This museum of local prehistory was founded in 1919 and taken over by Rennes University in 1947. It stands by the beach of the desolate Anse de la Torche where 'it should be remembered that too venturesome tourists have been swept away by the sudden, engulfing waves'.

Inside, the rectangular building is divided into two rooms, each containing interesting collections of prehistoric material including axes, pottery and weapons. There are some reconstructions of graves and photographs of important sites on the Penmarch peninsula.

Outside, at the front and side of the museum there is a bewilderment of Iron Age stelae, including that from Kerviltré, phallic menhirs and the re-erected passage-grave of RUN-AOUR (94b), which was brought from the commune of Plomeur 3 km to the NE.

94b Run-Aour Outside the museum is an extraordinary monument. The passage-grave was already ruinous when it was excavated in

Run-Aour (94b), reconstructed passage-grave outside St Guénolé museum.

75

(Above) St Guénolé (94c), stelae outside the museum.

(Below) Ploneour-Lanvern (94d), stele by the church.

1880 but the imperfect records gave enough details for its original form to be reconstructed when it was moved to the museum from Plomeur.

It consisted of a circular, drystone-walled chamber which was approached from the S by a long, straight passage, 16.5 × 1.5 m wide, built of local granite slabs. Just before it joined the chamber a second passage led off it to the E, 12 m long, 2.1 m wide and 2.2 m high, much bigger than the first. A sillstone, 40 cm high, separated it from its partner to the W.

Finds from this odd tomb were plentiful and informative. Three complete round-based bowls were discovered and sherds of carinated Kerugou ware and the base of a 'Pôt-de-Fleur'. There were adzes of flint, dolerite and fibrolite, flint blades, polishers and piercers, all products of the Late Neolithic period.

The architecture of Run-Aour appears to derive from the allée-coudée forms of passage-graves, but it is a very local and atypical development. It now stands amongst a clutter of megaliths at the front of the museum.

94c Also outside the museum is an assemblage of Iron Age stelae, including that from **Kerviltré** Halstatt/La Tène cemetery, and some low, domed Celtic phallic menhirs.

94d At Ploneour-Lanvern, 10 km to the

NNE, another stele, **Le Mât de St Éneour**, has been set up by the church. This elegantly smoothed cone is topped with a ball like those on the masts of sailing ships. The stone is supposed to be the mast of the boat in which the saint sailed from Ireland to Brittany. On the day of his Pardon, the second Sunday in September, young people would dance around the stele to be sure of having children.

St Guinec. Menhir (see 50b HUELGOAT)

95a   Ty-ar-Boudiquet, Brennilis. *Passage-grave*
26 km NE of Châteaulin, 24 km S of Morlaix. From Morlaix take the N21 SW for 5 km, turn S (L) onto the D785. In 16 km turn E (L) onto the D764. After 7½ km turn S (R) towards Brennilis. In 2 km, at Bellevue, turn E (L). Tomb is 200 m on S (R) of lane.

Ty-ar-Boudiquet, 'the House of the Fairies', is a well-preserved V-shaped passage-grave, strangely isolated in the centre of Brittany from the other passage-graves to the S. Standing in a big, oval mound the SE-facing passage, only 90 cm wide at the entrance and 1.2 m high, lacks a capstone. 5 m long, it leads towards a widening and rising chamber 8.4 m long and ultimately 1.8 m high and 2.8 m

wide. It is covered by three capstones of which the last is an enormous granite slab, 5.5 × 5 × 0.7 m thick, weighing around 40 tons. In the middle of the chamber, but aligned asymmetrically to the SE–NW axis of the tomb, is a freestanding pillar perhaps analogous to the stelae or 'figurines' known in other passage-graves such as ÎLE GUENNOC (52).

No finds are recorded from this tomb, whose architecture suggests it is a transitional form between the classical passage-graves and the later, rectangular allées-couvertes.

There is a folk-story that dwarfs built the tomb for their home. They are reputed to have been at constant war with the giants living in the allée-couverte of MOUGAU-BIHAN (82), 10 km to the WNW.

95b   Two settlements of forty to fifty houses each are known at **Reuniou** 9 km NE, possibly Late Neolithic in date.
4 km to the E there is the 8.5-m-high menhir at ST GUINEC (50b).

96a   Ty-ar-C'horriket, Poullan-sur-Mer. *Allée-couverte*
23 km WNW of Quimper, 4 km W of Douarnenez. From Douarnenez cross the S bridge to the D7 towards Poullan. After 2½ km pass

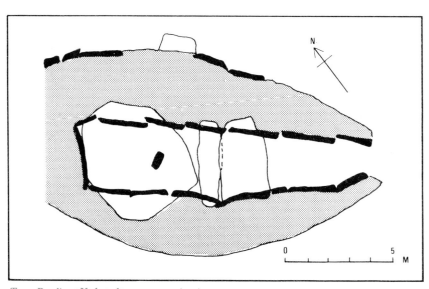

Ty-ar-Boudiquet V-shaped passage-grave (95a).

77

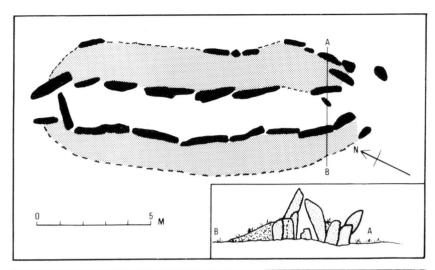

Ty-ar-C'horriket allée-couverte arc-bouté (96a), plan and view from the SE.

*over Tréhel crossroads and in 2¼ km turn N (R)
on road between woods. In ¾ km, at T-junction,
turn E (R). Tomb is 200 m on N (L) down a
narrow, hedge-lined footpath.*

This weird arc-bouté chambered tomb should
be seen for its architecture, the stones of the
chamber leaning together like a child's house
of cards. The monument, crowded by bushes,
stands in a long oval mound, 14 × 5 m, with
kerbing still visible on the eastern side. A
short vestibule at the SSE has a small
transverse slab marking the entrance to the
chamber which is rectangular, 12.3 × 1.6 m
wide but curving gently to the N. It is
composed of thin, flat slabs of local
granodiorite whose tops are propped against
each other to give the chamber a triangular
section up to 2 m high. At the NW end there is
a terminal cell, 1.2 m wide and 1.3 m long,
kinked a little to the NW. Beaker sherds have
been found in the tomb.

Comparable sites are rare and those worth
visiting even rarer, there being only three
others in Finistère at COAT-MENEZ-GUEN
(43), at CASTEL-RUFFEL (42a) and at GOULET-
RIEC (46a) and one in Morbihan at KERFILY
(143). There may once have been horizontal
stones capping these oddly-constructed allées-
couvertes but, if so, they have nearly all been
removed.

Other sites near Ty-ar-C'horriket include:
96b Kerdanet, a ruined allée-couverte
3½ km to the SW, 2 km S of Poullan at the N
end of a wood.
96c A menhir at **Kermenhir,** 2 km to the
WNW.
96d 750 m to the NNW the 'petit dolmen-

simple de Tréota' has been destroyed.
The allée-couverte of KERBANNALEC (56a)
is 6 km W.

97a Ty ar C'huré, Morgat. *Stone rows
30 km WNW of Châteaulin, 18 km S of Brest,
3 km SSW of Crozon. In the fields on the E
outskirts of Morgat between the Points de Morgat
and St Hernot. On the E 910 of the D255 before
reaching Montourgar.*
These ruined rows have sometimes been
mistaken for a cromlech. Like other
complexes of stone rows on the Crozon
peninsula Ty ar C'huré, 'the House of the
Vicar', had various extensions to it, but the
major part consisted of a roughly rectangular
setting characterized by a double line of large
and small stones in pairs decreasing in height
towards the centre. The rows have been badly
mutilated and are now in very poor condition.
97b At **Leuré,** 4 km N of Morgat and
2½ km NNW of Crozon, just to the N of the
hamlet of St Jean, there were once two lines of
standing stones at right-angles to each other.
They have been destroyed.
97c Across the Anse de Morgat, and 6 km E
of that town, there were the remains of two
lines of stones, again at right-angles to each
other, near the Plage de l'Aber at **Raguénés.**
These also have been removed.
97d Rostudel. *5 km SSW of Morgat and
immediately on the E of the D255, 150 m N of
the lane on the W to Keravel hamlet.* Here there
is a dolmen with a big but neat capstone of
granite supported by three metre-high pillars.
There is no sign of a mound.

Menhirs cut into crosses at Cap St-Mathieu, Finistère: a 19th-century view.

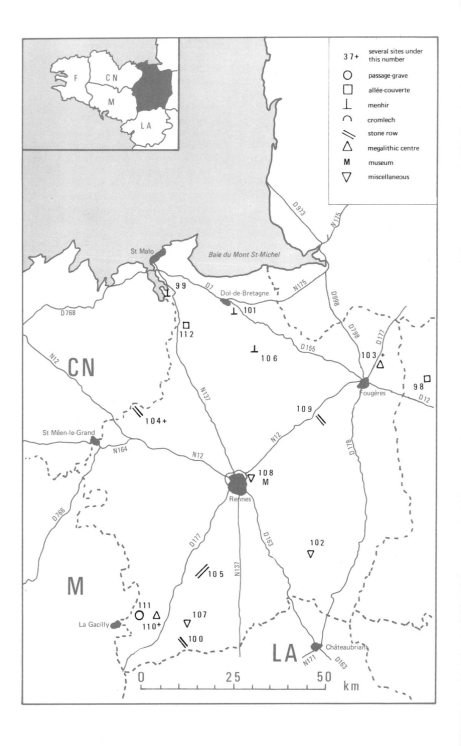

several sites under this number **3 7+**

○ passage-grave

□ allée-couverte

⊥ menhir

∩ cromlech

∕∕ stone row

△ megalithic centre

M museum

▽ miscellaneous

Ille-et-Vilaine

Maps: *Yellow Michelin 1:200,000, nos. 58, 59*
   Green Carte Touristique 1:100,000, no. 16

There are some excellent examples of the rectangular allée-couverte in this eastern part of Brittany and there is also one of the best standing stones, the shapely, soaring menhir at Dol (101). The chambered tomb at Tréal (111) and the carved allée-couverte at Tresśe (112), 'the Rock of the Fairies', would disappoint no one interested in Late Neolithic tombs and sanctuaries. Nor would the ponderous Loire dolmen at Essé (102), a monster of massive blocks and slabs with a neatly-symmetrical entrance of worked stones.

   Yet it is surely the stone rows, little-known but generally in good condition, that are one of Ille-et-Vilaine's chief megalithic attractions. There are the staggered lines at Lampouy near Médréac (104), with menhirs to their north and south; there is the sinuous line of the Cordon des Druides (103a) near Fougères, not far from two allées-couvertes and the medieval delights of the great castles of Fougères and Vitré, for which reason Fougères itself (103) would make a good centre, and a suggested itinerary has been provided for it; and, above all perhaps, there is the alignment at St Just (110d). Here there are lines, menhirs, chambered tombs and a collapsed cromlech, a collection of monuments that stands comparison in its variety with the more famous complexes at Carnac.

   St Just itself is small but the attractive town of La Gacilly, M (131), is only 10 km to the west near the Loire dolmen of Les Tablettes (162), and would make a fine centre for visiting the St Just sites and others near them.

Sites 98-112

Alignements du Moulin. *Stone rows (see* 110d ST JUST)

Château-Bû. *Mound and stones (see* 110g ST JUST)

Chenôt, Menhir de. *Menhir (see* 104c LAMPOUY)

98   Contrie, La, Ernée. *Allée-couverte*
19 km E of Fougères, 3¹/₂ km N of Ernée. From Ernée take the D31 N. In 1¹/₄ km turn NE (R) onto the D220 and after 2¹/₄ km the tomb is on the W (L) of the road about 200 m into a field.
This is an allée-couverte, average in size, which is still in good condition. It stands at the

end of a valley and faces NE. Its stones are of local dolerite and enclose a chamber 9 m in length. There is no sign of a covering mound, nor are there any portal stones. The width and height of the chamber, as is quite usual in these tombs, are about the same. The little end-cell at the SW end has no capstone to it. Excavations in the 19th century discovered the interior of the chamber was entirely floored with large, flat slabs. No finds were recorded. The tomb is also known as the Caveau du Diable.

Cordon des Druides, Le. *Stone row (see* 103a FOUGÈRES)

Croix-St-Pierre. *Tertre and cromlech (see* 110h, i, ST JUST)

99 Dent de Gargantua, La, St Suliac. *Menhir*

10 km S of St Malo, 15 km W of Dol-de-Bretagne. From St Malo take the N137 S and in 8 km, 2½ km S of St Jouan-des-Guerets, turn W (R) towards St Suliac. In 2 km, before outskirts of village, turn S (L). Menhir is 1½ km just beyond Chablé farm on W of lane, 100 m SW of the farm.

This fine standing stone on the eastern slopes of Mont Garrot is a coarse and heavy block of whitish stone with reddish blotches all over it. Square at its base it rises over 4 m, its sides measuring 2 m wide at N and S but only 1 m thick on the rough, narrower E and W ends.

The area around St Suliac has yielded several important Palaeolithic discoveries. Mammoth and horse bones dating back to the last glaciation have been found and also flint tools, possibly Mousterian, made by people using Levallois techniques of knapping.

100 Desmoiselles, Les, Langon. *Stone rows*

35 km W of Châteaubriant, 18 km ENE of Redon. From Pipriac take the D59 SSE. Cross the D177. After 7 km turn E (L) onto a minor road signposted 'La Marqueraie'. After 2 km the menhirs will be seen on the N (L) of the road on the outskirts of Langon.

Interrupted by gorse bushes and bracken but in good condition the rows stand on a gentle slope rising to the NW. Some twenty stones of granite and quartz, some of them startlingly white, stand in six roughly parallel rows on a SE–NW axis. Maybe half a dozen are between 1.5 and 2 m in height but the majority are about 1 m high. Some have fallen. Like many menhirs and standing stones in Brittany they have their broader faces at right-angles to the lines and in this they are different from the rows in the British Isles.

30 m to the NW, through the bushes, there are seven more stones, now encircled by conifers, in an irregular oval measuring approximately 10 × 6 m. They are to be found at the crest of the ridge. It is said that at the beginning of this century there was a concentric cromlech at the head of the rows and these stones may be the only evidence of its former existence.

The name, Les Desmoiselles, derives from the belief that these were girls turned into stone for dancing on the Sabbath.

Desmoiselles, Les. *Standing stones (see 110f* ST JUST)

Les Desmoiselles (100), rows from the SE.

101 Dol, Champ-Dolent, Dol-de-Bretagne.
Menhir
23 km SE of St Malo, 2 km SE of Dol-de-Bretagne. From Dol take the D795 towards Combourg and in 1½ km turn E (L) at crossroads. Stone is in field on S (R) of lane 200 m after turning.
This magnificent pillar of granite stands in a grassy enclosure surrounded by picnic tables. 9.5 m high it is one of the most beautiful of the Breton menhirs and also one of the tallest. In plan it is almost square, its base measuring 1.8 m wide at the SSE; 2 m, E; 1 m, WSW; and 1.5 m on the NNW.

The slender stone was erected on a schistose plateau and its source was probably from the granite massif 4 km to the S. Moving such a ponderous pillar weighing fifty tons or more must have involved the efforts of a greater part of the population. Then, having dragged it to the site, the people smoothed its sides, using heavy stone mauls to remove the rough lumps and give the stone some protection from crumbling. Such a practice was more common in West Léon, Finistère, where dressed menhirs such as KERLOAS (67a), and KERGADIOU (63), stand over 200 km to the W of Dol.

Its name is sometimes interpreted as *campus*

Dol (101), menhir from the E.

doloris, 'the Field of Sadness', which is interestingly paralleled by *Kerloas*, 'the Heath of Sadness', but *Champ-Dolent*, prosaically, probably means nothing more than 'the Field of Dol'.

A legend claims that it fell to earth to separate the warring armies of two brothers. Another story says that it sinks a little each year or that the moon eats a small portion of it nightly and that when it finally disappears the world will end.

102 Essé (La Roche-aux-Fées). *Loire dolmen*
28 km SE of Rennes, 25 km N of Châteaubriant, 2¾ km SSE of Essé. From Châteaubriant take the D178 N for 15 km to Martigné-Ferchaud and, beyond the lake on the E, take the D94 NNW for 9 km to Rétiers. Take the D41 W for 1 km and turn N (R). Tomb is 2¾ km on E (R) of road.
This isolated monument of cumbrous schist blocks is one of the megalithic wonders of Brittany for, despite the roughness of its stones, the structure has a balanced symmetry that belies the heaviness of its slabs. There are enigmas. It was built at the edge of an area of good stone and it is likely that its dark-red Cambrian schists, several of them weighing over forty tons, had to be dragged over 4 km to the site. Secondly, although Essé looks like a typical Breton allée-couverte, it is not. Furthermore, although it resembles a chambered tomb, neither bone nor sherd nor artefact has been found in it.

It faces SE towards a low horizon in the direction of midwinter sunrise. 19.5 m long and 6 m wide it has thirty-two orthostats, including three internal septal slabs, and nine enormous capstones, the westernmost being a monster of some forty-five tons. Yet despite this grossness the entrance is a marvel of architecture, two squat, shaped pillars 3.2 m apart and only 1.4 m high supporting an equally well-smoothed lintel that is perfectly horizontal, despite weighing some twenty-five tons. Great care had been taken over this entrance. The remaining stones are undressed and contrast starkly with the fastidious finish of these portals and lintel.

They give access to a short antechamber hardly 1 m high. At its NW two transverse slabs 1.1 m wide permit entry into the main

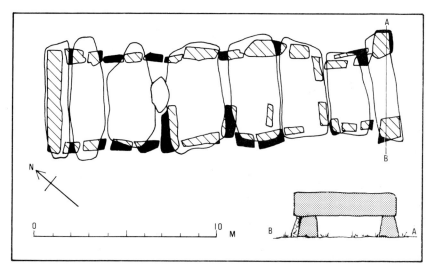

Essé (102), Loire dolmen plan and view from the S.

chamber 14.3 m long, 4 m wide and 2 m high. This spacious gallery had been subdivided into four side compartments by three projecting stones jutting from the SW side to create cells respectively 2.6, 1.7, 2.4 and 5.4 m long.

The architectural features at Essé link it with a series of huge megalithic sites between Angers and Saumur 150 km to the SE. They are known as Dolmens Angevins à portiques. The biggest of them at Bagneux on the outskirts of Saumur, Seine-et-Marne, is 18 m long, with four titanic limestone capstones. Its incredible size made it famous hundreds of years ago. In the late 17th century John

Aubrey, the British antiquarian, knew of it, 'an ancient Monument neer the high-way, called Pierre couvert. The perpendicular stones are, at least fower foot high from the ground'. Excavations in 1775 found nothing. Nor is there any sign of a covering mound to protect the dead from predators. Professor Glyn Daniel has considered this problem. 'I must perforce conclude that these great Loire galleries were never in barrows, and I am therefore forced to ask: if so, were they ever collective tombs, or tombs at all?'

This may be true also at Essé. It has the architecture of a tomb but was possibly raised at a time in the Late Neolithic when these

Le Cordon des Druides (103a), row from the SW.

monuments were becoming shrines for the living rather than burial-places for the dead. What ceremonies were performed in them must remain unknown, although one might speculate about an ancestor cult connected with the rising of the sun or moon.

Tradition has it that Essé was the home of fairies who were buried there and whose plaintive cries can still sometimes be heard. It is reputed that until recently young men and girls would go there at the time of the new moon to count the stones, the girl clockwise, the man in the other direction. If they agreed within a count of two the omens were propitious for their happy marriage.

Two other sites in Morbihan are akin to Essé, although much smaller, one at LES TABLETTES (162), 57 km to the WSW, the other at LA MAISON TROUVÉE (151a), 72 km to the W.

103 Fougères, Forêt de, Fougères.
Megalithic centre
48 km NE of Rennes, 8 km N of Fougères.
To the N of the old but rather dull town of Fougères, with its amazing 13th-century castle, there is the lovely expanse of the Forêt de Fougères. In it there are allées-couvertes, at least two of them worth visiting, and there is a good example of a stone row. It is suggested that the following itinerary would make a

pleasant afternoon's excursion. The orange Carte Touristique, 1:50,000 map, no. 1317, covers the area.

103a Cordon des Druides, Le. *Stone row.*
From Fougères take the D177 N for 10 km. In the forest turn E (R) at the Chiennedet crossroads which are signposted, 'Le Cordon des Druides'. The row is 500 m farther on to the N (L) of the road. This is an attractive line of quartz blocks and, as prehistoric rows are scarce in this part of Brittany, it is well worth visiting. It extends on both sides of the road but only the northern section is well preserved. Here the stones run in a SW–NE direction for some 240 m, ending with a massive terminal menhir. They are all of quartz, in contrast to the allées-couvertes of granite slabs nearby, many of them silkily white and veined with dark-red and black lines. None has been shaped and most are ragged with sharp shelves and shoulders where the stone has fractured.

There are twenty-three large stones, the majority about 1 m high, with others, mostly smaller, lying out of line to the E. The row leads up a quiet incline for about 75 m to the biggest stone of all at its crest, a tall pillar 1.8 m high with sides measuring 2 × 1 m. Its broader sides face E and W. Beyond it the land falls slowly away and the row curves subtly towards the NNE for another 170 m to the final huge quartz block.

S of the road there is almost nothing to be seen. 100 m S of the N row's end there are some roundish quartz blocks around a rectangular pit with a big granite slab 20 m to the NE. It is reported that there was once a small, squarish cromlech in this area with another, even smaller, close by. Of these questionable structures there is now no trace.

In the N row the position of the tallest stone at the top of the ridge suggests that this was the focal point of the complex, with two lines of stones approaching it from the NE and SW. What astronomical alignments there were in these rows may have been to the major northerly risings and southerly settings of the moon. The specific choice of quartz for the stones in these rows, of lunar whiteness, could therefore be of symbolic significance.

103b   Pierre de Trésor, La. *11½ km NNE of Fougères. From the Cordon des Druides return to the Chiennedet crossroads. Turn N (R). In 400m there is a footpath to the E (R). Bordering a wide and shallow ditch it leads in 200 m to the remains of an allée-couverte.* This is a much mutilated monument. Its former capstone now lies on the ground like an upturned plate, 2 × 3 m in size and nearly 1 m thick at its centre. By its S and SE edges are two of the original sideslabs, 1.2 m long and 1 m high. Two smaller ones stand by them. There are three more on the W side and another, 1 m long and 50 cm high, to the N. The ruin of this tomb was probably caused by the rumour that there was treasure concealed in it.

La Pierre Courcoulée (103c), allée-couverte from the W.

103c   La Pierre Courcoulée. *Return to the Chiennedet crossroads and turn W (R) for 1 km to the Serfilières crossroads. Here take the first road to the SW (L). In 1 km come to a clearing near the junction of several forest tracks. That on the E (L) leads 200 m to the allée-couverte.* This is in a charming part of the forest with chestnuts, pines, beeches and spruce growing alongside the path. The tomb is now in cleared ground. It is believed that the woodland was formerly the Iron Age 'druidical' forest of Scissy.

The ruined long megalithic tomb once stood in an earthen mound of which traces can still be noticed. It was erected on a slight slope down to the E and this is the direction that the monument faces with an axis of about 71°. The chamber is some 6 m long and 1.3 m wide but only 60 cm high. The twelve sideslabs and the capstone are all of local granite. The latter was once an enormous slab measuring 4.3 × 2.1 m and 90 cm thick and must have weighed twenty tons or more. Regrettably, it has been smashed by vandals whose wedge-marks can still be seen and only the western third of its length remains *in situ*. The rest of the gigantic slab now lies prostrate by the tomb.

103d   Also in the Fougères forest is the wreckage of a third allée-couverte, the **Pierre des Huguenots**, 3 km ENE of La Pierre Courcoulée and 1¼ km ENE of the Pierre de Trésor, deep in the forest.

103e   Le Rocher-Jacquot, St Germain-en-Coglès. *From Fougères take the D17 NW for 6 km. Take the first road W (L) 100 m beyond the lane to the W to La Bressais. The allée-couverte is 300 m along the road on the N (R) side just before a wood.*

The well-preserved allée-couverte of LA CONTRIE (98) is 19 km E of Fougères.

Four-Sarrazin, Le. *Chambered tomb (see 110j ST JUST)*

Grémel. *Round tumuli (see 110a ST JUST)*

104   Lampouy, Médréac. *Stone rows 34 km WNW of Rennes, 15 km NE of St Méen-le-Grand. From the centre of Médréac take the D220 E for 200 m and then turn N (L) onto country road. In 2½ km, after two lanes on the E (R), turn W. In 300 m the rows will be visible in* *the field on the S (L). There is a place to park just beyond.*

Despite their ruinous condition these are, perhaps, the most important rows in Brittany after those at Carnac. Here there are the remains of four lines, very unusually arranged, apparently having as their focus a tall menhir to their N with another, brilliantly white, on the level lowland to their S. The rows stand on the Crête des Roches, the Ridge of Stones.

Because of their tumbled state and because of the trees, hedges and brambles that grow between them it is hard to appreciate the relationship of the lines, whose disposition is unlike any other in Brittany. From the air they might be compared to four rowing skiffs racing towards the winning post of the northern menhir, on which they vaguely converge. The westernmost row is in the lead, two others to its E close behind with the bow of the third almost touching the stern of the second just to its E. Trailing well behind them and farther away to the E is the fourth and finest of the rows.

They were erected on a slope rising gently to the NNW, and it is noteworthy that the southernmost stone of the fourth row stands just where the land levels out, as though it were necessary for the lines to be on a gradient. They are known respectively as Les Longs Points, Le Clos de Rocher, Les Bergeons and La Grande Épinée. The individual components of the complex at Lampouy are best seen in the following order.

104a   La Roche Carrée. 200 m N of the road is the isolated menhir, reddish in colour and shining with mica crystals. It leans slightly to the E and its cracked and crumbling sides, about 1.8 × 1 m, rise to a pointed top 5 m high. Its broader faces are oriented towards the NW and SE.

104b   300 m SSW of the menhir and across the lane on the southern side of the hill is a row of nine stones, of which only one stands, a glittering white pillar, 2.5 m high, near the centre of this 35-m-long line of fallen blocks and slabs. The orientation is roughly N–S, not quite in the direction of the menhir.

60 m to the SE but separated from the first row by ditches, trees and brambles, is a second row also about 35 m in length and also with nine stones of which four are still erect. From N to S there is a standing stone 1.8 m high, two nearby fallen stones, a stone 1.5 m high, another 3 m tall with a broken stone to its E, another 2 m high and then three broken stones to its S. The row is oriented just W of N.

Immediately to its E, but with the most southerly stone in line with the head of the second row, is a third setting of seven fallen stones, many of them very large, the biggest being 4 m long. The length of the line is similar to the others. Tradition has it that a Roman general is buried under one of the slabs.

By far the most spectacular of the four rows

Lampouy (104), East row, La Grande Épinée, from the WNW.

is that at the extreme E. It is 200 m SE of the third row and divided from it by a low hedge. In the row, which is over 40 m long and aligned SSE–NNW, there are three fine stones still standing, of which that at the N is a starkly white 3.5-m-high pillar and that at the S is a great triangular block 4 m high with a deep reddish sheen. The row also contains four fallen stones.

104c In the flat fields to the S of these rows is the **Menhir de Chênot**. It is 500 m SE of the northern menhir, La Roche Carrée, and there is a local belief that from La Roche the midwinter sun can be seen rising over this glittering white block. Standing alone in the fields of Chênot farm the conspicuous, squat stone is 2 m square at its base and tapers only a little to its flat top. It is over 4 m high.

Sometimes known as the 'Stones of Three Colours', the varihued pillars of the Lampouy assemblage may have come from a source near Guitté, 1 km to the W.

The settings, despite the wreckage of time and man, appear to have been carefully planned, as the similarity in their lengths, their orientations and the number of stones in them indicate. The major elements in the group seem to be the single menhirs, red to the N and white to the S. What rites took place around them must now almost be a matter for guesswork, because what other structures, maybe of wood, also stood here is unknown. If the sun or the moon were involved in the rituals the approximate bearings to their northerly settings in the W would be 306° and 315° respectively, and 128° and 137° to their southerly risings. Even remembering the local tradition about the midwinter solstice, whether such orientations existed at Lampouy must now remain controversial.

Maison-des-Feins, La. *Allée-couverte* (*see* 112 TRESSÉ)

Museum (*see* 108 RENNES)

105   Perrons des Grées, Les, Messac. *Stone row?*
35 km WNW of Châteaubriant, 28 km NE of Redon. From the centre of Messac take the road NE between the school and the church. In 500 m by the railway veer E (R). Beyond a small quarry

on the left is a larger quarry. First stone is on the slope to the R of the quarry.
This is a tall menhir, 3.8 m high, with a triangular top. Its base measures about 2 × 1.5 m. 60 m away on the left of the road at the entry to the small quarry is a fallen stone, 2.5 m long and 1 m thick with a rounded top. 20 m farther on and standing side by side are two small stones, 1.5 and 1.8 m high. As the second of these four stones is fallen it is uncertain whether this group of whitish pillars was ever an alignment. They are almost on a SW–NE line.

Pierre Courcoulée, La. *Allée-couverte* (*see* 103C FOUGÈRES)

106   Pierre de Lande-Ros, La, Bazoges-la-Pérouse. *Menhir*
30 km W of Fougères, 17 km SE of Dol-de-Bretagne, 2½ km W of Bazoges-la-Pérouse on the D796 to Combourg. 2 km from the crossroads at Trois-Croix. On S side of stream between Bazoges and Noyal.
This impressive 5-m-high menhir is sometimes known as La Pierre Longue. It is triangular in shape, its sides measuring 1.2 × 1.8 × 2.2 m on the W. On its flattish top

La Pierre de Lande-Ros (106), Christianized menhir.

a small cross has been carved. The stone stands at the roadside and has 'Combourg' inscribed on it.

It is said to have been raised when St Michel and the Devil were arguing over the ownership of the Mont Tombe. Agreeing that it should belong to the one who built a marvel there first, Satan uprooted the two most massive stones he could find and returned to the hill only to find that St Michel had already erected an abbey on its summit. In amazement Satan dropped one stone and threw the other away. The first stone, the Menhir de Noyal, is this stone, the other is the towering pillar at DOL(101), 17 km away.

Another legend claims that the stone is the memorial of a great batttle but, say the natives of the neighbourhood, it is obvious that the first account is the true one because you can still see the depression on the stone where the Devil carried it on his back.

Pierre de Trésor, La. *Allée-couverte* (*see* 103b FOUGÈRES)

Pierre des Huguenots, La. *Allée-couverte* (*see* 103d FOUGÈRES)

107   Porte de la Roche, La. Langon.
Memorial
35 km W of Châteaubriant, 20 km NE of Redon. At the crossroads between the D56 W of Grand-Fougeray and the D127 S to Langon, immediately W of the River Vilaine.
Here there is a small, modern megalithic complex erected in commemoration of villagers shot by the German army in 1944. From a stone 1 m high two short lines of low stones extend to NW and SW. Between them, in line with the first stone, is a pillar of grey granite and a brilliant column of white quartz, both 2 m high and aligned E–W. The small stones are engraved with names of the dead.

2 km to the S are the rows of LES DESMOISELLES (100).

108   Rennes. Palais des Musées. *Museum*
In the city centre on the Quai Émile-Zola on the S bank of the River Vilaine. Palais des Musées for Fine Arts on the 1st floor; Musée de Bretagne, ground floor. Open 1000–1200, 1400–1800. Closed Tuesdays and holidays. Admission 3.50 Fr.
In the Musée de Bretagne there are attractive displays in a series of interlinking rooms. There is a good audio-visual map-board of the

La Porte de la Roche (107), memorial from the NE.

geology of Brittany and a very small section of cases devoted to Breton prehistory. There are excellent exhibitions, evocatively lit, of medieval material.

Roche-aux-Fées, La. *Loire dolmen* (*see* 102 ESSÉ)

Roche Carrée, La. *Menhir* (*see* 104a LAMPOUY)

Rocher-Jacquot, Le. *Allée-couverte* (*see* 103e FOUGÈRES)

109   Roches Piquées, Les, St-Aubin-du-Cormier. *Stone row*
26 km NE of Rennes, 16 km SW of Fougères. In the Forêt de Haut-Sève. From St Aubin take the D194 SE and in 2 km turn E (L) onto the D226. In 1 km turn N (L) onto the D103. In 600 m and 50 m W (L) of road there is a very high rock, La Roche Piquée, almost 20 m in height.
Here there is a line of four menhirs, arranged NW–SE, with two others nearby.

110   St Just. *Megalithic centre*
46 km W of Châteaubriant, 15 km NNE of Redon. 10 km E of La Gacilly.
So many megalithic monuments are concentrated in the area around the village of St Just that rather than listing sites individually two itineraries are suggested, the first to the E by car, the second to the W mainly on foot along well-marked paths. The

orange Carte Touristique 1:50,000 map, no. 1120, covers the area conveniently.

The countryside, today heathland with pines and gorse, is formed of a long E–W ridge of schists on which menhirs, stone rows and chambered tombs survive, the relics of what must have been a great Neolithic cult centre. It is reported that as late as the 19th century the inhabitants of the hamlet of Le Rocher just E of St Just refused to go onto the heath at night 'for fear of the horrible things to be seen there'.

EAST ITINERARY

110a   Gremel. *From St Just take the D54 E for 100 m and turn S (R) for 250 m. Turn W (R). Tumuli are in heath on N (R) of road. Five* small round mounds lie in the undergrowth. They are arranged in a crude Y open to the E. The two at the W forming the foot of the Y have small, deepset stones on their tops. Two others on the S arm have flat stones on them. The fifth is plain. All probably belong to the Early Neolithic period.
110b   Sévéroué. *Return to St Just. Turn E (R) onto D54. 1 km to Bignon crossroads. Take SE (R) fork. In 100 m there are huge schist outcrops in vegetation on N (L).* Just off the road on private land are many outcrops, including two stones supporting a third. This is a 'folly' constructed by enthusiastic antiquarians in the 19th century. A huge overgrown boulder, La Roche Mathelin, lies

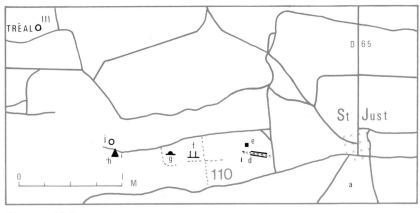

Sites around St Just (110).

Alignements du Moulin (110d), south row from the ESE.

just to the S. Similar deposits and laminations can be seen nearby, including seven or more massive blocks 20 m to the S. The site is known as 'L'Atelier de Sevéroué', rather fancifully, because it was thought to be the place where menhirs had been shaped. A Christian cross stands by it.

110c Les Trois Colonnes. *Return to Bignon crossroads and go straight across to N. In 200 m there are menhirs alongside farm to NE of the W (L) turning. Drive W 1 km to St Just.* At the D65 are three artificial caves dedicated to saints. The menhirs are opposite. On the W of the road the three tall menhirs, equally spaced, stand in line. They are covered in ivy and at a casual glance look like dead trees.

WEST ITINERARY

The Grée de Cojoux to the W of St Just contains one of the most interesting megalithic complexes in Brittany. Even today, mutilated by agriculture, land reclamation, stubble-burning and roads, there are still many monuments to be seen on it, most of them easily accessible after a short walk.

110d Alignements du Moulin. *From St Just take the D65 W but after 100 m drive straight on on minor road towards La Vieille Bourg. After 600 m turn N (R). In 250 m the rows are just to W (L) on open heathland.* There are three rows here. Two run ESE–WNW, slightly uphill and roughly parallel to each other. The third, 40 m to the W of the S row, is less

conspicuous, only 12 m long and aligned almost N–S at right-angles to the others (*see also* 74 LAGATJAR).

The S row is rather irregular in line, just over 30 m long, and is composed of a mixture of twelve thin quartz and grey pustular pillars of schist. The tallest, over 2 m high, is near the centre. The longer row, some 13 m to the N, is nearly 60 m long and is straighter. It consists of nineteen spectacularly white, squat quartz boulders, the tallest standing at the E. This juxtaposition of lines of thin pillars and low blocks has been considered by some as a representation of male and female principles. More certainly, the contrast between a line of pillars to the S and a row of low stones to the N can be compared with similar pairings in some unchambered Neolithic long mounds or tertres tumulaires where they jut from the body of the barrow or cairn and form an enclosure around the burials within. There are examples at the nearby LA CROIX-ST-PIERRE (110h), and at NOTRE-DAME-DE-LORETTE, CN (18), 66 km to the NE. Such a distant cultural connection is not improbable, for Notre-Dame is close to the principal axe-factory in Brittany at SÉLÉDIN, CN (31), whose products were distributed all over the Armorican peninsula.

Rescue excavations in 1978–80 revealed recent damage to the rows, some stones having been cut up when the adjacent windmill, now ruined, was built. The positions of the missing stones were identified by the packing-stones left in their holes. Some holes, however, were too small to have held pillars and it was supposed that posts had stood there, at least four being surmised to have occupied the long gap in the S row. Another break in the same row had been filled with a little freestanding ring of posts or by a flimsy hut. A hearth had burned in it. Sherds and flints strewn haphazardly in the vicinity of the row indicated its existence in the Middle Neolithic around 3800–3200 BC.

The rows were still functioning early in the Bronze Age, for three fine beakers of Rhine Basin style were found here. Later still, in the Middle Bronze Age around 1800 BC, when the rows were lapsing into disuse, a small round cairn was heaped over a fallen stone in the N row. It held two short cists. Finally, the cremated ashes of an adult were buried in a huge urn, 55 cm high, alongside the S row. The 'horseshoe' handles showed it belonged to the Éramecourt series, well-known in the Paris Basin but rare in Brittany.

The purpose of rows like those at St Just remains obscure, although in an area with so many burial places it is likely that they were associated with funerary practices, a belief made more probable by their architectural affinities with the lines of stones found in the earlier long mounds of the tertres tumulaires. That such practices were also associated with the sun or moon is also feasible. At the latitude of St Just and with a low horizon to the WNW the rows, which converge on an unmarked point 45 m to the WNW, appear to have been oriented, rather casually, on the equinoctial sunsets of March and September (*see also* 203 MÉNEC, CA; 104 LAMPOUY).

110e Le Vieux Moulin. *From the rows a footpath leads N to the ruined mill.* At its base there is a stone with a round hole in it. 50 m to the SW there are traces of a rectangular ditched and banked enclosure, 18 × 12 m, with a line of five tiny stones at its NW angle. Two stones at right-angles terminate the line.

110f Les Desmoiselles. *Return to the car and drive N on the minor road to the first turning W (L). Go past old farm. In 1 km a footpath to the S (L) is signposted, 'Pointe de Vue'. 200 m down it a path to the W (R) is signposted, 'Les Desmoiselles'. 150 m walk.* Two great quartz blocks, conspicuously placed on the hillside but half-engulfed in gorse, are each about 3 m

high and are 3 m apart. They are aligned E–W, the taller to the E. From them the CHÂTEAU-BÛ (110g), can be seen to the WNW. Les Desmoiselles are also known as Les Roches Piquées, 'the Worm-eaten Stones'. A third stone, 3.1 m long, lies nearby.

110g Château-Bû. *Continue 400 m W in car. The mound is 200 m S of the road on the heath. Best approached by footpath curving to SE. The area can be marshy.* The mound at the Croix des Garinais is oval, 46 × 26 m and 2 m high. It is constructed of a mass of small stones, now overgrown, and there is a deep, untidy pit just W of the cairn's centre. Around this cavity stand three large quartz stones at the corners of a square from which the SE stone is missing, possibly being the slab now lying 2 m away on the side of the mound. The tallest of the standing stones is at the NE. Smaller, upright stones, 1 m high, are set in line between it and the NW pillar, and stumps of others project from the mound on the E and W sides of the rectangle.

Such a site appears to be unique in Brittany but, paradoxically, it is very like the Four-Posters of northern Britain, which are rectangular settings of four stones, many with cremations and urns of the Bronze Age. Some of them have a pair of standing stones near them rather like LES DESMOISELLES (110f) to the ESE of Château-Bû.

Tradition has it that each year in ancient times a young girl was sacrificed on the mound on an altar specially built for the occasion. The meaning of 'Château-Bû' is obscure, but 'bû' may derive from the Breton for 'cattle', bulls having an important role in the religious celebrations of Brittany.

110h Tertre de La Croix-St-Pierre. *By car follow the same minor road W.* In just over 100 m there are fallen and standing stones on the S (L). These are the remains of a U-shaped cromlech open to the E. Of the nine stones only the third is erect. It is 1.6 m high. A tenth stone lies isolated 45 m to the E of the semicircle.

110i Immediately to the W is a low, overgrown tertre tumulaire, a Neolithic long mound excavated in 1953. It measures 20 × 15 m and is aligned E–W. In it were two parallel lines of stones, 5 m apart, containing twelve large quartz blocks leaning outwards on the S side, dark schist pillars on the N, an arrangement already noticed in the Alignements du Moulin. A large slab at the eastern end of the mound covered burials whose bones had been eroded in the acid soil. They had been surrounded by a line of little stones and with them were a few flint flakes and some nondescript sherds. Just to the W of the mound was a 1-m-high menhir.

On the northern side of the road in the gorse and bracken are other long mounds also having southern lines of quartz and northern of schist inside them.

110j Le Four-Sarrazin. *This chambered tomb is half-hidden in gorse. To find it from La Croix-St-Pierre cross the road and walk 50 m into heath. At cupmarked rocks turn W (L) for 50m. Site stands on a little rise.* This interesting although badly damaged megalithic monument is at the extreme W of the Grée de Cojoux. Its architecture is difficult to make out, but it is important for two reasons: it almost certainly had a lateral entrance and it stands on a well-preserved long mound with an internal setting of stones.

The long, rectangular chamber of the tomb measures about 9 × 1.5 m. It is aligned SE–NW. Only three capstones remain and the W end of the tomb has virtually disappeared. The entrance would have been at the far E on the S side where a capstone now leans. The passage-grave stands on an enormous mound, 28 × 13 m, in which there is still visible a rectangular setting, 24 × 7 m, of small dressed stones. These internal arrangements of stones and the frequent proximity of lateral entrance passage-graves to the unchambered mounds, Le Four-Sarrazin being only 100 m NW of LA CROIX-ST-PIERRE (110h) reveals the close cultural associations between them. Le Four-Sarrazin is likely to be the later.

There are the remains of other stones and mounds in the area, but for the chambered tomb most worth visiting, TRÉAL passage-grave (111), 1¾ km NW, it is necessary to return to St Just.

Severoué. *'Atelier' and outcrops (see 110b ST JUST)*

111 Tréal, St Just. *Passage-grave*
15 km N of Redon, 47 km W of Châteaubriant. 3½ km WNW of St Just. From St Just church

Tréal (111), passage-grave from the SE.

take the D54 NW for 500 m, turn W (L) through
Poubreuil and ¾ km beyond it take N (R) fork to
La Rohulais. Road curves to W. At Tréal farm
junction follow the metalled road W for 300 m.
Opposite barn on S (L) below road follow R fork
of footpath NNE up steep, wooded slope for
150 m to gigantic schist outcrop at crest. Tomb is
30 m NW in a clearing.

At first sight this fine megalithic tomb looks
like an allée-couverte arc-bouté with inward-
leaning sideslabs, but this is an illusion. It is,
in fact, a lateral entrance passage-grave in
which the southern sideslabs have fallen
inwards. Some capstones have slipped
between the orthostats. The entrance is at the
SE. Standing as it does on a level site in an airy
forest, the site provides a pleasant and
peaceful atmosphere for the visitor to look at
the ruined tomb whose grey, splintered slabs
are blotched with white patches of quartz.

It is 15 m long, just over 1 m wide and 1.3 m
high inside its chamber. Almost all its rough
schist stones remain, twenty-four sideslabs
and fifteen capstones, although many are now
displaced. The long chamber, aligned ESE–
WNW, has a tiny vestibule and an entrance
with two stones at right-angles to the southern
side at the extreme SE of the chamber. In this
it is similar to, but in better condition than, LE
FOUR-SARRAZIN (110j).

There is a folk story that the monument was
deliberately wrecked by fairies. It is
sometimes known as La Grotte aux Fées.

112   Tressé (La Maison-des-Feins), Le
Tronchet. *Allée-couverte*

20 km SSE of St Malo and 13½ km ENE of
Dinan, in the Forêt de Mesnil. 11 km SW of
Dol-de-Bretagne. From Dol take the D176 SW
for 12 km then turn SE (L) onto the D73. In
2½ km take turn SW (R). After 500 m, at T-
junction, turn W (R). In ¾ km lane bends
sharply N and then W. At head of this short bend
there is a parking space in the trees on N (R) of
lane. Follow footpath N over a little, wooden
footbridge, through forest for 300 m.

This superb allée-couverte, in the attractive
setting of a dry and spacious forest, was
excavated in 1938. Built on level ground near
the edge of a terrace falling away to the SE, its
entrance faced in that direction.

The rectangular chamber, 10.8 × 1.4 m

Tressé (112), 'breasts' in the terminal cell.

wide, was built of granite stones possibly from
an outcrop 20 m to the ESE. Seven capstones
are in position, the largest weighing over a
ton. The paved chamber rises in height from
about 1 m at the entrance to 1.4 m at the NW
end, where there is a big transverse slab.
Beyond there is a terminal cell open to the
NW and to the sky. Eight little breasts have
been carved here, two pairs on the NW face of
the transverse stone and two pairs on the
sidestones to its SW. In each case the
righthand pair is larger than that to its left and
it has a necklace lightly engraved beneath it.
In this the art is like that of PRAJOU-MENHIR,
CN (22a). Regrettably, at Tressé the carvings
on the end-stone were brutally smashed in
1961.

Remains of a skeleton were found under a
paving-stone at the NW end of the chamber
and this, with the discovery of some late
prehistoric sherds, persuaded the excavator
that Tressé had been built in Iron Age times,
'erected in the 1st century AD, probably in the
reign of Domitian'. Reassessment of the
primary artefacts, however, has shown this to
be a mistaken view. Sherds of SOM affinity,
transverse flint arrowheads and blades of
Grand Pressigny flint demonstrate that
Tressé, like other Breton allées-couvertes, was
a product of the Late Neolithic period.

Legend has it that fairies lived in the tomb's
ruins. When their cow trampled on some
crops they compensated the farmer with a

magic loaf, saying that it would never grow less or harden as long as he kept its origin secret. Forgetting his promise the farmer boasted of his prize one day and the loaf instantly became as hard as a brick.

Trois Colonnes, Les. *Menhirs* (*see* 110c ST JUST)

Vieux Moulin, Le. *Enclosure* (*see* 110e ST JUST)

A fanciful 19th-century view of Essé (102).

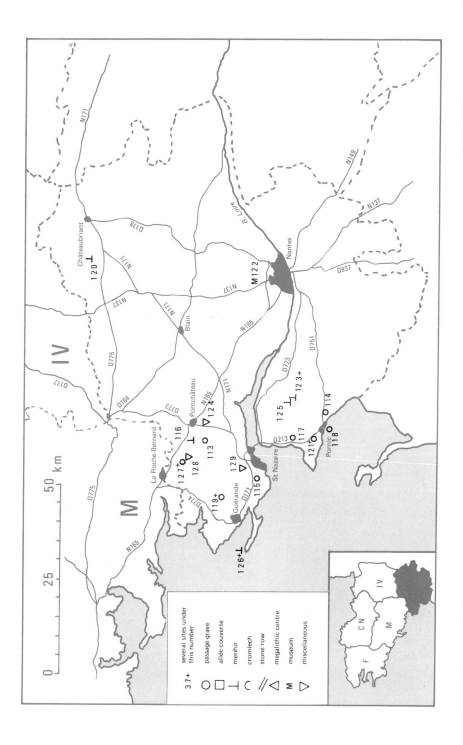

Loire-Atlantique

Maps: *Yellow Michelin 1:200,000, nos. 63, 67*
       Green Carte Topographique 1:100,000, no. 15 for west, no. 16 for north,
       no. 24 for major part of département

The south-east corner of Brittany, with its seaside resorts and commercial city of St Nazaire, might not seem a good region for the prehistorian, but this is not so. It is true that there are only a few fine sites left, but those that do exist are remarkable. Not ignoring the odd little group of reconstructions in St Nazaire itself, there is an excellent area of menhirs and chambered tombs around Herbignac 20 km north of that city, one of the best sites being the passage-grave at Kerbourg (119a), with a brilliant quartz standing stone in the fields to its west.

It is the transepted passage-grave tradition around Pornic, however, that distinguishes this part of prehistoric Brittany. Although many of these tombs are now in grievous disrepair and others such as St Michel Chef-Chef have been destroyed, one can still visit and enter Les Mousseaux (121a), at Pornic, examine its chambers and speculate about the cupmarks around the edge of the stone at its north entrance.

There is also the fenced-off splendour of Dissignac (115) on the other side of the wide Loire estuary. Readers must be warned that there is a toll bridge over this unavoidable river. Seen from a distance the bridge is like a rainbow, a parabola of engineering splendour, but the car driver's admiration will turn to dismay when he pays the toll. It is 30 Fr. – each way.

Sites 113-129

Arbourg. *Stone rows* (*see* 127b RIHOLO, LE)

113 Barbière, La, Crossac. *Passage-grave 15 km NNE of St Nazaire, 6 km SW of Pontchâteau. From Crossac, 6 km SW of Pontchâteau, take the D4 SE for 500 m. On N side, against lane to La Mioltais, is a footpath signposted, 'Dolmen'. Tomb is 150 m on W side of track.*
This is a ruined passage-grave which still has its huge capstone in position resting on three orthostats. It measures about 4 × 3 × 0.7 m thick and must weigh in the region of twenty tons. Many of the other stones have fallen. The entrance was probably at the E where four big stones may be passage remains.

Just to the N, on a hillock, is a Christian cross on a crude base. In the nearby wood is a 2-m-high menhir.

La Barbière (113), passage-grave from the S.

97

114 Boudinardière, La, Pornic. *Passage-grave*

From Pornic, 20 km SSE of St Nazaire, take the D13 E and in 1½ km at the Place Quatorze-Juillet turn S (R). In 400 m there is a parking space near the cliffs. Take the high but pleasant cliff path E for 500 m to the ruined tomb.

Known variously as Pré d'Air and La Pierre Creusée this is a collapsed example of a Pornic transepted tomb. The tumbled passage, facing SE, has a transept on either side of it and a small, square end-chamber over which is a very large capstone. There are fallen capstones in each of the transepts and in the passage. The stones are sandstone erratics and not of the local schists which can be seen in the cliffs immediately to the S. Excavations in 1875 recovered two Grand Pressigny flint daggers from this wrecked site.

LES MOUSSEAUX (121a) is 3½ km WNW and LA JOSELIÈRE (118) is 850 m to the W. There are some stones of another chambered tomb at La Maison Blanche 300 m ENE.

115 Dissignac, St Nazaire. *Passage-graves*

13 km ESE of Guérande, 5 km W of St Nazaire. From the centre of St Nazaire turn W off the Boulévard Gambetta onto the Rue du Commandant Gaté and go straight along onto the Rue de l'Hôpital. In 1 km pass under the D492. In 2½ km turn S (L) onto lane to Dissignac, Ste Margarite and St Marc. Tumulus is 1½ km on W (R). Short walk along track.

The tombs are closed off within a wire fence but good views may be obtained of the mound, the façade and the entrances. Dissignac is one of the great sites of megalithic Brittany and even though there is no access for the public enough can be seen of its construction for it fully to merit a visit. It was excavated in 1873 and again in 1970 when it was restored.

People had settled on this low, rocky knoll before the tombs were built. Microlithic flints, round-based sherds like Carn ware, cereal pollen and charcoal yielding dates of 4300 ± 150 bc, 3990 ± 150 bc and 3830 ± 150 bc, with an average of about 4900 BC, suggest that at some time at the Mesolithic/Neolithic transition a community had occupied this spot, growing cereals in a cleared area beyond a heavy inland forest of oaks and hazels. Nothing can be seen of their activities, only

the later mound, overgrown, 30 m in diameter and 3 m high. It was pillaged in historic times for building materials.

Beyond it, to the SE, the land slopes steadily down to the coast 5 km away. It was from there that huge blocks and slabs of granite and quartz were dragged by Neolithic families for two passage-graves that were set up, side by side, parallel, facing SE. Both had impressively dressed stones for their uprights upon which thick blocks were perched to support the even more ponderous capstones.

The tomb at the SW was possibly the earlier. Its 7-m-long and 1-m-wide passage led to a rectangular chamber only 1.9 m wide but 3 m long. In it no fewer than 400 sherds of early Castellic ware were found, highly decorated and quite different from the usual passage-grave Carn pottery. There were also some beads, including two of sericite, some 700 flints, six petit-tranchet arrowheads, scrapers and points. The underside of the capstone at the entrance to the chamber of this Neolithic treasure-house had been carefully smoothed and on it had been pecked out carvings of shepherds' crooks, axes and a superbly large hafted and thonged axe. This sanctified, dark tomb had an additional significance. Its passage faced directly towards the midwinter sunrise whose rays 'illuminate the chamber with a pale, orange gleam'.

The second chamber, to the NE, had a passage, slightly kinked, also 7 m long, 1.1 m wide and the same height but rising up to 2.5 m at the entrance to the chamber. This was P-shaped with a spectacular roofing of overhanging blocks in a series of inverted steps. The chamber was 3.3 m long, the same at its widest, and 3 m high, a truly megalithic vault for the dead.

Over these admirable tombs a neat cairn was constructed, 14 m in diameter with two concentric drystone walls in it, the inner enclosing the chambers, the outer encircling the passage-ends with a lining of big, contiguous blocks of granite and quartz. Visually this was magnificent, but when some of the kerbs began to topple outwards the cairn was enlarged, the passages lengthened by 4 m, and the cairn surrounded by unimposing walls of local gneiss. The only setting of granite stones now was a short stretch between the entrances.

In front of this later façade was a mass of Middle Neolithic sherds, the broken pieces of pots left as funerary offerings that had fallen from the low wall as others had done at LES MOUSSEAUX (121a), LARCUSTE, M (149a) and other tombs. These Colpo sherds, much influenced by the Chassey tradition, were probably related to the second phase of the Dissignac cairn, as a charcoal sample of 2990 ± 140 bc, around 3750 BC, appeared to confirm.

116   Fuseau de La Madeleine, La, La Madeleine. *Menhir*
18 km NNE of St Nazaire, 3½ km W of Pontchâteau. From La Madeleine turn S at the café, and beyond the Calvary take the 2nd lane to the E (L). Stone is in field on N (L), 200 m beyond the corner of the lane.
This is a tall, tapering stone, its roughly wrinkled surface like an elephant's hide. It is known as the 'Spindle of Ste Madeleine', a sinner who repented and who persuaded other villagers to abandon their heathen practices. It is a 5-m-high menhir, leaning a little to the NW. It is a pretty stone, whitish in colour, and it stands on a NW–SE axis, its sides measuring 2 × 1 m.

La Fuseau de La Madeleine (116), menhir from the S.

117   Grand-Carreau-Vert, Le, St Michel Chef-Chef. *Passage-grave*
12 km SSE of St Nazaire, 44 km WSW of Nantes and 11 km N of Pornic.
In this popular and built-up holiday resort there used to be a transepted megalithic tomb on the low land between the sea and the village. Such transepted monuments are a characteristic of this coastal area of south-eastern Brittany.

Le Grand-Carreau-Vert, 'the Great, Green Square', was a localized form of passage-grave with side-cells that were not apparently connected to the passage of the tomb but open to the sky. Limited excavations in the already ruinous monument recovered some beaker sherds and others of Middle Neolithic, thin-walled bowls. The site has been completely destroyed.

Nearby there were three standing stones, 'Les Pierres Boivres'. They also have gone.

118   Joselière, La, Pornic. *Passage-grave*
From Pornic take the D13 E and after 300 m E of the junction with the D213 turn S (R) onto the Rue du Château. From it turn E (L) onto the Rue de la Joselière. At the Rue de la Plage de La Joselière turn S (R). Walk down left fork of side road and turn L at end. Tomb is near coast 300 m to the E of road's end.
Standing on a SW slope near the sea this transepted passage-grave was in ruins in 1984 but being restored. It has a quartz stone at its entrance like the nearby tombs of MOULIN DE LA MOTTE (121b) and LES TROIS SQUELETTES (121c).

The tomb faces SE. In plan it is similar to the S tomb at LES MOUSSEAUX (121a), with two side-cells and a long rectangular chamber at the end of the passage like a megalithic T. There is a heavy capstone over each of the side-chambers and at the end of the short passage. Here there is a large and elongated terminal cell. The monument originally stood in a circular mound some 13 m in diameter.

119a   Kerbourg (Kervinche), Kerbourg. *Passage-grave*
16 km NW of St Nazaire, 6 km NE of Guérande. From Guérande take the D51 NE for 6 km and just after the D48 crossroads turn N (L) towards Kerbourg. 500 m along lane there is a lane to the E (R) signposted, 'Les Pierres

*Druidiques'. Tombs are 100 m on S of road,
200 m along track in field.*

The splendid passage-grave of Kerbourg or
Kervinche faces SE downhill and stands at the
crest of a low slope with good views to E and
W. The tomb is 8 m long with a narrow
entrance, only 40 cm high below its lintel, but
the passage widens and rises in height up to a
pear-shaped, asymmetrical chamber, 3.5 ×
3 m in dimensions, appreciably higher than
the passage. Its eight sub-rectangular blocks
support a heavy capstone. Beaker sherds have
been found at this site.

119b 100 m to its S, on the other side of the
track, is a ruined tomb, facing SSE, also about
8 m long but with its capstones fallen on the
toppled sideslabs. All the stones are large.

Legends claim that the two tombs were
connected by an underground passage filled
with gold and that they were the scenes of
druidical sacrifices.

119c 500 m SW of the Kerbourg passage-
grave, on the W of the lane leading to the D51,
is a beautiful white, domed menhir of quartz.
It is clearly visible in a field about 200 m from
the lane.

120 Louée, La, St-Aubin-des-Châteaux.
Menhir
*31 km NE of Blain, 10 km W of Châteaubriant.
From St Aubin take the D34 W towards Sion but
almost immediately, and before leaving St Aubin,
take S (L) road towards La Chapelle. In 150 m
take central of three roads. In 300 m stone is in
field on R.*
This is a gross and coarse block, 3.5 m high,
its sides measuring about 2.7 m on the N and
S by 1 m on the E and W. Many fables are
attached to this menhir, one claiming that
when Gargantua was sitting on the steeple of
Ruffigné with one foot in St Aubin and the
other in Sion this 'pebble' fell from his left
shoe. According to another story, if one puts
an ear to the stone it chimes will be heard. It is
also said that at midday the stone's shadow
points to a buried treasure.

Moulin de la Motte. *Tumulus (see* 121b
MOUSSEAUX, LES)

121a Mousseaux, Les, Pornic. *Passage-
graves*
*1 km W of Pornic town centre. Go W through
archway from town centre onto Avenue de*

*Général de Gaulle. Pass under and over two
bridges. 1 km from centre turn N (R) onto Rue
Mermoz. At top of hill turn E (R) onto Chemin
de la Motte. Monument is on S (R) of road,
signposted, 'Pierres Druidiques'.*

The two passage-graves here have been known
since 1840 when they were dug into. Nothing
is recorded of any discoveries. The site was re-
excavated and restored 1975–7.

These are fine examples of the Pornic
transepted passage-graves which have been
compared with the Notgrove transepted long
tombs of the Cotswold-Severn group in
England. Several other cruciform-planned
sites are known along the coastline of south-
eastern Brittany (*see* 114, 115, 118).

The Les Mousseaux sites were built at the
head of a slope down to the S to the Pointe de
Gourmalon. Their passages and chambers
were constructed of sandstone and
puddingstone probably from the Pays de Retz
inland to the NE but the covering cairn was
composed of local friable schist. Measuring
24 × 20 m in extent and standing 2 m to its flat
summit its succession of internal retaining
walls gives it the appearance of a stepped
pyramid. It has a neatly fashioned peripheral
wall.

In its straight SE façade are the entrances to
two parallel passage-graves, the southern
being T-shaped with an extra pair of lateral
chambers creating a ground-plan like a cross
of Lorraine. The northern tomb has a plan
like a distorted letter F. Capstones cover the
passages but the long, rectangular chamber at
the end of the southern tomb is now open to
the sky and may originally have been
corbelled. The righthand portal stone of the
northern tomb has a vertical line of dainty
cupmarks along its edge.

Between the two entrances sherds of vessels
akin to Chassey ware lay on the ground where
they may have tumbled from the wall of the
façade on which they had been placed as
funerary offerings.

121b Moulin de la Motte. A few metres to
the E of Les Mousseaux but on private land
are the remains of a huge tumulus once 70 m
long and 30 m wide but never excavated
because of the buildings, including a mill,
standing on it. It was aligned E–W. It is
supposed to have contained at least six
megalithic structures. The mill, which dates

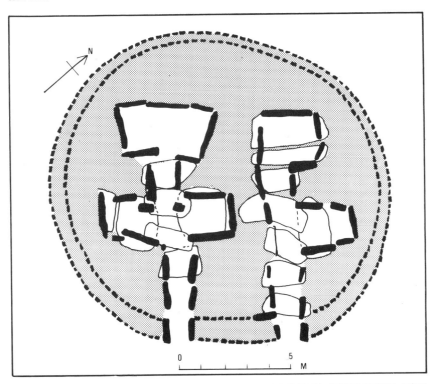

Les Mousseaux passage-graves (121a), plan and view from the S.

back to 1720, is composed of stones taken from this massive cairn. Eight tubular gold beads are said to have been found here. From the rear of the garden at the E of the house a quartz block is just visible at the entrance to one of the megaliths.

121c Les Trois Squelettes. 60 m to the E of the tumulus, in the same private garden, are the stones of a chamber excavated in 1875. From it came Chassey artefacts of the Middle Neolithic. They are now in NANTES MUSEUM (122). Sometimes known as the 'Dolmen de la Croix' it was transepted like Les Mousseaux. Two quartz blocks can still be glimpsed at its entrance with a fig tree growing in the neglected chamber.

Museum (see 122 NANTES)

122 Nantes. Musée Archéologique Régionale. *Museum*

In Nantes on the Rue Voltaire, 1¼ km WSW of the Château Ducal via the Place Royal. It is in the gardens of the Palais Dobrée. Open 1000–1200, 1400–1800. Closed Tuesdays and holidays. Admission 5 Fr.

In this attractive, modern building the prehistoric collections are on the first floor and are mainly concerned with material from south-east Brittany. Although the displays are not extensive they range from the Palaeolithic down to the Iron Age and are especially interesting about the Bronze Age.

123a Pauvredrie, La, St Père-en-Retz. *Menhir*

19 km SE of St Nazaire, 10 km NE of Pornic. From St Père take the D58 E and in 2½ km turn SE (R) onto the D5. In 1 km turn W (R) to hamlet of La Pauvredrie and, ¾ km beyond it, turn NW (R) to La Caillerie hamlet. Stone is on W (L) of lane.

This huge tapering block stands on a false crest on the grass verge opposite the cottage of La Croterie. It is over 4 m high and playing-card in shape, 1.5 m thick but 3.5 m wide on its NNE and SSW sides. There is a possible cupmark at the bottom right of its western face. It is of local sandstone. Another stone, perhaps the partner of an original pair, is prostrate immediately to the N. Where the menhir stands the land falls to the NW and SE but rises towards the E.

123b From this menhir it is possible to walk to the remains of a three-stone row. *From the menhir walk SE then, before the sign to La Tondonnerie, turn NE (L) onto farm track. In 250 m on the NW (L) three large fallen stones lie in line behind the hedge.* All of them have fallen or been pushed over in an E–W direction but the row originally had a NNE–SSW axis. The bulkiest of these sandstone pillars is at the NNE, its dimensions being 5.8 m long × 3.5 × 1.8 m thick. The row is now some 20 m in length. From it the land falls slightly to the NE and SW but rises to the E and, ultimately, to the W also suggesting that the NNE–SSW axis was the important one, providing as it does a view to a distant horizon.

Not far away is the PIERRE LE MÂT menhir (125).

124 Pierre à Berthe, La, Besné. *Dolmen*

17 km NE of St Nazaire, 5 km S of Pontchâteau. In a field N of the cemetery of the village.

There are three smallish stones here, equally spaced in a triangle, the Devil's Tripod. A treasure is said to lie at the centre. Originally La Pierre à Berthe was part of a dolmen which was said to cure gout if one approached it on one's knees. Up to the 19th century pilgrims would go from the fountain by the church to make their devotions at the stone. The dolmen was blown up around 1850 by the owner who was convinced that riches were to be found in it. Only this one stone remains standing.

In Besné a road near the cemetery leads to the Chapelle St-Friard where one can see one of the finest Celtic crosses in Brittany, its cross enclosed in a circle like many of those in Ireland.

125 Pierre le Mât, La, St Père-en-Retz. *Menhir*

18 km SE of St Nazaire, 10 km NE of Pornic. 3 km SSE of St Père-en-Retz. From La Caillerie (see 123a) continue NW for 1 km and just before a little road sign, 'La Pierre le Matz' the menhir is 50 m along farm track and on its W (L) side.

This is a square-based pillar, tapering, and leaning slightly to the N. It is about 4 m high, its narrower ends to NNW and SSE. There are fine views to the SSE.

On the other side of the track, almost

opposite the menhir, there are some prostrate stones with possible cupmarks on them.

126a Pierre Longue, La, Batz-sur-Mer. Menhir
23 km W of St Nazaire, 7 km SSW of Guérande. On rocks behind the breakwater on the beach of St Michel.
This is an impressive menhir 3 m high. A treasure is supposed to be hidden at its foot.
126b Another menhir, 2.4 m high, stands on the SW coast of the Croisic peninsula just to the W of Batz-sur-Mer.

127a Riholo, Le, Herbignac. Passage-grave
21 km NNE of St Nazaire, 7 km SSE of La Roche-Bernard, 2½ km ENE of Herbignac. From Herbignac take the D774 N for 2 km and then turn E (R) onto the D2. In 2 km take the SE (R) fork. After 2 km the tomb is on the N (L) side of the road just after a lane on the same side.
This monument, very badly ruined, is on private land behind a steepish bank. It has to be approached through high gorse bushes. It stands on a low knoll. The stones of the passage and chamber lean, some have collapsed but the capstone covering the central space is still *in situ*. The stones are local. Others, and similar, exposed bedrock, litter the ground nearby.

The site is known variously as Le Riholo, the Moulin-de-Gué and Le Haut-Langâtre. It is a transepted passage-grave with two side-chambers and a third at the end beyond a central space. It stood in an oval mound about 26 × 16 m and was oriented to the SSE.

Hardly anything remains of the passage. There is one stone standing on its eastern side and a bigger, 1.7 m from the SW chamber, at the W. On either side of the central space, some 2 m square, there was a chamber of which that at the SW is wrecked. The NE transept is in better condition with three capstones on it covering a cell about 3 m long and 2 m wide. Directly in line with the passage and to the NNW of the central space there is a fairly well-preserved end-chamber, trapezoidal in shape, 1.2 m wide at its entrance and widening to 2 m at its end. It is about 3.5 m long.

Such a site has clear affinities with other transepted tombs in south-eastern Brittany

such as LES MOUSSEAUX (121a), and LA BOUDINARDIÈRE (114).

Little is known of the prehistoric contents of this despoiled megalith but in 1869 the Rev. W.C. Lukis found a man living inside it, shifting his bed from one chamber to the other according to the direction of the wind. 'By filling the interstices between the stones he was able to protect himself against the inclemency of the weather.'

5 km SSW of Herbignac is the fine passage-grave of KERBOURG (119a).
127b In the 19th century there were stone rows at **Arbourg**, 5 km S of Herbignac. Some fifty-seven stones stood in seven lines, but these have now been totally removed.

128 Roche-aux-Loups, La, Le Bas-Bergon. Dolmen
20 km N of St Nazaire, 22 km NE of Guérande. From Herbignac take the D33 E for 4½ km to La Chapelle-des-Marais. Turn NE onto the D50 for 3 km to l'Angle-Bertho. Turn SE (R) onto the D4 and in 2 km, beyond the turn on the S to Le Bas-Bergon, take S (R) unmetalled road, all right for cars, signposted, 'La Roche-aux-Loups'. Dolmen is ¾ km along track, on W.
This is a grand example of a denuded dolmen with a huge capstone supported by three chubby pillars, the single one at the S being 1.5 m high. Two others stand side by side at the N at the edges of a triangular chamber about 4 × 4 × 1.2 m. Around the stones are vague traces of a circular mound.

LE RIHOLO passage-grave (127a) is 4½ km WNW.

La Roche-aux-Loups (128), dolmen from the SE.

St Nazaire (129), megaliths in the city centre.

129 St Nazaire. *Megaliths*
Near the city centre, 600 m E of the Boulévard Victor Hugo which runs N–S through St Nazaire. Stones are in a little public garden in the angle between the Rue Jean-Jaurés and the Rue du Dolmen.

Almost in the middle of this busy city a 4-m-high menhir has been erected. Its original provenance is unknown. Near it is a little dolmen with a 3.3 × 1.6 m capstone on two uprights, each about 2 m high and bulky, rather like a miniature Stonehenge trilithon. No reason is provided for this megalithic surprise.

Trois Squelettes, Les. *Passage-grave* (*see* 121C MOUSSEAUX, LES)

Christianized menhir in a 19th-century scene.

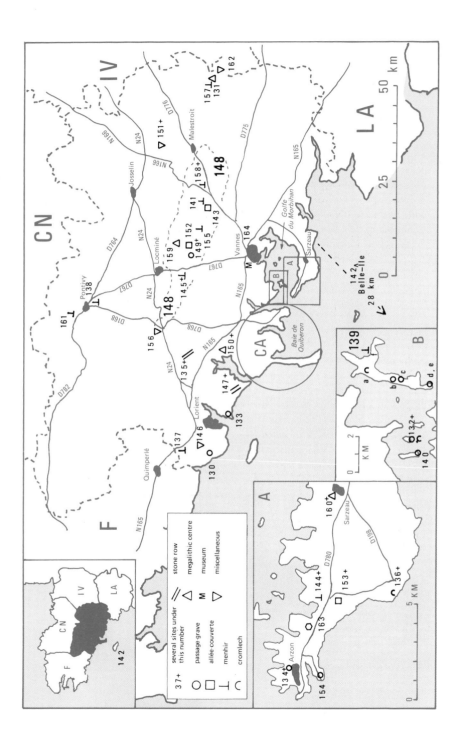

Morbihan

Maps: *Yellow Michelin 1:200,000, no. 230 for whole département*
Green Carte Touristique 1:100,000, nos. 16 for NE; 14 for NW, 15 for
majority of département
Blue Carte Touristique 1:50,000, no. 501 for Gulf of Morbihan

Meaning, 'the Little Sea', the name refers to the Gulf of Morbihan, now an
expanse of water with small islands on which there are several passage-graves
but, in early prehistoric times, an undulating and fertile plain, watered by slow,
wide rivers and densely populated by Neolithic farming groups who built their
tombs on the low hills above their settlements. Today the ornate Gavr'inis
(132a) can be visited by motor launch from Larmor-Baden, with the bonus of a
circumnavigation of the private island of Er-Lannic (132b) with its two stone
circles. One can also cross to Île aux Moines (139) with its cromlech and
passage-graves. The Arzon peninsula at the east of the Gulf holds lesser-known
but splendid monuments, the mutilated, desecrated Petit-Mont (154), now
under reconstruction, the finely-carved Grah-Niohl (134a), and many other
tombs and standing stones.

It was not only around the Gulf, however, that prehistoric people lived.
Although there are no spectacular rows far from Carnac, there is a
concentration of sites around Colpo, inland, with the paired passage-graves of
Larcuste (149) near the decorated menhir of Kermarquer (145a). On the
Landes de Lanvaux (148) there are many menhirs and there are heavy Loire
dolmens at La Maison Trouvée (151a) and Les Tablettes de Cournon (162). It
should, moreover, only be shortage of time that prevents one from going to the
angled passage-grave of Goërem at Gâvres (133), with its carvings of 'figurines'
along its low, black passage and chamber.

A visit to the museum at Vannes is a megalithic imperative. It is a simple
delight to enjoy the delicacy and beauty of the ceremonial axes, discs, beads and
pendants on display in this pleasantly laid-out building.

Good centres for those wishing to stay for a day or two to see sites at leisure
might be Locoal-Mendon (150) in the west, St Jean-Brévelay (159) in the east,
and Sarzeau (160) on the Arzon peninsula.

Sites 130-164

Bois, Menhir de. *Menhir* (see 158b ST
GUYOMARD)

Brouel. *Menhirs* (see 139f ÎLE AUX MOINES)

Colého. *Menhir* (see 159a ST JEAN-
BRÉVELAY)

130a Crugellic, Ploemeur. *Passage-grave*
15½ km SSE of Quimperlé, 9 km W of Lorient.
From Ploemeur take the D162 W for 4 km
towards Fort-Bloqué. Turn N (R) on lane
towards Lannenec reservoir. Tomb is 1 km E of
Fort-Bloqué on the S-facing slope of a low hill
before the reservoir.
This finely-restored tomb was used as an anti-
aircraft gun emplacement in the Second
World War and, later, had material removed

from its rectangular mound for banks and earthworks. It was excavated and restored in 1974–5.

In the kerbed cairn, 23 × 15 m, the SW-facing passage led to four transepted cells and an end-chamber. The passage, now open to the sky, is 9 m long and 1 m wide. Halfway along there are the SW and SE cells, each about 2 m square, and beyond them are two more transepts at the NW and NE of the same size. At the end of the passage is the fifth chamber, rather narrower than the others. Only this chamber and that at the NW have most of their capstones surviving.

In the excavations two decorated stones were discovered. One was a passage slab between the SW and NW cells. At its centre was a complex carving of what appears to be a 'figurine', with a vertical line down its middle and some possible cupmarks inside it. A broken stone was also found with a somewhat similar design.

Finds included two dolerite axes, thirteen steatite beads, a flint blade, votive pendants and sherds of Chassey round-based bowls, beaker fragments and collared flasks of the Crech-Quillé/Le Mélus tradition.

130b There are several menhirs in the region around Ploemeur. At **Courégant**, 4 km SW, there is a 5-m-high stone. Another stands on the **Pointe du Talut**, 4¾ km S. At **Kerbénés** hamlet, 2½ km E, a menhir was thrown down because of the unseemly activities of women and girls around it.

Er-Lannic. *Stone circles* (*see* 132b GAVR'INIS)

131 Gacilly, La. *Megalithic centre*
47 km ENE of Vannes, 20 km ESE of Malestroit.
This quiet and attractive town by the River Oust is a good centre for several types of menhir and chambered tomb, including LES ROCHES-PIQUÉES (157), 500 m W of the centre; the Loire dolmen of LES TABLETTES (162), 1 km SSE; and, farther E, in Ille-et-Vilaine, TRÉAL passage-grave (111) and the profusion of sites nearby at ST JUST (110), 13 km E, where there are tertres tumulaires, stone rows, menhirs and passage-graves.

For the general location of the sites around La Gacilly the visitor will find the orange

Carte Touristique maps, nos. 1020 and 1120, useful.

132a Gavr'inis, Larmor-Baden. *Passage-grave*
14 km SW of Vannes, 11 km WNW of Sarzeau. From Vannes take the D101 SW. At Le Moustoir the road becomes the D316 to Larmor-Baden. At the village turn SE (L) and then S (R) to the quayside. Motor launches to Gavr'inis run half-hourly between 15 May and 15 September. Other times by application in the village. Fare 12 Fr. Trip is 20 minutes each way. Usually no time limit on one's stay on island except when busy. Motor-boats also operate from Locmariaquer. Though the tomb is lit a torch is helpful.
On its 'Island of Goats' this is the most lavishly decorated megalithic tomb in Europe. Its chamber, rectangular, 2.7 × 2.3 m, of six slabs covered by a heavy granite capstone, was erected at the summit of a hillock from which the ground sloped steeply downwards towards the SE. On this gradient Neolithic people in the centuries around 3500 BC put up twenty-three slabs to make the longest passage in Brittany, 11.8 m in length, 2 m high but only about 1.5 m wide. It was paved with flat stones

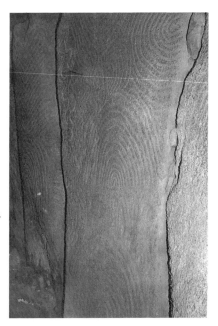

and a third of the way along a sillstone was set upright in the soil. At the entrance to the chamber there was another. The well-designed structure was finally covered under a large, sub-circular cairn, 60 × 54 m, stepped like an early pyramid, 8 m high.

The passage-grave may have been known to a medieval community of Red Monks, some of whose members were buried in the mound, although not in the tomb itself, but it was not until 1832 that the chamber and passage were delved into. There is no record of any finds. There have been subsequent excavations in this century by le Rouzic and le Roux.

It is for its art that Gavr'inis is famous. No fewer than twenty-three of its twenty-nine upright stones have been carved, not in single or isolated motifs but in a profuse series of compositions so that stone flows into stone or is mirrored by another in patterns engraved in low relief. The art is balanced in panels horizontally and, vertically, in symbols of which the main elements are concentric arcs and axes. These latter implements have splayed cutting edges like the big, prestige axes from the Carnac Mounds such as MANÉ-ER-HROEK, CA (195), suggesting that

Gavr'inis (132a): (above) axes and 'serpents' on base of Stone 8; (left) arcs on Stone 4.

Gavr'inis belongs to the same Middle Neolithic period. Also to be seen are the wavy lines of 'serpents', rectangular 'figurines', shepherds' crooks and fir-tree patterns.

Moving anti-clockwise from Stone 1 at the entrance there are twelve stones on the right-hand side, numbers 1, 2 and 7 being undecorated. Stones 13–18 form the chamber and Stones 19–29 make up the left-hand side of the passage, with the last three, 27–29, being plain. As well as the abundance of elegantly engraved arcs, many carvings of crooks can be seen on Stones 8 and 25; 'U's, perhaps yokes, on 15 and 16 at the back of the chamber; 'figurines', probably anthropomorphic representations of a female 'guardian-spirit', on 8, 24 and 25; 'serpents' on 4 and 8; and axes on 6, 8, 10, 16, 21 and 24. Stone 7, without art, is a fine slab of white quartz. At the base of Stone 8 is a group of serpents and axes recalling a similar juxtaposition by the menhir of the MANIO I ertre tumulaire, CA (183c), where it was suggested that the serpent represented the earth, and the axe, fire.

The sill at the entrance to the Gavr'inis chamber has arcs on its upper surface and chevrons on both its vertical faces. Intriguingly, during the recent excavations it was recognized that two incomplete loops carved on the back of an end-stone in the chamber had once been part of an axe-carving whose greater section was now on the top of a broken capstone in the passage-grave of the TABLE DES MARCHANDS, CA (175c), 1¾ km to the W. The two fragments of stone were pieces from a decorated menhir that had been deliberately broken for use in the passage-graves, perhaps dragged from the vicinity of Île Longue when the Gulf of Morbihan did not exist. Such iconoclasm is evidence of the indifference prehistoric people could have for the handiwork of earlier societies.

As with the monumental Loire dolmen of ESSÉ, IV (102), it has to be asked whether Gavr'inis was a tomb or shrine or sanctuary. There is an enigmatic niche in Stone 18 where three horizontal, hand-sized holes have been pecked into the slab, about 10 cm deep, the rear of their sides hollowed out together to make a small shelf like the piscina by the altar of a church. Axes and arcs surround this strange phenomenon. A somewhat similar

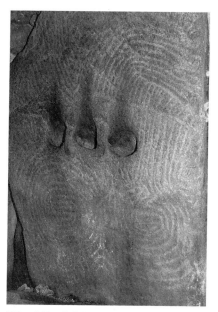

(Above) Gavr'inis (132a), triple niches in Stone 18.

(Below) Newgrange, Co. Meath, Ireland: carvings on kerbstone 52 of the passage-grave. Gavr'inis and Newgrange have several features in common.

arrangement occurs on the NW kerbstone, number 52, of the Irish passage-grave of Newgrange. There, three sets of three deep cupmarks are contained inside cartouches and surrounded by axes and concentric arcs.

The possible association between the two 'tombs', 400 km apart, is all the more interesting because of other connections between them. Gavr'inis is the only Breton passage-grave to contain carvings of spirals, a motif common amongst the Irish passage-graves of the Boyne Valley. There are four at Gavr'inis, two on Stone 18 just below the three perplexing holes, and there are others on Stones 11 and 25. The fact that Newgrange was designed to face the midwinter sunrise is now an archaeological truism. Gavr'inis also faces in that direction and the chevron decoration on Stone 30, the sill at the entrance to the chamber, is very like the patterns carved on the lintel of Newgrange's 'solar' roofbox.

The length and spaciousness of the Gavr'inis passage-grave, the absence of finds and the profuse ornamentation of the stones are indications that this may have been as much a ritual centre as a tomb. Astronomically it is interesting. Looking from Stone 19, at the left-hand entrance to the chamber, towards Stone 1, the bearing is 128°, almost perfectly in line with the midwinter

Gavr'inis (132a), axes and zigzags on Stone 21.

sunrise. The main axis of the passage is 134° towards the low-lying Arzon peninsula and the orientation is close to that of the major southern moonrise. It has been calculated that the two alignments, one solar, the other lunar, intersect halfway down the passage level with Stone 7, the white quartz slab whose undecorated surface may have been illuminated by the light of the rising sun and moon.

132b Er-Lannic. 500 m to the S of the island of Gavr'inis are the remains of two stone circles on the islet of Er-Lannic. They are now half-hidden beneath the waters of the Gulf of Morbihan, but in pre-Roman times they stood on a little hillside with a river flowing to their S. Er-Lannic is now privately owned and cannot be visited, but the motor launches to Gavr'inis pass around it on the return journey so that the N circle stones can be seen. The southern ring is submerged.

Between 1923 and 1926 Zacharie le Rouzic

excavated here, discovering that the rings had been built on the site of an earlier settlement in which there was both Middle Neolithic and later Conguel vessels, suggesting that the circles were unlikely to have been erected much before 3000 BC. The southern setting may have been horseshoe-shaped like other cromlechs in Morbihan (*see* 136a, 139a), 61 m across and open to the E.

If le Rouzic's reconstruction can be trusted the N ring was a flattened circle, 65.8 m in diameter with a straightish north-eastern arc. Its stones, 2 to 5.3 m high, are almost contiguous. Two outlying stones, 136 m apart, stand almost E–W of each other at a tangent to the ring's northern corner. Le Rouzic found that the pillars of the ring stood in a low, rubbly bank and that around each there was a small cairn of stones with scatters of bone, ox teeth, flint flakes, quartz, mauls and sherds, the débris from the earlier settlement and re-used as packing to keep the stones vertical.

On the inner faces of two stones at the NW and one at the E are carvings of unhafted axes and a yoke. One of the packing-stones of the tallest stone at the NW had nine cupmarks arranged in a pattern which le Rouzic likened to the constellation of Ursa Major.

133 Goërem, Gâvres. *Passage-grave*
45 km W of Vannes, 6 km SSE of Lorient.
7½ km W of Plouhinec from which take the
D158W along the coast road through military
installations to the centre of Gâvres. Turn S (L)
along the Avenue des Sardinières and, in 200 m,
at the Place de la Mairie on the W (R) walk
along alley at its NW corner to the Rue du
Tumulus. Tomb is to the N (R) cramped between
the houses. A torch is necessary.

Discovered by chance under the dunes on the W shore of the Anse de Goërem, this is a splendid example of a Morbihan angled passage-grave or allée-coudée. Excavated between 1964 and 1967, it was found to lie beneath a sand-covered tumulus of blackish earth, 34 × 24 m, under which was a cairn shaped like the inverted head of a golf-club that had been built over the passage and chamber of the tomb.

The entrance at the SSE had been blocked with small stones. From it a 9-m-long passage, 1.2 m wide and 1.6 m high, had sides of drystone walling alternating with granite

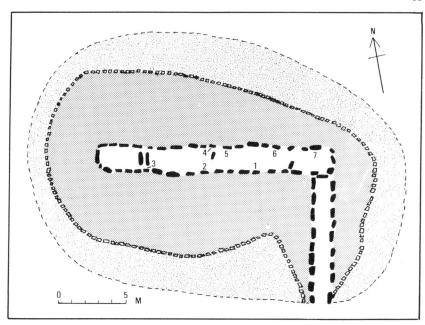

Goërem, Gâvres, passage-grave (allée-coudée) (133). The numbered stones are discussed in the text.

orthostats in a 'post-and-panel' arrangement. It was capped with heavy slabs. Charcoal gave a date of 1910 ± 200 bc, about 2400 BC, for the time when the tomb was abandoned.

On both sides of the passage the second stone from the entrance bore carvings, the one on the right having a motif like an imperfect M, that on the left a simplified 'figurine'. The nature of the rough granite had prevented these carvings, like others in the main chamber, from being well executed.

At the far end of the passage a 'door' was formed of a huge granite slab. From this point the passage turned at right-angles towards the WNW to create a long chamber which was divided by sideslabs into four compartments, 3.4, 6.8, 5.5 and 3.6 m long respectively from E to W.

In the easternmost cell there was a carving of a figurine on the stone (7) facing down the passage. The second chamber had four carvings, three on the N wall (4, 5, 6), the other being a typical allée-coudée figurine with incurved head and two small breasts (1). The third chamber had one decorated stone (2) with conjoined cartouches, one with

concentric circles inside it (3). Charcoal provided an assay of 2150 ± 140 bc, about 2750 BC.

The end-chamber was different from the others. It had been completely sealed by two slabs, back to back, with drystone walling between their edges and the sides of the tomb. The chamber had been used for only a short while and the discovery of Kerugou pottery left in it suggested that this terminal cell had been the focus of funerary or dedicatory rites undertaken when the tomb was completed. A date of 2480 ± 140 bc, or 3200 BC, gives an excellent indication of the age of this intriguing late Neolithic sanctuary.

Over a thousand years later Beaker squatters broke into this chamber, leaving some shattered pots, a copper awl, two arrowheads and four small plaques alongside a burial. The time of their intrusion may be indicated by the presence of a Conguel pot found in the passage at their point of entry and by a C-14 determination, obtained from charcoal in the end-chamber, of 1520 ± 120 bc, the equivalent of about 1850 BC.

Despite its claustrophobic situation and the

modern litter that disfigures its interior,
Goërem is a site to be visited for its
architecture, its art and the evocation of rituals
inside its dark recesses.

134a   Grah-Niohl, Arzon. *Passage-grave*
16 km SSW of Vannes, 9½ km WNW of
Sarzeau. From Arzon church take the road N
towards Bernon, turn E (R) onto the Rue du
Presbytère and almost immediately turn N (L) up
the Impasse de Graniol. Tomb is 300 m along
lane on the W (L).

Sometimes known as La Pierre Men Guen,
this is a fine passage-grave with a single S
transept. The tomb is noteworthy for its art
and a torch is recommended.

Just outside the oval mound, 25 × 18 m, a
menhir stands at the ESE entrance to a
12-m-long passage that is still in good
condition. Six stones stand on either side and
at the end there is a sub-rectangular chamber.
Two-thirds of the way along the passage there
is a damaged S transept 2.7 m deep. Four
capstones, two of them large, cover the major
part of the tomb, which has been unhappily
restored by the addition of unattractive stone
blocks and mortar. In plan Grah-Niohl is akin
to the N tomb at LES MOUSSEAUX, LA (121a).

There are five carved stones. From the
entrance the fourth on the S has a worndown
motif, but its partner opposite has much
deeper carvings of a yoke and a 'boat' pattern.
Stone 7, at the N entrance to the chamber and
somewhat askew of the passage, has several
fine crooks on it. The underside of the final
capstone bears a magnificent hafted axe,
54 × 22 cm, with two looped links on its
handle. A little crook has been carved
alongside it. The end-stone of the chamber has
an anthropomorphic 'figurine' on its inner face
looking down the passage. The carving is
28 cm high and 25 cm across. It has 'handles',
probably wizened arms, on either side.

Excavations in 1890 produced artefacts
typical of the Morbihan passage-graves,
Neolithic sherds with horizontally-perforated
lugs, small axes, callais beads, a fragment of a
gold tube and flints. This and the Period II art
suggest that Grah-Niohl was in use around
3500 BC.

134b   Graniol *cromlech. 120 m to the N along*
the lane there is an uncultivated stretch of land
thick with gorse and uninviting brambles. This

was once the site of a large cromlech. Until
quite recently some stones still remained
alongside a garden wall to the N of this
wilderness, but they have been removed. In
1930 a low bank, about 1 m wide and 80 cm
high, could be seen forming the NW arc of a
ring perhaps 50 m across. Two stones stood in
it with two others to their S. Nothing is left.

135a   Grand Resto, Le, Languidec. *Stone*
rows
17 km ENE of Lorient and 25 km SSW of
Pontivy. From Languidec take the D102 SSE
but almost immediately turn SE (L) onto the
D189 for 3 km to St Jean. Continue straight on E
for 2½ km to the crossroads at Penhoët. Turn N
(L). Rows are by the road between Penhoët and
Le Grand Resto 1½ km to the N.

At one time this must have been an important
collection of rows of standing stones with
several tertres tumulaires in the vicinity.
There were three lines, well enough spaced
out to have contained over 300 stones and
blocks. Today the remaining stones are low
and unimpressive. They are said to be the
petrified bodies of soldiers who were pursuing
St Cornèly. Deserters from their army can be
seen lying in the fields around them.

135b   At Les Orgu, 1 km N of Languidec,
five connected and subterranean chambers of
the Iron Age were discovered, the largest
about 2 × 3 m in size. Sherds and ox-bones
were found in them.

135c   At Kernli or Kervili there is a
Christianized menhir set in a wall.

136a   Grand Rohu, St Gildas-de-Rhuys.
Cromlech
16 km SSW of Vannes, 5½ km W of Sarzeau.
There was once a notable collection of huge
cromlechs around the Gulf of Morbihan: ER-
LANNIC (132b); GRANIOL (134b); KERGONAN
(139a); KERLESCAN WEST and NORTH, CA
(180a, c); MÉNEC EAST and WEST, CA (203a,
c) and KERBOURGNEC, CA (204b). Many of
them are now either badly damaged or
destroyed.

According to Merlet, who in this century
made a special study of these cromlechs, there
was a vast U-shaped enclosure, open to the
NE, at Grand Rohu 600 m S of the hamlet of
La Saline and 2½ km NNW of St Gildas-de-
Rhuys. All but one of the stones has gone and

the cromlech's exact position is uncertain. There are now cultivated fields in its general area. It was probably 330 m ENE of the old blockhouse 1 km W of Kerpont and 500 m WNW of Kerpont itself. There were still twenty-two stones when Merlet saw it, most of them on the cromlech's SW side. It measured about 180 m from NW to SE, and Merlet suggested that it contained an alignment towards the midsummer sunset along its major axis. Today only one stone can be seen NW of Kerpont in a field N of the lane leading W from the D198.

136b   Men Platt. *750 m S of St Gildas, passing the village of Kerfago to the Plage de Port Maria.* Here there is a dolmen consisting of a large capstone supported by six low stones.

4½ km NW of Grand Rohu another cromlech existed at GRANIOL (134b).

Graniol. *Cromlech (see* 134b GRAH-NIOHL)

137   Guidel. *Menhirs*
10½ km WNW of Lorient, 10 km SSE of Quimperlé. From Lorient take the N165 W for 10 km, turn S (L) onto the D306. 1½ km to Guidel.
There are two impressive menhirs in the neighbourhood of Guidel, both of them moved from their original sites. One was taken from Cantus to the square of the new Mairie at Guidel. Another is 7 km to the NE near Park just S of Pont-Scorff, where it was transported to act as a memorial to the Free French of the Second World War.

Other menhirs in the region have disappeared. One was near the Chapelle St-Fiacre. Another, which had carvings on it, was at La Saudraie. Today it is under the road.

138   Houssaie, La, Pontivy. *Menhir*
33 km WNW of Josselin, 1½ km SE of Pontivy. From Pontivy take the D764 E and after 1 km turn S (R). Take the first E (L) fork towards Remungol to the Chapelle de La Houssaie.
The La Houssaie stone stands near the fountain of the chapel and is set in a wall. This is a Christianized menhir which is 4 m high. Rumour has it that it was once much smaller, perhaps no bigger than a milestone or even a pebble. It is now growing, the legends claim,

because each Easter it goes down to the River Blavet on the W to drink. This is the time, if one is in a state of grace, when it is possible to seize its treasure, although one must be quick because the stone is gone for only a second.

If one is not in a state of grace then the heavy slab will crush you.

139   Île aux Moines, Gulf of Morbihan. *Megalithic centre*
10 km SW of Vannes, 10 km NW of Sarzeau. The island can be reached by passenger ferry (no cars) from Port-Blanc 3 km NE of Larmor-Baden. The ferries run every half-hour between 0700 and 1930 daily. Fare 3 Fr. single. The ferries run to the N end of the island which is 5 km long from N to S.

139a   Kergonan *cromlech. 1¼ km S of ferry landing stage, 1 km S of Locmiquel village, on W (R) of road S towards Nioul.*
Because its stones stand in several private properties and amongst walls and hedges it is difficult to discern the shape of this enormous enclosure, which is open at its SE end like an excessive horseshoe. The land falls steeply here. Thirty-six tall menhirs, varying in height from 2 to 3.5 m, still stand and it is said that there was once a line of closely-set stones across the 90-m-long empty side. They would have completed a D-shaped setting whose major axis of 126° would have been in line with the midwinter sunrise. Perhaps significantly the cromlech is also known as the Cercle de la Mort.

According to le Rouzic one of the stones has a carving of an unhafted axe.

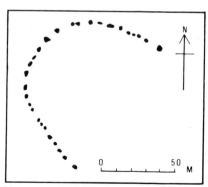

Kergonan cromlech (139a).

139b Kerno. *From Kergonan continue walking S for 3 km. After 1 km pass Kerno passage-grave on the W (R) of the hamlet. A road, twisting between the houses, leads to it.* Offering fine views to the sea this little passage-grave still has a great capstone in position over the chamber which is defined by three sideslabs.

Just S of Kerno hamlet some stones survive of **Roh Vras** *passage-grave. Take E (L) old road, opposite the Pointe de Sperneguy, up to a fork. Stones are against a little wall in a field to the left.* This little and devastated passage-grave had a square chamber and is possibly very late in the chambered tomb series. Beads and pendants have been found in it.

139c Penhape. *Follow the main road S from Kerno. At the crossroads just beyond Penhape hamlet turn W (R) onto track up a steep climb. In 200 m at the top a drystone wall indicates the position of the nearby megalith.* Known as the Pierre des Sacrifices, this is a well-preserved P-shaped passage-grave with a short, 3-m passage leading to a sub-rectangular chamber offset to the right. It measures 2.5 × 2 m and has a great, mushroom-like capstone over it. The site was excavated, without result, in 1877. It once stood in a mound over 80 m long containing several other megalithic tombs on the same axis as Penhape, but all this has gone. It may once have resembled BARNENEZ, F (40). The easternmost tomb once had a stone standing on it and it is possibly this stone that now lies in the field against Penhape.

The passage-grave has several carvings. The left-hand stone at the entrance to the chamber has representations of a hafted axe and two anthropomorphic 'figurines', domed rectangles, one with four pairs of breasts. The left backstone has three axes on it. Three other carvings, possibly axes, can just be made out on the backs of other stones.

139d Pen-Nioul. *At the extreme S of the island on the Pointe de Nioul. Walk S from the road along footpath half-obscured in gorse. Dolmens will be seen on a rise amongst the bushes.* Here there is the wreckage of two passage-graves, the northern P-shaped, the southern almost ovoid and with a fallen capstone. They face the sea and both were contained in circular cairns of which traces are still apparent.

139e Nioul. *100 m to the N, on private land near some kennels,* are the stones of two more passage-graves, also once in a circular tumulus. The passages and chambers are undifferentiated. Both face SE as do those at Pen-Nioul.

139f At **Brouel,** *2 km ESE of the ferry quay at the N of the island and just SE of the village.* Here there is a short line of three stones. Excavations at their bases recovered some coarse sherds, charcoal and animal bones.

Île de Locoal. *Re-used menhir (see 150d* LOCOAL-MENDON)

140 Île Longue, Gulf of Morbihan. *Passage-grave*
15 km SW of Vannes, 11½ km WNW of Sarzeau. Although only ¾ km SW of Gavr'inis, this island is not readily visitable because it is now privately owned.

At the southern end of this 1-km-long island is a ruined passage-grave with some excellent carvings. Facing ESE an 11.5-m-long and exceptionally high passage with a sill at the entrance leads to a q-shaped chamber, 3 × 3 m, with a diagonal SW corner. It was once roofed with a towering 5-m-high vault of drystone walling, and similar walling is interspersed with granite orthostats in both the passage and the chamber. The whole was enclosed in a 20-m-wide, circular cairn in which there were three concentric retaining walls of flat slabs. There was a funnel-like approach to the tomb's entrance.

Five stones are decorated, unusually all of them in the passage, and it is the anthropomorphic 'figurine' that is the dominant motif. The second and fourth capstones have this device on their undersides, somewhat triangular in shape and with attached arcs round part of the outer edges. The sixth capstone has this device on their undersides, somewhat triangular in shape and with attached arcs round part of the outer edges. The sixth capstone has this device that looks like an archer's bow across its face. The first orthostat on the right of the entrance has a large and rectangular figurine with a little domed head. The broad slab, second on the left, has a great domed outline, 'handles' or arms on either side and arcs around its head. Such figurines are rather like the carving on the end-stone of the TABLE DES MARCHANDS, CA (175c).

Île Longue passage-grave was reconstructed in 1907.

Jean Babouin (141), carved male stone from the SSE.

Jeanne Babouin (141), carved female stone from the W.

141   Jean and Jeanne Babouin, Elven.
Menhirs
19 km NE of Vannes, 15 km WSW of Malestroit. From Elven take the N1 N and after 5 km take the SE (R) country road from Le Rodouer. Road ends in 1 km. A forest track leads ENE and in 200 m a small sign on S (R) side of track misleadingly points NE. Stones are in wood, opposite the sign, on NW (L) of track, 200 m at the end of a woodcutter's path.

There are two carved stones here, both of granite. The larger, to the W, is 2.5 m high and has a crude face carved at its top. 20 m to its E is the smaller, Jeanne, only 1.5 m high, but with a clearer carving of a human face. It has been suggested that such stones date from the Iron Age and are representations of male and female principles, the taller, Jean, being a phallic symbol.

2 km to their SSW is the ruined allée-couverte of KERFILY (143).

142   Jean and Jeanne Runelo, Belle-Île.
Menhirs
On Belle-Île, 49 km SW of Vannes, 18 km S of Quiberon. Ferry from Quiberon, 45 minutes each way. 30 June to 15 September, 10 trips daily, otherwise 2 to 8 trips daily depending on the time

of year. Return passenger fare (1984), 50 Fr. Cars, 100–240 Fr. according to length, advance reservation essential (6 Fr.). Cars and bicycles can be hired on the island at the landing place of Le Palais.

3 km S of Sauzon the D25 passes between two menhirs 300 m apart. One is in the angle of the junction between the D25 and the road to Port de Donnant. The other is to the E, just S of the D25. The western menhir, Jean, is a raddled, thin pillar of red schist, 4 m high. Jeanne to the E is a smaller menhir of granite.

Legend has it that these are two petrified lovers whose intended wedding was disapproved of by the Druids because Jean was a bard. A fairy is supposed to release them occasionally. In this folk story there may be memories of the thin pillar and the lower squat block being representations of the male and female principles.

Kerallan. *Passage-grave (see* 159e ST JEAN-BRÉVELAY)

Kerara. *Menhir (see* 145c KERMARQUER)

Kerdramel. *Menhir (see* 159b ST JEAN-BRÉVELAY)

143   Kerfily (La Loge aux Loups), Trédion.
Allée-couverte
22 km SE of Locminé, 17 km NE of Vannes.
From Elven take the D1 N and in 3¾ km there is a little sign to the Loge aux Loups in the woods on the E (R) of the road opposite the old house of La Perche. Follow a footpath SW for 250 m, skirting the bracken-thick Bois de Kerfily.

This is an example, rare in Morbihan, of an allée-couverte arc-bouté in which the sideslabs do not support capstones but, instead, lean inwards to form a ridgelike structure. The remains of the surrounding tumulus can still be seen.

In the best-preserved section of this collapsed monument there are capstones which are supported, not on the inclined slabs of the chamber, but on secondary pillars outside them. Such architecture undoubtedly added to the complications of building the allée-couverte, but was perhaps intended to give strength to the chamber and prevent its collapse. Similar tombs exist in Finistère at TY-AR-C'HORRIKET (96a), where the surmounting capstones have gone, and at COAT-MENEZ-GUEN (43) and CASTEL-RUFFEL (42a).

Kergonan. *Cromlech (see* 139a ÎLE AUX MOINES)

144a   Kermaillard, Sarzeau. *Menhir*
15 km S of Vannes, 6 km W of Sarzeau. On Arzon peninsula. From Sarzeau take the D780 W and after 5½ km turn WNW into Kermaillard hamlet. In 500 m take N road towards Le Logeo. After the first house take the lane on the E (R). Stone is at N edge of the field by a gorse-covered bank.

This is a magnificent though fallen stone, 5 m long and measuring almost 8 m around its broad, cylindrical body. Today it lies like a tailless but contented dolphin basking in the sun. On its upper surface is a group of eighteen cupmarks. On the other side there is a groove which seems to be marking out a square cartouche of the kind often found in the Morbihan passage-graves.

144b   Returning eastward towards the D780, in ¾ km, just S of the road, is a little menhir standing almost exactly N of the LE NET allée-couverte (153a) and perhaps associated with it.

145a   Kermarquer (Mein Bras), Moustoirac.
Menhir
20 km NNW of Vannes, 7 km S of Locminé. From Colpo go W on the D115. After 3 km turn N (R) past Kerara on the E. Take 1st lane W (L). Stone is in angle of 1st lane on S (L) opposite the turn to Kermarquer de la Lande, on the slope of a small wood.

This is a standing stone of granite brought from Lanvaux 5 km to the W. It is 6.7 m high and leans to the W. It is a 'playing-card' slab, flat-topped, with its longer faces towards the NW and SE and its corners at the cardinal points.

It has the distinction of being the first menhir to be recognized as having carvings on it. In 1847 two carvings in the shape of shepherds' crooks were noticed on its SE face. Since then, and as recently as 1967, further motifs have been recorded and it is now known that three sides have art, only the NW face being left plain.

Much time had been spent laboriously grinding its four sides to almost perfect smoothness. On the SW side two crooks can be seen low down at the eastern corner, one above the other, the upper having its crook to the left, the lower to the right. Each is about 40 cm long. The NE side has five carvings in low relief. On the left-hand edge are three crooks, one above the other, all facing left, and low down near the middle are two small ones on their sides, one lying on the other. The SE side has two crooks side by side low down in the exact centre of the stone. One on the left faces left, its partner faces right.

These motifs are very like those from the coastal passage-graves of Morbihan at PETIT-MONT (154), GAVR'INIS (132a), MANÉ LUD, CA (199b), and others, and from this it seems likely that the menhir of Mein Bras was erected no later than the early 3rd millennium BC and probably many centuries before then.

145b   150 m to the W is the smaller **Kermarquer** menhir in a hollow.

145c   Another menhir stands 180 m to the SSE at **Kerara**.

6 km to the ESE are the fine passage-graves of LARCUSTE (149).

146   Kerméné, Guidel. *Statue-menhir*
9 km WNW of Lorient and 12 km SE of Quimperlé. From Guidel take the SE road past

Kerouarch for 2¼ km towards Mané Guen.
At Kerméné hamlet on a hillside overlooking
the nearby woods there is a tumulus 18 m in
diameter and 2.8 m high. Excavations in
1957–8 found it contained no megalithic
structure but was composed of layers of earth
capped with small stones. Under it were
masses of broken objects including querns and
three granite fragments of a female statue-
menhir.

Most of this stele was missing, but the
domed and faceless head was found, the right
shoulder with a thin arm placed under the
breast, and a small piece of the left side.

Such a stone is similar to the stele from the
allée-couverte of CRECH-QUILLÉ, CN (9), and
to another now standing in the churchyard of
Catel in Guernsey. The incorporation into a
ritual monument of such a broken idol is also
reminiscent of the re-used stones at TOSSEN-
KELER, CN (34). From Kerméné also came
Late Neolithic sherds of flat-based pots.Two
C-14 assays produced determinations of
2440 ± 140 bc and 2080 ± 110 bc averaging
around 2900 BC.

Kerno. *Passage-grave (see* 139b ÎLE AUX
MOINES)

Kervelhué. *Stone row (see* 147b KERZINE)

147a Kerzine, Plouhinec. *Stone row*
11 km ESE of Lorient, 35 km W of Vannes.
1 km S of Plouhinec on W (R) of road between
Le Gueldro and Kerzine.
Here, 17 km ENE of the great rows at Carnac
and only 9 km from those at KERZERHO, CA
(187a), are the remnants of another set of
megalithic lines. They have been much
disturbed but appear to have consisted of eight
rows, about 45 m in length and oriented
WNW–ESE. No more than forty almost
haphazard stones survive of the complex.
147b At **Kervelhué** nearby there is a single
line of eight stones.

148 Landes de Lanvaux. *Megalithic*
monuments
Until recently this 70-km-long stretch of
inhospitable moorland was one of the most
desolate regions of Brittany, with schistose
rocks and acidic, thin soils. It extends at its
NW end from Baud, 31 km NW of Vannes,
across to La Gacilly at the ESE, 48 km ENE of
Vannes. On the heaths around St Germain,
17 km NW of Vannes, there are several
megalithic sites, difficult to find but worth
visiting. The blue 1:25,000 maps, nos. 0920
Est and Ouest, are necessary. The D764
between La Chapelle, 7 km S of Ploermel, and
St Gravé, 19 km SE, also has many menhirs
near it, most of them fallen and
inconspicuous, especially in the area near the
Bois de Brambien to the N of St Gravé.

Of particular interest in this rich prehistoric
region are, from E to W: the Grée de Cojoux
(ST JUST, IV (110d–j)), with its rows, tertres
tumulaires, standing stones and chambered
tombs; the passage-grave at TRÉAL, IV (111);
the Loire dolmen at LA MAISON TROUVÉE
(151a); the menhirs at ST GUYOMARD (158a);
the statue-menhirs of JEAN AND JEANNE
BABOUIN (141); KERFILY allée-couverte arc-
bouté (143); the decorated menhir at
KERMARQUER (145a), with other menhirs
near it around Colpo; the paired passage-
graves at LARCUSTE (149); and the fantastic
VENUS DE QUINIPILY (156), near Baud.

Also worth a visit for the dedicated tourist
are two wrecked chambered tombs, one at
SOURNON (158c) near St Guyomard, 10 km
WSW of Malestroit and 8 km NE of Elven.
This is a badly damaged and small passage-
grave. There is another at KERALLAN (159e)
near St Jean-Brévelay.

Lann Douar. *Menhir (see* 159c ST JEAN-
BRÉVELAY)

149 Larcuste, Colpo. *Passage-graves*
18 km NNW of Vannes, 8½ km SSE of
Locminé. From Locminé take the D767 S for
9 km through Colpo and in ¾ km to S turn E
(L). In 150 m take the SE (R) fork for 1½ km to
Larcuste. Lane to the N of the hamlet leads in
200 m to the tombs 150 m E on a little rise.
Once there were four cairns here, one of them
excavated in 1885, but today only two remain.
They were excavated in 1968–72. The cairn to
the N contains two small passage-graves and
the cairn to the S has a single, transepted
tomb.
149a *North Cairn* In the gently concave
façade of this oval cairn, 13 × 10 m, with its

three internal walls and aligned NE–SW, are the entrances to two passage-graves. That to the N, though used for many years, had been ransacked by treasure-hunters and few artefacts remained. The SE-facing passage, only 3 m long, led to a little circular chamber. Dressed stones lined the passage and chamber but the capstones of both were supported on drystone walls. A well-preserved double-yoke carving was found in the chamber on the stone that faced down the passage.

The southern of the two tombs faced ESE and had a rather longer passage. At its end the ovoid chamber may have been corbelled. Two stones, immediately on the right in this chamber, had faint carvings of yokes and crooks or hafted axes. Burnt flint flakes and sherds of a large vessel were discovered on the rough paving. A rusticated, footed bowl was found behind the wall that separated the two passages and under the roots of an oak tree in front of the façade there were many other sherds from about eighteen shouldered bowls and vases, some of the sherds reddish and decorated with triangles. Such 'cooking pots' of the Souch tradition suggested a local adaptation of Chassey styles. The pots had probably been placed on the outer wall between the entrances as offerings and had fallen and broken as the cairn decayed.

149b *South Cairn* 2 m to the SSW of the North Cairn was another oval mound, this time aligned WNW–ESE but with a façade in line with its predecessor. Measuring about 15 × 13 m, it had been badly damaged by looters. Within it a 9.7-m-long passage had three pairs of transepted chambers that diminished in size the farther they were from the entrance, the pair at the western end being only about 1.5 m in diameter. All were drystone-walled, with dressed slabs set intermittently along their sides. Six granite capstones survived.

An assay of 3540 ± 120 bc, about 4400 BC, came from charcoal in the passage. Three other charcoal samples, two from outside the façade, gave dates of 2660 ± 110 bc, 2110 ± 120 bc and 2030 ± 110 bc, hinting at a span from 3450 to 2650 BCfor the later centuries of the tomb's use.

Lobo, Le, Caro. *Allée-couverte* (*see* 151b MAISON TROUVÉE, LA)

150 Locoal-Mendon, Auray. *Megalithic centre*
27 km WNW of Vannes, 20 km E of Lorient. There are many menhirs in the neighbourhood of Locoal-Mendon, not all of them easy to find. Most of them have been Christianized, probably by the Knights Templar who once owned much of the land here. The orange Carte Touristique 1:50,000 map, no. 0820, is a useful guide.

150a By the cemetery of Locoal-Mendon is a stone, the **Men-ar-Menah** or the 'Stone of the Monks'. It is only 1.4 m high, but on it is a large cross inscribed in a circle.

150b From Locoal-Mendon take the W minor road towards l'Île St Goal. Near the calvary is the Iron Age stele or cross of **Prostlon** like a truncated horn, 2.2 m high and measuring 2.5 m around its base. Two Maltese crosses have been carved on it.

150c Near Plec hamlet there are two other Christianized stones called **Wegil Brehed** and **Goured Brehed**, the distaff and spindle of Ste Brigitte. One is 3 m high, the other a mere 75 cm with a carving, perhaps of Jesus, on it.

150d At the Templar chapel of St Jean on the Île de Locoal, 3 km WSW of Locoal-Mendon, there is a re-used, carved menhir. Above the lintel of the door is a stone with the carving of a hafted axe on it. Set in a hollow the carving has its blade to the left, edge down, and the haft has a loop of thonging hanging from it. It is possible that this stone was taken from a destroyed passage-grave in the vicinity and built into the chapel.

150e There are the remains of two passage-graves in the neighbourhood, both called **Mané-er-Hloh.** The first, also known as **Mané Bihan,** stands in a mound 28 × 25 × 2 m high. It has a flat façade of drystone walling and alternating small blocks. The S entrance to the tomb leads to a 10-m-long passage which curves to the NNW to join a chamber, lying E–W, 7 m long, 1.2 m wide and 1.5 m high. This allée-coudée had Kerugou sherds.

150f The other **Mané-er-Hloh,** known also as **Mané Bras,** had a 9-m-long passage leading from the SSE to a P-shaped chamber, 3.5 m in diameter, with a large capstone which is unusually supported by two uprights in the chamber itself.

4 km to the S of Locoal-Mendon is the passage-grave of LOCQUELTAS, CA (191).

Loge aux Loups, La. *Allée-couverte* *(see* 143
KERFILY)

151a Maison Trouvée, La, La Chapelle.
Loire dolmen
*14½ km ESE of Josselin, 8½ km N of
Malestroit. From Ploermel take the D8 for 7 km
to Monterrein. Turn W (R) for 3 km and take
side road to N (R) signposted La Ville au Voyer.
At the farm turn E (R) for 200 m. A track
signposted 'Dolmen' leads N for 250 m. Tomb is
on E (R) in a coppice 50 m from the track.*
This is a diminutive version of the gigantic
tomb at ESSÉ, IV (102). It stands in the
remains of a circular mound. Unusually facing
WNW it has a short and narrow vestibule 1 m
wide and 1.5 m long which leads to a
rectangular chamber 5.5 × 2.3 m wide.
Although the entrance to it is only 60 cm high,
the ground inside is lower and the height of
the chamber is about 1 m. Over it there is a
single, massive capstone which has been
squared at its western end to create a
symmetrical entrance.

Excavations have recovered no grave-goods
and like ESSÉ, IV (102) and LES TABLETTES
(162) this may have been a shrine rather than a
tomb.

151b 5½ km to the SE, at **Le Lobon**near
Caro, there is a ruined allée-couverte with
indications of a terminal cell.

Mané-er-Hloh (Mané Bihan). *Passage-grave*
(see 150e LOCOAL-MENDON)

Mané-er-Hloh (Mané Bras). *Passage-grave*
(see 150f LOCOAL-MENDON)

152 Mein-Goarec, Plaudren. *Allée-couverte*
*18 km N of Vannes, 10½ km SSE of Locminé,
4½ km SSW of St Jean-Brévelay. From St Jean
take the D778 S. After 2½ km pass Kerdramel
menhir (see 159b) on W. In 2½ km more turn W
(R) onto lane to Colpo. In 500 m tomb is 150 m
to S (L) on N slope of low hill.*
This short allée-couverte was excavated in
1967. It is 7 m long, aligned E–W, with a
possible lateral entrance at the SE corner.
There is one capstone remaining at the W end
where there may have been a terminal cell
from which the sidestones have gone. The
outer face of the end-stone here has two
breasts carved in relief inside a faint
cartouche.

The ruined passage-grave of KERALLAN

La Maison Trouvée (151a), Loire dolmen from the W.

(159e) was 100 m away with a fine carving of a hafted axe. Interestingly, at the allée-couverte of MOUGAU-BIHAN, F (82), carvings of breasts and axes were juxtaposed. From Mein-Goarec came sherds of Crech-Quillé/Le Mélus ware of the Late Neolithic.

Men-ar-Menah. *Menhir (see* 150a LOCOAL-MENDON)

Men Platt. *Dolmen (see* 136b GRAND ROHU)

Museum (see 164 VANNES)

153a Net, Le, St Gildas-de-Rhuys. *Allée-couverte*
16 km SSW of Vannes, 5½ km W of Sarzeau. From Sarzeau take the D780 W and in 5½ km the tomb is visible to the S (L) of the road. To approach take next lane immediately to the W.
Surrounded by hawthorns, gorse and bramble but fairly clear in its gallery, where there are several fallen stones, this is a very long allée-couverte, 21 m from WNW to ESE where its entrance is concealed by repelling vegetation. It is 1.6 m wide. At the WNW there is a big capstone, split in two. A fallen stone near it has six possible cupmarks on its upper

surface. There is a western chamber 6 m long demarcated by two transverse slabs forming a porthole entrance.

Excavations in 1921 recovered Gallo-Roman material indicating the monument's re-use. There were also sherds of beaker as well as Late Neolithic arrowheads, two pendants, a Grand Pressigny dagger and other flints.

40 m to the S of the tomb is a tall menhir, 3 m high, aligned N–S.

153b Across the lane to the W, in a field of many bushes, is the **Men-ar-Palud** menhir, a jagged slab of granite also 3 m high.

Nioul and Pen-Nioul. *Passage-graves (see* 139e, d ÎLE AUX MOINES)

Penhape. *Passage-grave (see* 139c ÎLE AUX MOINES)

154 Petit-Mont, Arzon. *Passage-grave*
18 km SW of Vannes and 10 km W of Sarzeau. From Sarzeau take the D780 W for 9½ km and turn S (L), following the road for 1 km, past the marina, continuing straight up the hill to Petit-Mont at its crest. Signposted. Car parking.
Towards the N end of a huge cairn, 60 × 46 × 6 m high, are the remains of a

(Above) Calderstones, Liverpool museum. Carvings of feet on stone from probable passage-grave.

(Left) Petit-Mont (154), cast of stone with carvings of feet. Cast is in Carnac museum, CA (166).

passage-grave in which were some of the most splendid carvings in Brittany. The mound rises dramatically on a hill above the waters of the Baie de Quiberon. Unfortunately, this monument, partly excavated in 1865 and restored in 1905, was almost wrecked by the insertion of two concrete blockhouses during the Second World War and today some of the decorated stones are smashed and others have disappeared. Casts of some can be seen in CARNAC museum, CA (166). Further restoration and repair of the site was taking place in 1984.

The tomb, facing SE, had a passage 4.4 m long, only 60 cm wide at the entrance but widening, rising in height and curving slightly southwards to a chamber about 2 m square. The art is concentrated at the NW end of the passage and in the chamber itself.

The style is somewhat different from that of the classic Breton passage-graves. Here the dominant motif is the chevron, often in multiple, horizontal bands. Although crooks and axes appear there are also spoked 'suns', meanders, cupmarks and the soles of a pair of feet, side by side, toes upwards. Two triangular axes, hafted, were carved on a lost stone half-blocking access to the chamber; a fine 'sun', 50 cm in diameter with a cupmark at its centre, was on a stone to its S in the chamber; and the paired-foot stone was at the NW corner. At its top-left corner was a 'figurine' resting on a long, upcurved line which has been interpreted as a boat for the souls of the dead, not implausible in a tomb overlooking the sea.

The Petit-Mont art has been compared with that in the Anglesey passage-grave of Barclodiad-y-Gawres, also on a rocky cove by the sea. Here there were chevrons thought to represent a 'Mother Goddess' or guardian spirit. Interestingly, chevrons also occur on the pillars of the Calderstones in Liverpool, possibly the dismantled orthostats of another passage-grave built on the coastline of the seaways of western Europe and only 110 km E of Barclodiad-y-Gawres. It may be significant that feet were carved on these stones also. At Bryn-Celli-Ddu, a passage-grave on Anglesey 18 km E of Barclodiad, the untypical freestanding stone in its chamber has been likened to the anthropomorphic stelae known in some Breton passage-graves such as ÎLE

GUENNOC, F (52).

Middle Neolithic finds from the 1865 Petit-Mont excavations of stone axes, axe-hammers, sherds, including one of a vase-support, flint arrowheads and callais beads are now in VANNES museum (164).

Alexander Thom suggested that the mound of Petit-Mont could have acted as a backsight for observations towards the GRAND MENHIR BRISÉ, CA (175a), 5 km to the NW, in line with the major northern moonset.

Plec. *Christianized stones* (*see* 150c LOCOAL-MENDON)

155 Quenouille de Gargantua, La, Plaudren. *Menhir*
16 km SE of Locminé, 15 km NNE of Vannes. From Plaudren take the D133 E towards Trédion and in 800 m turn N (L) onto the D126 towards Plumélec. After 1½ km, at La Croix Pleinte, the menhir is 170 m to the W at the edge of a pine wood.

This 'distaff' or 'spinning rod' of Gargantua is, in fact, a neatly shaped rectangular block, 7 m high. Standing at the place sometimes known as the Croix des Pins, it has an almost square base and a domed top.

5 km NW of Plaudren is the allée-couverte of MEIN-GOAREC (152).

156 Quinipily, Venus de, Baud. *Statue*
33 km NW of Vannes, 15 km WSW of Locminé. From Baud take the N24 W towards Hennebont. After 1¼ km turn S (L) past the mill and after 500 m take two left turns to the farm of Quinipily. Statue is in the meadow to the R of the farm buildings. Ask permission.

The farm stands in a large enclosure, all that is left of the château of Quinipily. The 'Venus' is a crude, 2-m-high semi-naked female figure on a high, arched pedestal above a granite cross. Below it is a fountain. It is a rare representation of a Gallo-Roman statue. On the pedestal, which was erected in 1696, is the inscription, *Venus armoricum oraculum, Caius Julius Caesar*, 'Venus, oracle of the Bretons, under Julius Caesar'.

The Venus has been known under various names: *Gwreg Houarn*, 'the woman of iron'; the Virgin; and *Coarda ar Guarda*, the 'Witch of La Couard'. The history of the statue provides an insight into the strength of pagan tradition even in the late 17th century AD.

Originally the figure stood some 12 km to the N at Castennac by the site of the ancient Gaulish settlement of Sulim. Well into the Middle Ages pagan rites were performed around the statue and, in 1661, angered by this the Bishop of Vannes ordered it to be thrown into the River Blavet. Peasants recovered her three years later. With the rites continuing the bishop, in 1670, commanded that she be smashed into pieces. One tradition says that this was done, others that the workmen being fearful of the statue's powers broke off only an arm and a breast and once again dropped the rest of the figure into the river. Others say that the destruction was thorough but that in 1696 a crude replica was made.

Whatever the truth, in 1696 either the original or a copy was set up in the grounds of the château of Quinipily and despite further protests by the church it has remained on the spot ever since.

It is possible that this was a representation of the Egyptian goddess, Isis, her cult introduced into Brittany by Roman legionaries.

157 Roches-Piquées, Les, La Gacilly. *Menhirs*

48 km ENE of Vannes, 19 km ESE of Malestroit. From La Gacilly take the D777 W and in 300 m a footpath on the SE (L) of the road is signposted to the stones. There are steps provided for the 50 m climb up the hillside.

Originally there was a pair of enormous standing stones here, about 3 m apart on a WSW–ENE axis. The taller, an immense granite pillar with a surface pitted and rough like sandpaper, still stands, 5 m high with sides measuring 3.3 × 1 m. Its longer faces are to WSW and ENE.

The second stone lies fallen to the NW. Its dimensions are about 2.5 m in length by 1.3 × 1 m. The stones were erected laterally to their axis on a steep slope falling towards the N. Around them some of the packing stones are still apparent.

158a St Guyomard, Malestroit. *Menhirs*

19 km S of Josselin. From Malestroit take the D776 SW for 7 km then turn W (R) onto the D112. It is 5 km to St Guyomard.

In the commune of this village there are the remains of two chambered tombs, a large tumulus and two menhirs in the woods to the E. In the village itself, at the Chapelle-St-Maurice-des-Bois, there are two stones reputed to have healing powers. One of them is actually set in the wall of the chapel. This is the Pierre Droite and it is 5 m high. The other, lozenge-shaped, is behind and it is said that to be cured one must pass between the stones. Sufferers afflicted with rheumatism would drink water from the fountain and then rub themselves against the Pierre Droite. It was until recently the custom, on the feast of St Maurice, to dress the two stones with freshly-cut branches.

158b There are two larger menhirs in the woods just to the E of the village. One of them, the **Menhir des Bois**, is over 7 m high and is strangely rectangular all the way up its length so that its flat summit is no smaller than its base. The other stone, deeper in the woods, is 6.5 m tall and is patched with weathering and lichen as though it had been decorated with vertical stripes.

158c On the heath of **Sournon**, close to St Guyomard, are the collapsed slabs of a little passage-grave that once had a stone, now missing, with indistinct carvings on it.

159 St Jean-Brévelay. *Megalithic centre*

20 km N of Vannes, 10 km ESE of Locminé.
Within some 5 km of St Jean, and mainly to its SW, are some fine menhirs and two ruined chambered tombs. The name of the little town is a corruption of St John of Beverley who, as Bishop of York, consecrated Bede. He died in AD 721 and was buried at Beverley. Some of his relics were brought to Brittany by refugees.

7 km WSW of St Jean is Colpo around which are the important megalithic sites of the LARCUSTE passage-graves (149), the decorated menhir of KERMARQUER (145a) and several others. To find them the blue Carte Topographique 1:25,000 maps, Elven 0920 Est and Ouest, give detailed coverage of the area. Less informative but still helpful is the orange Carte Touristique 1:50,000 map, no. 0920.

Near St Jean, predominantly on the still desolate heaths of the Lande de Lanvaux, the stones most worth visiting are:

159a Colého. *From the D778 take the side road to the W (R) signposted Colpo. The menhir is 1½ km along this lane just before the S turning to Poulgat. It is 100 m NE of the junction.* This leaning pillar, 5½ km SSW of St Jean, stands on typical heathland of bracken, gorse and bramble. It is 5 m high, a rectangular rough pillar of granite, its longer side 1.3 m, its narrower 75 cm long. It stands on a NW–SE axis.

159b Kerdramel. *2½ km SSW of St Jean immediately W of the D778 opposite Kerdramel farm. Halfway up a slope in the first field.* This is a massive, rectangular block of granite, over 5 m high, with a tapering top. Around it the skyline is level to NNW and SSE, the latter being the direction to which the flatter face of the stone is pointing.

159c Lann Douar. *2½ km SW of St Jean and most easily found by taking the D778 S and in 2 km, having crossed the River Claie and passing a lane to the W (R) just beyond it, take the next lane SW 100 m after a bend to the S. Pass the 1st turn W (R) to Kervenic and Lann Douar. In 150 m turn W (R) past Kercado. Menhir is ¾ km farther on immediately to the N of the lane.* The stone stands in a shallow hollow with the horizon level to the NE and rising to the E and W. There is a noticeable

hill just to the SW on the major axis of this heavy granite pillar.

159d Also to be seen near St Jean but not always easily accessible or impressive are the menhirs of: **Goh**, 4½ km to the SW of the town; and **Menguen-Lanvaux**, 4½ km SSE. There are overgrown or ruined chambered tombs at **Kerhern-Bodunan**, 3½ km SSW of St Jean but very difficult to find in the marshy woods; **Kerjadu** dolmen 4 km WSW of St Jean; and KERALLAN (159e).

159e Kerallan. *Passage-grave. 5½ km S of St Jean and 1 km S of Kerallan hamlet. 500 m W of the D778 in the 2nd field S of the lane.* This little tomb is important for the carving of a hafted axe which was noticed in it. The site is now a mass of stones and the decorated slab has been removed for safety. From the passage-grave were recovered some Late Neolithic artefacts including some beaker sherds, two tubular beads and a plano-convex archer's wristguard of Beaker affinities. All these seem to have been secondary intrusions.

100 m away is the small allée-couverte of MEIN-GOAREC (152).

160 Sarzeau. *Megalithic centre*
15 km S of Vannes on the Arzon peninsula.
The town itself is pleasant with its tiny square and fine church, and to its W is a sprinkle of

Colého (159a), menhir from the SW.

Kerdramel (159b), menhir from the SSE.

excellent sites most conveniently seen in the
order of: LE NET (153a), 5½ km from Sarzeau;
KERMAILLARD decorated menhir (144a), 6
km; TUMIAC Carnac Mound (163),
8 km; PETIT-MONT passage-grave (154), 10
km; and GRAH-NIOHL passage-grave with
carved stones (134a), 10 km WNW. Also in
the area but not described in the gazetteer is
the menhir at **Larguéven**, 3½ km W of
Sarzeau, and the dolmen of **Lannek er Men** at
Brillac, 3½ km NW. 3 km E of Sarzeau is the
magnificent menhir at **Corporh**.

The Carte Touristique 1:50,000 map, no.
501, *Golfe du Morbihan*, covers the area.
There is also a useful guidebook,
*Locmariaquer: aperçu de la pensée mégalithique
dans le golfe du Morbihan*, compiled by the
Association Archéologique Kergal, Fontenay-
le-Fleury, 1981.

Sournon. *Passage-grave (see* 158c ST
GUYOMARD)

161   Stival, Pontivy. *Menhir*
*25 km NNW of Locminé, 2½ km NW of
Pontivy. The village of Stival is on the D764.*
Close to its church of St Mériadac is a
Christianized menhir 1.5 m high. It has a cross
carved on it. On the reverse side is a deep
mark, 'the hoof of the devil'. It is said that
Satan turned himself into a goat to distract St
Mériadac from his devotions. Furious at the
interruptions the holy man kicked the goat
which in turn kicked out and damaged the
stone.

162   Tablettes, Les, Cournon. *Loire
dolmen*
*50 km ENE of Vannes, 22 km ESE of
Malestroit, 1 km SSE of La Gacilly. From La
Gacilly take the D773 S, cross the river and in
150 m turn E (L) onto lane signposted, 'Dolmen
des Tablettes'. In 300 m a footpath on S (R)
leads through wood to tomb on W (R) signalled
by red and white marks on tree.*
One can scramble inside this roughly restored
monument and appreciate its similarity to its
enormous counterpart at ESSÉ, IV (102). Here,
two big capstones, the one at the WNW split,
are propped on big stones variously of
Cambrian puddingstone, sandstone and
quartz. Additional support is provided by
modern iron and concrete pillars. The tomb is
about 8.5 m long and 4 m wide. Inside,
somewhat below ground level like the other
Loire Dolmen at LA MAISON TROUVÉE (151a),
it is about 1.7 m high. A wide slab at the ESE
marks the entrance and just inside there is a
low transverse stone forming an embryonic
vestibule.

163   Tumiac, Arzon. *Carnac Mound*
*16 km SSW of Vannes, 8 km W of Sarzeau.
From Sarzeau take the D780 W. Mound is on N
(R) of road, clearly visible, 200 m past the lane
on the N to Beninzé. Layby. Track on N leads to
the monument which is closed.*
This is a huge, slightly oval barrow, about
50 m in diameter and still 15 m high. It
dominates the skyline. Lukis observed that
'the great tumulus of Tumiac will always come

Tumiac (163), Carnac Mound from the S.

into view, and like the Loadstone Mountain in
the Arabian Nights' Entertainments, be the
attractive power which will draw [the
traveller] onwards.' It is known as the Butte
de César and it is popularly believed to be the
vantage point from which Julius Caesar
watched the naval battle between his Roman
ships and the Gaulish Veneti in 56 BC.

Beneath this colossal barrow there was a
central cairn, 28 m in diameter, concealing a
closed chamber at its SE edge. It was
excavated in 1862 and has since been restored
but cannot be seen today. Under a big, quartz
capstone the chamber was 4.8 m long,
narrower to its SE where the granite sideslabs
of the NW were replaced by drystone walling.
There was no passage. The chamber had a
wooden floor and on it, placed in neat groups,
was a rich variety of grave-goods. At the S
corner were fifteen small broken stone axes,
three of them perforated, and where the
drystone walling gave way to the first granite
orthostat there were fifteen more, larger and
intact. In the NW corner were 107 stone beads
and nine callais pendants. Altogether in this
confined tomb there were eleven jadeite axes,
twenty-six of fibrolite, pendants, 249 beads
and some flint flakes, a luxurious
accompaniment for the dead on the way to the
afterlife. Such wealth is typical of the Carnac
Mounds and quite unlike the paucity of
artefacts to be found in the passage-graves of

Morbihan. Conversely, the carvings in
those tombs are not repeated in the Carnac
Mounds.

Alexander Thom considered that near, but
not at, Tumiac there had been a backsight
towards the GRAND MENHIR BRISÉ, CA
(175a), 6½ km to the WNW. The
astronomical orientation would have been
towards the minor northern moonset.

164   Vannes. Musée Archéologique.
Museum
*The museum is in the old Maison du Parlement,
the Château Gaillard on the Rue Noé 150 m E of
the Place de la République and a similar distance
SW of the cathedral. Open 0930–1200, 1400–
1800. Closed Sundays and holidays. Admission
6 Fr.*

This museum is in an attractive part of
medieval Vannes and is housed on the first
floor of a house of historic interest. The
Parlement of Rennes met here from 1456 to
1532.

The archaeological collections on display
are magnificent and come mainly from 19th-
century excavations, from 1853 onwards, of
the Morbihan megalithic monuments. On
display are Neolithic vessels, hoards, callais
beads and collars, and an amazing
accumulation of polished stone axes, including
those from MANÉ-ER-HROEK, CA (195). There
is also a small amount of literature for sale.

Measuring a menhir in the Morbihan in 1834.

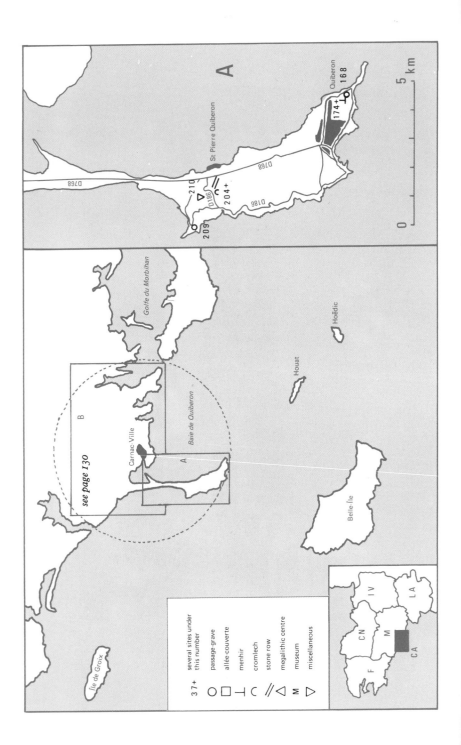

A

St Pierre Quiberon

Quiberon

174+

168

210

204+

209

D186

D768

D768

D186

C

0   5 km

see page 130

B

Carnac-Ville

A

Baie de Quiberon

Golfe du Morbihan

Île de Groix

Houat

Hoëdic

Belle-Île

37+   several sites under
       this number

○   passage grave

□   allée-couverte

⊥   menhir

C   cromlech

∥   stone row

△   megalithic centre

M   museum

▷   miscellaneous

F   CN
IV
M   LA
CA

Carnac

Maps: *Yellow Michelin 1:200,000, no. 63*
Green Carte Touristique, 1:100,000, no. 15
Blue Carte Touristique 1:50,000, no. 501. Golfe du Morbihan Belle-Île
Blue Carte Topographique 1:25,000, no. 0821 Est, Auray Quiberon. This
gives detailed coverage of the whole area in this section of the gazetteer

There is such a concentration of well-preserved monuments within a 12-km radius of Carnac-Ville that the area demands a section to itself. Visitors may find it convenient to divide even this small region into four parts: Erdeven to the north-west; the Quiberon peninsula to the south-west; Locmariaquer to the south-east; and Carnac-Ville at the centre. The best bases for exploring the district are probably Carnac-Ville (165) and Locmariaquer (190), although accommodation at Carnac-Plage, Erdeven or La Trinité-sur-Mer may be just as satisfying. Some visitors might prefer the busier town of Auray a few kilometres to the north-east. It is easiest to travel by car, but bicycles can sometimes be hired. Enquire at the local Syndicat d'Initiatif. That at 74, Avenue des Druides, Carnac-Plage, is open throughout the year.

Some of the sites in the vicinity of Carnac are the most famous of the Breton megaliths. They include the striking rows of Ménec (203), Kermario (183), and Kerlescan (180), close to Carnac itself. To the west are other rows at Kerzerho (187a), the unique quadrilateral at Crucuno (171b), and other lines, menhirs and chambered tombs along the thin finger of the Quiberon peninsula. Nor should the bulky Carnac Mounds such as Le Moustoir (205a) be ignored, but the visitor should be warned that the guided tour inside the Tumulus St-Michel (215a) can be archaeologically disappointing.

At Locmariaquer are the megalithic marvels of the Grand Menhir Brisé (175a), the passage-graves of Mané Lud (199b), the Table des Marchands (175c), and Les Pierres-Plats (208), with its 'figurine' carvings and the white steps of its veering capstones.

Following surveys in the 1970s Professor Thom argued for two important astronomical observatories near Carnac. He concluded that the Manio (202a) and Grand Menhir Brisé (175a) menhirs had been erected as foresights towards the eight major risings and settings of the moon. Several sites, he believed, could have been the backsights from which observers would have seen these lunar events: for Manio, 167b, 178, 180b, 181, 183c, 197b, 200; and for the Grand Menhir Brisé, 154, 163, 174a, 185b, 205b. Omitted from the gazetteer are some non-megalithic (or non-existent) sites. There are good reasons for doubting the astronomical function of many stones in the two 'observatories'.

Not to be forgotten in this prehistoric wonderland is the museum at Carnac-Ville (166). The objects on display, from the flints and the pots to the casts of carved stones, are vividly revealing of the lives of the people who erected and used the menhirs, the rows and the tombs.

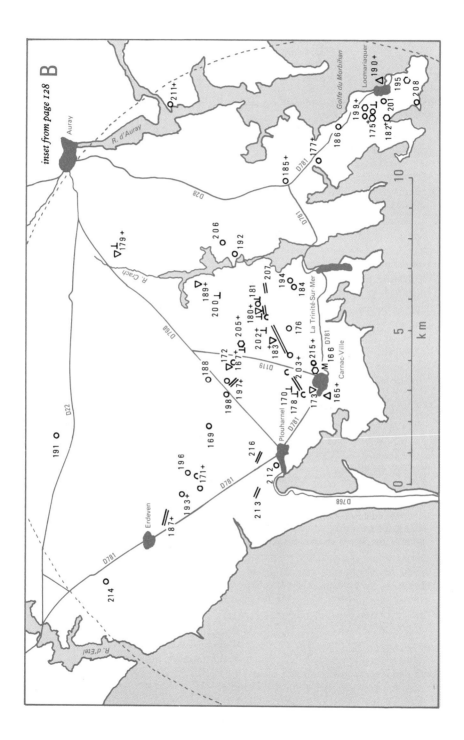

inset from page 128 B

Auray

R. d'Auray

R. d'Étel

Erdeven

Plouharnel

Carnac-Ville

La Trinité-Sur-Mer

Golfe du Morbihan

Locmariaquer

211 +

185 +

179 +

206

192

189 +
200

180 + 181
205 +
202 +
183 +
176
194
207
184

172
167
215 +
203 +
166
165 +
173

188

197 +
198

169

216

193 +
171 +
196
187 +

191

214

212

213

177 +

186

199 +
175
182 +
201
190 +
195
208

D28

D781

D768

D22

D781

D119

D781

D768

R. Crach

km

0   5   10

Sites 165-216

165 Carnac-Ville. *Megalithic centre*
26 km WSW of Vannes, 12 km SSW of Auray.
Probably the best-known of the Breton
megalithic monuments are the astonishing
lines of huge standing stones just N of the
little town of Carnac. These are worth seeing
for themselves but near them are other sites –
cromlechs, menhirs, passage-graves – which,
with the rows, would make a splendid day's or
days' programme for the energetic walker.
Each of the rows (MÉNEC (203b), KERMARIO
(183b), KERLESCAN (180d), and PETIT-
MÉNEC (207)) is listed separately in the
gazetteer, but the enthusiast may wish to
follow an itinerary starting at Ménec and
concluding with Petit-Ménec 3¾ km to the E.
Allowing for deviations to adjacent
monuments, the walk would be about 5 km to
the far end.
The rows, only 2¼ km N of the sea, stretch
W–E almost across the width of the Carnac-
La Trinité peninsula, with the majority of the
chambered tombs to their N. Amongst other
functions the lines may have acted as
territorial markers. As their terminal
cromlechs were erected on level ground with
the rows running uphill towards them it is
probable that the rings were earlier and that
the lines were put up gradually over
succeeding centuries.
In Carnac-Ville itself there is the great
mound of the TUMULUS ST-MICHEL (215a)
which can be entered for a fee; the
Christianized dolmen of CRUZ-MOQUEN
(173); and the MUSEUM (166), with its
evocative collections of prehistoric material.

**166 Carnac-Ville. Musée Archéologique
James Miln–Zacharie le Rouzic.** *Museum*
*The contents of this museum were moved in 1984
to 10, Place de la Chapelle, just N of the Maison
de la Presse near the Mairie. Open from Easter to
15 October, 1000–1200, 1400–1700. June and
September, 1800. July and August, 1900. Closed
1 May. Admission 4 Fr.*
Until 1984 these fine prehistoric collections
were housed in a small, two-roomed building
at the foot of the Rue St Cornèly. They have

now been taken to more spacious
accommodation in the town centre.
The museum is named after two famous
Carnacian archaeologists, James Miln, a Scot
who excavated around Carnac from 1874 until
his death in 1881, and Zacharie le Rouzic
(1864–1939), who also excavated here up to
the beginning of the Second World War. On
Miln's death his brother had the small
museum built to display the material Miln had
gathered together, and when le Rouzic died
fifty-eight years later his name was added to
that of Miln. The museum is a tribute to the
work of these indefatigable men.
It contains some of the most attractive and
exotic prehistoric artefacts in Brittany.
Amongst the hundreds of objects are scores of
polished stone axes, flint tools, pottery of all
periods, including some of the delicate vase-
supports from le Rouzic's excavations at ER-
LANNIC (132b), callais beads, and weapons.
Inspection of the ordinary domestic
implements such as spindle-whorls, scrapers,
and querns for grinding corn provides a
necessary reminder that the builders of the
fascinating ritual monuments were men and
women who also had to live an ordinary,
humdrum existence as country people.
Yet there is also an intriguing set of casts
taken from the decorated stones in the
passage-graves around the Carnac region.
Postcards and literature, including some
excavation reports, are for sale.

167a Champ de la Croix, Crucuny.
Cromlech
*4 km N of Carnac-Ville, 3¾ km NE of
Plouharnel. From Carnac take the D119 N for
4 km and turn W (L) for 300 m to Crucuny
hamlet. At the T-junction turn S (L). The
cromlech forms the wall of a garden. A lane leads
to it just after the last house.*
Only the western arc, 45 m long, of thirty
stones survives of what must once have been a
great ring. The arc now stands alongside a
cart-track to its W. The site is known also as
Parc-er-Groez. The stones were re-erected in
1926–7. Three of them have carvings.
167b 78 m to the E in the same garden is an
isolated 2-m-high menhir, almost square in
plan but roughly aligned NNW–SSE. This is
Thom's Stone Y which he thought might have
been a backsight for the MANIO menhir

(202a), 1940 m to the SSE. It would have defined an orientation to the major southern moonrise. The axis of the Crucuny stone, however, does not confirm this alignment.

CRUCUNY tumulus (172) is 400 m N of the cromlech.

168 Conguel, Quiberon. *Passage-grave*
23 km S of Auray, 2 km ESE of Quiberon. From Quiberon take the D186 S and in 500 m, at the crossroads, turn E (L) along the sea-front. In 2 km on the N (L) of the road there is a large menhir set in concrete at the entrance to a holiday camp. Tomb is nearby on R of camp entrance.
This is a small and inconspicuous passage-grave, and in poor condition, but it is important because of the pottery found in it.

Excavated in 1892, it had a cairn covered by the dunes and for one wall of the chamber the natural bedrock had been used. A short passage about 1.2 m long and oriented NE, perhaps in line with the midsummer sunrise, led to a rectangular chamber 4 m long and 1.7 m wide, angled to the NNE. Two occupation layers were discovered in it, separated by a 45-cm-thick layer of sterile sand. Unusually for a Breton tomb skeletons were found in these strata, preserved by the sand that covered them.

In the lower layer there were five skeletons, two in the passage and three in the chamber lying on a paving of granite stones. With them were flint and dolerite axes, some beads and sherds of round-bottomed bowls with half-ellipses, parallel lines and other motifs deeply incised in their walls. These vessels gave their name to the classic Late Neolithic Lower Conguel ware. Other pots belonged to the later Middle Neolithic Souch series.

On the sterile layer above was a second occupation band containing two more skeletons and three Upper Conguel pots, flat-bottomed biconical vases with a wide zone of bands incised around the body. With them were beaker sherds.

In its design the Conguel tomb belongs to the traditional passage-grave group, but the artefacts found in it point to a time late in the tradition, towards the end of the 4th millennium BC.

About 100 m to the N is the GOULVARCH menhir (174a), probably erected many centuries after the passage-grave.

169 Cosquer (Men-er-Roh), Plouharnel. *Passage-grave*
4½ km NNW of Carnac-Ville, 2½ km NNE of Plouharnel. From Plouharnel take the D768 NE for 2 km and then turn NW (L) for 1¼ km. Turn W (L) for 250 m to Cosquer hamlet. Tomb is 80 m N of the village by the side of the lane.
Standing on a slight rise this monument has a very short passage, facing southwards, and a polygonal chamber on which there is a huge capstone, about 4 × 2 m and 50 cm thick, supported on six orthostats.

170 Crifol, Carnac-Ville. *Menhir*
1¼ km NW of Carnac-Ville. From N corner of the Ménec West Cromlech a footpath leads N. After 200 m it veers NE. In 400 m the menhir will be seen, isolated in the fields.
The stone, 400 m NE of the KERDERFF menhir (178), stands 2.9 m high. Excavations at its base by James Miln in 1879 produced nothing. A fallen stone near it was destroyed in 1900.

The Crifol menhir appears as Stone T on Alexander Thom's 1978 plan of the Carnac alignments, but he made no astronomical claims for it.

171a Crucuno, Plouharnel. *Passage-grave*
5¾ km NW of Carnac-Ville and 3 km NNW of Plouharnel. From Plouharnel take the D781 NW and in 3 km turn NE (R) for ¾ km to Crucuno hamlet. Chambered tomb is in centre of village.
This is one of the most photographed megalithic tombs in Brittany. It stands alongside farm buildings, an impressive

Crucuno (171a), passage-grave from the S.

chamber now lacking all but one of its passage stones. The whole monument was nearly dismantled during the building of the village, but it was eventually taken into State care in 1882.

It once measured almost 24 m, with its long passage leading from the SE to the chamber which is almost square, 3.5 × 3.4 m and 1.8 m high, covered by a great capstone 7.6 m long and weighing over forty tons. There is no record of any finds.

The site has had a varied history. It was used by the German army during the Second World War and before then it had acted as a stable, an amusement stall, a hemp-bruising platform and, late in the 18th century, a village idiot had lived in it for ten years.

171b Crucuno Rectangle. *Immediately N of the tomb a small lane between the buildings leads E for 300 m to the Crucuno quadrilateral 100 m to the S in a field.* The field is called *Parc Vein Glass*, 'the Field of the Blue Stone'. The rectangle is almost impossible to inspect because of the gorse bushes growing thickly inside it. It is a perfect megalithic oblong which was restored in 1882, before which time only nine of its twenty-two stones were standing. The accuracy of the reconstruction has been questioned, but a plan by Dryden and Lukis, made in 1867, confirms that the restorer, Gaillard, had taken great care to erect the stones in the correct places. The tallest stone stands at the SE corner.

According to the Thoms who, with the Merritts, made a very accurate plan of the monument in 1970, the rectangle measures 24.9 × 33.2 m, the sides being in an exact 3:4 ratio with a diagonal 41.5 m long. These dimensions correspond almost exactly to 30 × 40 × 50 of Alexander Thom's megalithic yard of 0.829 m.

The longer sides are aligned neatly to E and W, so that looking to the W one would have seen the equinoctial sunsets of March and September nicely defined along the longer sides of the oblong. The Thoms recorded that 267 m to the W there lay the menhir of **Chaise du Pape**, 'the Pope's Chair', which could have acted as a foresight to these sunsets. To the E, because of a different skyline height, the alignment to the equinoctial sunrises was not so good.

It has also been claimed that Crucuno was

laid out as a rectangle, rather than a square, so that the diagonals could be used to define the positions of the solstitial sun. To this the Thoms added that there could have been orientations also to the eight 'standstill' positions of the moon, but they remarked that without distant foresights Crucuno 'could never have been more than a symbolic observatory'.

A possible Breton counterpart to this intricate site existed at Le Conquet on the Kermorven peninsula, Finistère, 21 km WSW of Brest, but the polygonal enclosure there has now disappeared except for a few displaced stones. Monuments with a closer resemblance to Crucuno exist in England at both the little-known King Arthur's Hall on Bodmin Moor (SX 129776) – a rectangle of standing stones, 48 × 21 m, inside a wide earthen bank: its long sides lie N–S – and at Stonehenge, where the Four Stations stones stand in a rectangle whose sides point to midsummer sunrise and the major northern setting of the moon. The diagonals are also astronomically significant.

If it is true that the open enclosures or cromlechs of Brittany derived their shapes from the earlier passage-graves then the oblong of Crucuno may have been influenced by the rectangular chambers of the nearby tombs not only of Crucuno itself but also of MANÉ GROH (196), 500 m to the N, and MANÉ BRAS (193a), 1¼ km NW.

From Crucuno hamlet the road to the NE leads in 500 m to the passage-grave of MANÉ GROH (196).

172 Crucuny, Plouharnel. *Tumulus 3¾ km NE of Plouharnel, 4 km N of Carnac-Ville. From Carnac-Ville take the D119 N for 4 km, turn W (L) to Crucuny hamlet and in 300 m at T-junction turn N (R). Tumulus is 250 m on the W of the road. Signposted.*
This overgrown mound, some 55 × 23 m, 13 m high and aligned NNE–SSW, was heaped up at the edge of a steepish slope. Excavations in 1922 uncovered several neatly-built cists and small standing stones in its complicated layers. Three skeletons were found in it with objects of copper, polished stone and flint axes, sherds and an intrusive Gallo-Roman statuette of Venus. On top of the mound, as at the tumulus of LE MOUSTOIR (205a), there is a menhir, here wretchedly thin

but 2.8 m high, with carvings of hafted axes at its base.

There are several tertres tumulaires in the neighbourhood.

173 Cruz-Moquen, Carnac-Ville. *Dolmen*
From the new museum in Carnac-Ville take the minor road N towards Cité du Runel. It is the road to the L of the D119. In 400 m, just after a little road to the W (L), a short path on the W leads to the dolmen.
Sometimes known as La Pierre Chaude, this is a ruined megalithic tomb whose thick capstone lies on three pillars about 1.5 m high. On it a Christian cross has been erected. It is said that at full moon women would raise their skirts in front of the dolmen in the hope of becoming pregnant.

Er-Grah. *Carnac Mound* (see 175b GRAND MENHIR BRISÉ, LE)

174a Goulvarch, Quiberon. *Menhir*
23 km S of Auray, 2 km ESE of Quiberon. From Quiberon take the D186 S and in 500 m, at the major crossroads, turn E (L) along the sea-front. In 2 km on the N (L) of the road there is a large menhir set in concrete at the entrance to a holiday camp. 200 km to its N, behind the building, is the menhir.
This is a fine granite pillar, slightly tapering to a flat top. It stands 6 m high and its playing-card sides measure 2.7 × 0.7 m. It stands on a NE–SW axis.

Alexander Thom suggested that a viewing-station towards the GRAND MENHIR BRISÉ (175a), 15¼ km to the ENE across the Baie de Quiberon, would have stood near here, although the menhir itself was not quite in the right place. He added that 'as seen from Goulvarh [*sic*] the sun at the winter solstice set over the reef', off the N end of Belle-Île, and now submerged, 'and there may have been a clearly defined projection to use as a foresight; it thus seems likely that Goulvarh was a solstitial backsight.'

174b The menhir at the front of the holiday camp has been moved here in recent times. It is prehistoric.

CONGUEL passage-grave (168) is 100 m to the S.

175a Grand Menhir Brisé, Le, Locmariaquer. *Menhir*
18 km SW of Vannes, 12 km SSE of Auray. From Auray take D28 S. After 8 km join D781

Cruz-Moquen (173), Christianized dolmen from the NE.

Le Grand Menhir Brisé (175a), broken menhir from the NE.

continuing S. Just before entering Locmariaquer take road to W (R) at the cemetery. Menhir is 100 m on R. Parking space.

If ever it were erect this would have been the tallest known standing stone in Brittany. It has various names including La Grande Pierre; Er-Grah; and Pierre de la Fée (Men-er-Hroeg). It now lies in four fragments, three of them in a 13.6-m-long E–W line, the base, 9.2 m long, to the W on a SE–NW axis. This latter stump is slightly tilted and it is twisted round from where it might be expected to have lain.

In its unbroken state the menhir would have measured 20.3 m. It was a tapering pillar, hexagonal in shape, 4.1 m wide from N to S, 2.3 m from E to W. Like many other Breton standing stones its intended alignment would have been at right-angles to its broader face, here in an easterly direction. The stone's weight has been computed as 342 tons if the volume is 134 cubic m, or 256 tons if, as a recent estimate calculated, the volume is only 96 cubic m.

This astonishing menhir was not of local granite but of a harder variety, possibly from near the abandoned quarry at Kerdaniel 3¾ km to the NNW. The task of moving such a ponderous block must have been almost beyond the powers of the prehistoric community especially as, having to avoid the bays and slopes of the coastline, the shortest distance to be travelled would have been over 4 km. The stone may have been shaped before removal. Inspection of the middle section, least affected by weathering and vandals, shows that it had been dressed and smoothed

with stone mauls. On the second section from the E there seems to be an eroded, indistinct carving of a Neolithic hafted stone axe.

The date of erection, the purpose and the time of its collapse have all been the subjects of controversy. From historical records it seems that it was prostrate before AD 1286. Excavations by le Rouzic found Gallo-Roman rooftiles and sherds underneath the overhang of its base, but these did not prove that the stone fell after Roman times. The material could well have been rubbish from an adjacent temple dumped in the convenient space under the leaning fragment. It was too dangerous for the excavators to examine the stonehole itself.

Alexander Thom claimed that this high pillar had been intended as a foresight on the major and minor risings and settings of the moon as observed from eight backsights from 3 to 15 km away, and that a date around 1700 BC was the most likely time for its erection. He added that from the top of the TUMULUS ST-MICHEL (215a), Carnac-Ville, the stone would have marked moonrise at the beginning of March and October. If true, Thom's theory would make the Grand Menhir the central feature of a very accurate Bronze Age observatory.

175b What has rarely been commented on is that the broken stone lies at the SSE end of a former Carnac Mound known as **Er-Grah**. This Neolithic tumulus has been destroyed. Even in 1872 Lukis commented on the massive 120 × 48m barrow, 'a greater portion of which has been carted away'. It had a kerbing of small stones. Le Rouzic wrote that the mound was aligned N–S, but from its 'dilapidated chamber' to the middle of the fallen menhir the alignment is about 160°, a NNW–SSE axis.

Near its original centre was the 'dilapidated chamber of no particular interest', and this megalithic structure can still be seen under a cypress tree at the far end of what is now a car park. With a line of trees separating it from the fallen menhir, the connection between the levelled mound (from which six Neolithic callais beads were recovered) and the stone is not readily apparent, but the association does suggest a Neolithic date and a function for the Grand Menhir Brisé. The incredible pillar was probably meant to stand at the SSE end of the tumulus as an 'indicateur' or even as an anthropomorphic stele like other menhirs against Carnac Mounds such as LE MOUSTOIR (205a), and MANÉ-ER-HROEK (195) and their probable progenitors, the tertres tumulaires like MANIO I (183c). For further comparisons see nos. 18, 134a, 110j, 208. The Grand Menhir Brisé, therefore, is almost certainly Neolithic and the astronomical 'date' of 1700 BC must be wrong.

It should be remarked, moreover, that of the eight proposed backsights three do not exist and of the five others the Carnac Mound at TUMIAC, M (163), is not accurately placed. The GOULVARCH menhir (174a), the field-clearance stone at KERRAN (185b), the Carnac Mound of LE MOUSTOIR (205b) with its menhir, and the passage-grave of PETIT-MONT, M (154), are too dissimilar in architecture and date to be convincing purpose-built Neolithic viewing-stations.

Whatever its purpose it is uncertain that the menhir ever stood. Arguments have been fierce about this, people claiming that the stone could not have fallen and smashed while being lifted upright because the four fragments would not have tumbled into the positions they now occupy. If, instead, the pillar had been standing an earthquake could well have caused it to tremble, rotate and split throwing its upper segments to the E but loosening its base which slumped to the NW.

There are, however, other entirely feasible explanations. The stone could have been pushed over by Christians. More probably, and in keeping with what is known of other decorated menhirs, it is arguable that while being heaved up it had dropped and broken

and perhaps only its stump was finally set upright. Whether or not this was done years later, the size and the shape of this base tempted Neolithic people to move it towards a newly-built passage-grave for use as a capstone. Other shattered stones are known to have been integrated in this way, their shape and size making them ideal roofing slabs. Examples are known at GAVR'INIS, M (132a), the TABLE DES MARCHANDS (175c) and at MANÉ RUTUEL (201). Even at Mané Rutuel, which has a gigantic block over its chamber, this capstone weighs little more than forty tons whereas the stump of the Grand Menhir is over 110 tons, more maybe than could be lifted onto the top of a chambered tomb and the attempt was abandoned leaving the fragment where it lies today.

Should this be correct then the Grand Menhir Brisé must be amongst the earliest megalithic monuments in Brittany with a date far back in the primary centuries of the Neolithic.

175c Table des Marchands. Only 50 m to the NE of the shattered menhir is a passage-grave fascinating for its art and its re-used stones. When it was excavated in 1811 its oval mound with inner retaining walls was completely removed, leaving the great capstone and pillars exposed. This 'dolmen' was lived in for a while around 1850. Since then the monument has been restored several times in 1883, 1905, 1921 and, finally, in 1937 when the cairn was reconstructed to protect the decorated stones.

The low entrance, facing SE, is only 1.3 m high. It gives access to a 7-m-long passage opening onto a big, polygonal chamber, 3.5 × 3 m and 2.4 m high. Stones are missing at the E. It is covered by a massive capstone, 6.5 × 4 m, and weighing some forty tons.

The art is astounding. In the passage the third stone on the left (S) has some 'serpents' on it, but these are trivial when contrasted with the astonishing block at the back of the chamber. This is an ogival slab of sandstone, all the other stones being granite, transformed into a lavishly-carved anthropomorphic figurine. On its surface are four horizontal bands of fifty-three shepherds' crooks, upright, arranged in two vertical left and right panels. Between them is a central space and in it can just be made out a 'U' with another

Table des Marchands (175c), passage-grave from the SE.

Table des Marchands (175c), axe-carving on underside of capstone.

touching its base. Below them is a weathered 'sun' symbol. Other cruder arcs run all around the rim of this huge 'guardian' stone that looks down the passage. Out of sight, below the earth, is a small circle and a ragged line of cupmarks near the base of the stone.

On the back of the stone, but accessible to visitors because of the way in which the tomb has been rebuilt, are central arcs and vertical lines with a possible, broken 'figurine' at the bottom right-hand corner.

The underside of the capstone has a splendidly carved hafted and thonged axe and to its left is a broken crook. The N end of the capstone has been fractured and it has been discovered that an incomplete carving on its upper surface fits the broken end of another motif at the GAVR'INIS passage-grave, M (132a), nearly 2 km to the E. There is a probability that both the end-stone and the capstone at the Table des Marchands were once freestanding menhirs that were pushed over and broken for re-use when this passage-grave was being erected.

Most of the human bone, sherds, flints, a fragment of gold and a flint axe discovered in 1811 are lost, but some are now in VANNES museum, M (164).

Kerascouet. *Stone rows* (*see* 187b KERZERHO)

Kerbourgnec. *Cromlech* (*see* 204b MOULIN DE ST PIERRE-QUIBERON, LE)

176 Kercado, Carnac-Ville. *Passage-grave 2¼ km NW of La Trinité-sur-Mer, 2¼ km*

ENE of Carnac-Ville. From Carnac take the D119 N and in 1¼ km turn E (R) onto the D196. In 2 km an avenue leads S (R) to the château. Before reaching the house, after 300 m a lane on the W (R) curves S for 250 m. The tumulus is on the E (L) surrounded by trees. Locked. To enter, apply at the château 200 m to the E.

In the peaceful setting of the pines this fine passage-grave which stands inside a damaged stone circle is an important monument in prehistoric Brittany. An assay of 3890 ± 300 bc from charcoal in its passage suggests that it was in existence as early as 4675 BC.

The tomb is covered by a neatly kerbed circular mound, 25 m in diameter and 5 m high, on top of which is a 2.2-m-high menhir. Outside the cairn are the remains of a ring of contiguous stones, good arcs surviving at the SSW–SW and W–WNW. A single pillar, 1.8 m tall, stands outside the ESE entrance to the passage-grave. Like many early rings in the British Isles, the Kercado cromlech was not perfectly circular. Its radius varies from 19 m to less than 18 m at the ESE where the stones are highest.

If the ring were earlier than the cairn and was circular then its centre would have been at the SW corner of the tomb's chamber and the cairn would have been inserted asymmetrically inside the cromlech. It seems more probable that the ring was a later addition, its stones roughly offset some 3 m to 4 m out from the kerbstones.

There is a funnel-shaped entrance to a stone-lined passage 6.5 m long, 1.2 m wide, rising in height from 1.5 m to 2.7 m in the

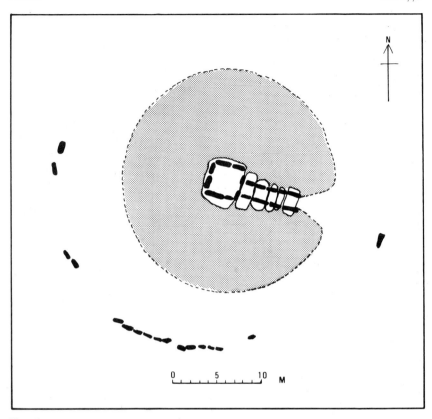

Kercado passage-grave (176).

rectangular chamber which is slightly offset to the N. Eight big stones line this central compartment, which is 2.9 × 3.2 m in extent with a great 3.8 × 5.3 m capstone. On its underside there is a carving of a big, thonged and hafted axe. A shouldered 'figurine' can be seen on a chamber stone and there are some geometrical motifs here and on the stones of the passage.

Kercado was excavated and restored in 1925. Before then other investigations in 1863 recovered a wide variety of objects including burnt human bone, dolerite and jadeite axes, serpentine and schist pendants, a perforated stone, barbed and tanged arrowheads, flint flakes, 147 callais beads, fragments of Souch bowls, and Kerugou, Upper Conguel and beaker sherds, all of which indicate the

continuing use of this imposing tomb into the Late Neolithic period. The finds are in VANNES, M (164), and CARNAC (166) museums.

177a Kercadoret, Locmariaquer. *Passage-grave*
3¾ m E of La Trinité-sur-Mer and 3½ km NW of Locmariaquer. From Locmariaquer take the D781 N. The monument is hidden behind a high and thick hedge on the W side of the road 50 m to the N of the lane on the E to Coët Courzo.
The stones of the passage have gone from the tomb leaving only the sub-circular chamber with its one big capstone. During the restoration in 1930 the chamber was found to be paved with small pebbles. Inside the tomb were Chalcolithic remains of a short copper

dagger and eight fine beaker arrowheads.
177b Along the lane opposite **Coët Courzo**
are the remains of a passage-grave with its
capstone leaning on five small supports.
Beaker sherds were found here.
177c In front of the farm near Kercadoret is
a low, domed Iron Age stele.

178   Kerderff, Carnac-Ville. *Menhir*
*1 km NW of Carnac-Ville. From the N end of
the Ménec West cromlech a footpath leads N
between hedges. Menhir is 200 m along path on
the W (L) in the NE corner of a field. It is set in
the high hedge.*
This is a heavy and impressive standing stone,
5.4 m high, and placed on a NE–SW axis, its
base measuring 4.7 × 1.9 m. James Miln
excavated here in 1879 but found nothing.

Alexander Thom suggested that from this
'Giant of Kerderff', his Stone L, one could
look towards the MANIO menhir (202a), 265 m
to the ENE, to observe the minor northern
moonrise. The axis of this 'playing-card'
stone, however, is some 20° too far to the N
and if it were aligned upon anything it is more
likely to have been the menhir at CRIFOL
(170), 400 m to the NE.

Keriavel. *Stone rows (see* 197b MANÉ
KERIAVEL)

179a   Kerivin–Brigitte, Auray. *Dolmen*
*8 km N of La Trinité-sur-Mer, 3½ km SW of
Auray. From Auray take the D768 SW and 2 km
SW of the junction with the D22 to the W take
lane SE (L) to Bourdello. In 250 m take 1st S
(R). Tomb is 200 m immediately on W (R) of
lane, 100 m in a field.*
This seldom-visited chambered tomb has a
huge remaining capstone, 6.7 × 3.4 m resting
on large supports, the one on the W being
4.9 m long. The monument is now overgrown.
179b In the woods opposite the lane leading
into the village there is a tall menhir.

180   Kerlescan, Carnac-Ville. *Megaliths*
*3 km NE of Carnac-Ville. From the town take
the D119 N and in 1¼ km turn E (R) onto the
D196, going past the Kermario rows. The
Kerlescan sites are 2 km to the E of the D119 on
the N (L) side of the D196 just beyond some
woods.*

Kerderff (178), menhir from the SE.

There are two cromlechs here, the largest
tertre tumulaire in the Carnac region, thirteen
impressive rows and a lateral entrance
passage-grave. It is also possible that the rows
at PETIT-MÉNEC (207) belong to this group,
but as the major setting there is nearly 400 m
to the E they have been given a separate entry
in the Gazetteer.
180a   West cromlech. This is the best-
preserved of the Carnac cromlechs with
upstanding stones along its E, S and W sides.
It is loaf-shaped with a flat eastern side
abutting the rows. Here eighteen towering
stones stand in a straight 78-m-long line and
from its S end a convex line, 74 m in extent,
and with ten or eleven stones, runs W to the
western side, also convex, where ten surviving
stones stand intermittently along a flattish arc

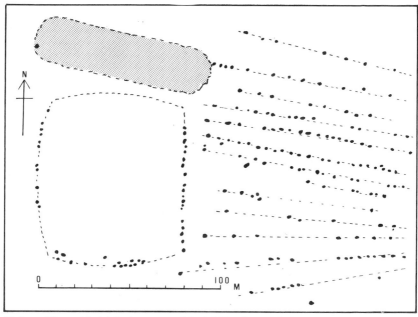

Kerlescan West cromlech (180a), tertre tumulaire (180b) and rows (180d).

Kerlescan (180a), west side of the cromlech.

some 83 m long. There are no stones left on the N side. The orientation of the E side is almost precisely N–S, and it is possible that this huge enclosure of 6400 square m, quite different in shape from the MÉNEC cromlechs (203a, c), was intended to define the equinoctial positions of the sun along the E–W axis. The shape of the cromlech is reminiscent of the MANIO III quadrilateral (202b), 300 m to its W.

180b   Tertre tumulaire. Just to the N of the cromlech's NW corner is a menhir at the western end of an overgrown tumulus, oriented WNW–ESE, 98 m long and widest at its E. The stone, 3.7 m high and oriented NNW–SSE, is Alexander Thom's Stone K and supposedly a backsight to the MANIO pillar (202a), 380 m to the WSW, for observations of the Candlemass and Martinmass sunsets in February and November. Standing as it does at the end of the tertre, the menhir was probably an 'indicateur' for the mound like the GRAND MENHIR BRISÉ (175a) and others. It is, however, unusual to find such stones at the W end of the mound (*but see* 18, 110i, 205b).

The Kerlescan tertre, restored in 1926, has been partly destroyed, for its smaller stones 'have been employed in the construction of the roads and fences'. Some thin flagstones can still be detected lining its N and S edges. From cists in the mound came fibrolite axes, some Neolithic sherds like those from the Middle Neolithic settlement of LE LIZO (189a), nearby, and, from upper levels, beaker-type sherds and a flat copper axe.

As with the KERMARIO tertre (183c), some of the Kerlescan stone rows encroach upon the mound demonstrating their later erection.

180c   North cromlech. Although most of the stones in this cromlech are large they are difficult to make out because of the trees and bushes amongst which they stand. The first stones of this great enclosure are 90 m NE of the tertre's menhir.

Lukis called this an irregular circle about 90 m in diameter, but the Thoms have planned it accurately and consider it to have been a flattened ring incomplete at its E. From SW to NE it measures 240 m and, across its open end, about 200 m. Thirty-six stones still stand and there are six more fallen. This is the biggest of the Carnac cromlechs. If its E end originally was indeed open then it would have belonged to the group of 'horseshoes' of Morbihan such as KERGONAN, M (139a), GRAND ROHU, M (136a) and perhaps CHAMP DE LA CROIX (167a).

180d   Stone rows. Thirteen monumental splayed rows extend from their widest, 140 m, near the West Cromlech, for 355 m ESE to the hamlet of Kerlescan, 'the House of Burning'. There are more stones in the village itself. Fifty-five pillars of granite stand in these lines and the packing-stones of thirty more have been detected. The rows have a general WNW–ESE orientation except for three stones at the S which lead WSW–ENE and which may be later additions. The tallest stones, as usual, are at the W by the cromlech.

The disrupted groups at Kerlescan and PETIT-MÉNEC (207) may once have been joined in an enormous complex 900 m long, curving and converging north-eastwards like a gigantic rhinoceros tusk. Today, however, there is a wide gap between the two sets of lines and it is best to treat them as separate assemblages.

180e   Passage-grave. *Halfway along the Kerlescan rows a footpath leads N for 100 m where one should turn E (R) into the wood for 50 m. Here there is an untidy, gorse-laden long mound, the mutilated survival of a passage-grave with a lateral entrance. A few of*

Kerlescan (180d), rows from the SE.

its kerbstones are visible. The tumulus is almost rectangular, 70 m long with curved 18-m-wide ends. It is aligned E–W. 3.5 m from its E end there is a narrow entrance on the S side. Here a short passage leads into the central chamber, 16.5 m long but only 1.6 m wide. Originally it was subdivided almost equally into two compartments, but it is now open to the sky, the transverse slabs removed and with only one capstone remaining at the W end. Access both to the passage and to the western sub-chamber had been provided by two 'portholes' constructed from pairs of adjacent slabs with semi-circles hacked out of their sides. These rare stones and many others disappeared in 1868 when material from the mound was sold for buildings. The monument was partly restored in 1887.

Excavations in 1858 'in a careless and partial manner' recovered dark coarse and fine red, ornamented Kerugou ware of the late 4th millennium BC. With these sherds were others of beakers. There were also flint arrowheads, a beautiful fibrolite axe and pendants.

The proximity of this Neolithic lateral-entrance passage-grave to the Kerlescan tertre tumulaire demonstrates the cultural affinities that existed between their builders, as at LE FOUR-SARRAZIN, IV (110j).

The rows of PETIT-MÉNEC (207), are 350 m E of Kerlescan hamlet.

181   Kerlescan hamlet, Carnac-Ville. Menhir

3¾ km NE of Carnac-Ville, 3 km NNW of La Trinité-sur-Mer. From La Trinité take the D186 N. Stone is 500 m N of Kerlescan hamlet at the S edge of a wood on W of road opposite turning to Kerlegad to the E.

This is a large menhir, 3 m high, almost rectangular in plan, its sides being about 1 m wide. It is Stone S of Alexander Thom's survey, 808 m ENE of the MANIO menhir (202a), and he suggested that looking from it towards the great pillar there would have been a good alignment on the midwinter sunset. What discernible axis the stone possesses does appear to point to the SW.

182a   Kerlud (Kerlut), Locmariaquer. Carnac Mound

11¼ km S of Auray, 9¼ km ESE of Carnac-Ville. 1 km W of Locmariaquer, from which take

the only road W and in 250 m take the NW (R) road at a Y-junction. Signposted, Kerlud. In 600 m monument is at the far end of the hamlet. This was once a massive Carnac Mound like those nearby at MANÉ-ER-HROEK (195), and MANÉ LUD (199a). Today the huge tumulus has been entirely removed and only a small megalithic chamber remains. It was restored by le Rouzic in 1928. The passage faced E. The chamber, covered by a large capstone, has walls half of orthostats, half of drystone walling. One stone, now missing, had carvings of a triangular axe with opposing crooks on it. The structure is presumably that of a tiny passage-grave that was incorporated into the mound as was the case in others of the Carnac Mounds. The Kerlud tomb is now overlain with nettles, bracken and brambles, but it stands opposite an old farm with lovely red roses on its walls.

182b   1¼ km W, on Pointe Er-Vil and ½ km NW of **St Pierre Lopérec** hamlet is the passage-grave of that name. Still in good condition, its front capstone has several cupmarks on its upper surface. The excavation of 1890 recovered axes, flint arrowheads and other artefacts now in VANNES museum, M (164).

183   Kermario, Carnac-Ville. *Megaliths*

1½ km NNE of Carnac-Ville. From the town take the D119 N and in 1¼ km turn E (R) onto the D196. The rows are 500 m farther on where the road bends to the S.

183a   Lann Mané Kermario. *Passage-grave.* The cromlech that once stood at the W end of the rows no longer exists and the granite plateau is now occupied by a car park. There is, however, a restored chambered tomb standing at the SW bend of the road in line with the southernmost of the Kermario rows. The tomb's mound has gone and the exposed passage and chamber are about 8.7 m long. From the SSE entrance, only 1.4 m wide and flanked by large sideslabs, the passage widens to 3.5 m at the end of the sub-rectangular chamber. Four capstones are in

Kermario (183): (above) passage-grave (183a) at the W end of the rows, from the S; (right) rows (183b), from the E.

place. Excavations around 1858 and 1878 recovered a broken diorite axe, a sandstone whetstone, flints and coarse sherds. The lack of differentiation between the passage and the chamber suggests that the tomb was built quite late in the passage-grave series in the centuries around 3500 BC, but well before the cromlech and the rows.

183b Stone rows. There are seven main lines with subsidiary ranks to their S in this complex which today contains 1,029 stones arranged on a WSW–ENE orientation. Stretching over 1128 m and running uphill and down dale these are the longest of the Carnac lines, but three slight changes of direction suggest that additions and extensions were made to a primary, shorter setting. The rows are 96 m wide at their W where the stones are highest, but only 36 m wide at the E where aerial photography has revealed the erstwhile existence of a cromlech. Three contiguous stones at right-angles to the others near La Petite-Métairie are the probable remains of a further line to the S. A ruined windmill, 500 m from the western end of the rows, provides a good viewing-station and photographic tower.

Excavations in the rows by James Miln in 1877 found flints, sherds, pebble tools, a stone axe, querns, fire-reddened stones, cinders and ashes at the foot of some stones. The name Kermario, 'the House of the Dead', may be a memory of funerary rites once performed in the cromlech.

183c Manio I. *Tertre tumulaire.*
500 m E of the windmill and near the end of the rows just before a pine wood. Near a bend in the road a tall pillar rises amongst the lower stones of the rows. It stands at the eastern end of a trapezoidal mound, 35 m long and 16 m across its wider E end. Only 90 cm high, it contained a sub-rectangular peristalith of little stones, and excavations in 1922 discovered over thirty tiny cists in it with others outside the tumulus. There were signs of burning but no human bones in them.

The menhir, 4.5 m high and with broader faces to N and S, is almost exactly S of the MANIO pillar (202a), 250 m uphill. On the W side of the base of the Kermario menhir five vertical 'serpents' were carved and can be seen today half-protected by a concrete slab. By them were four diorite axes with another

nearby close to a quartz pendant. Just to the W a gross capstone, 3.4 × 1.8 m and 90 cm thick, had a carving of a hafted axe on its upper side. Beneath it was a big pit with Chassey sherds of the Middle Neolithic period. As the Kermario rows pass over this long mound they must be later.

On the S side of the road, just beyond the rows' end, a lane leads to the KERCADO passage-grave (176). The KERLESCAN cromlech and rows (180) are 393 m to the W.

184 Kermarquer, La Trinité-sur-Mer. *Passage-grave*
3¼ km ENE of Carnac-Ville, 1¾ km NW of La Trinité. 180 m N of E lane to Kermarquer. Take footpath E (R) by the transformer, and walk 70 m uphill to the heath S of a little wood. Half-lost in vegetation today this passage-grave provided a wealth of objects from the excavations of 1866, 1867 and 1887. It was explored and restored by le Rouzic between 1905 and 1927.

The tomb stood in a neat, circular mound lined with drystone walling. Its ESE entrance, now lacking its capstones, opened onto a short passage at the end of which the main chamber had a side-cell at its SW. Amongst the material found here were Middle Neolithic sherds and a mass of Chalcolithic artefacts including beaker and pot-beaker sherds, pendants, triangular arrowheads and two globular gold beads. The objects are scattered in CARNAC (166) and VANNES, M (164) museums and the British Museum, London.

185a Kerran, Chat-Noir. *Passage-graves*
5 km NW of Locmariaquer and 3½ km ENE of La Trinité-sur-Mer. From La Trinité take the D781 E to the junction with the D28 and cross over. The tombs are 250 m along the lane opposite the D781, on the lane's S (R) side.
At Roh-Vras there are the remains of two passage-graves, one in good condition, the other half-collapsed in the gorse. A few sherds, now lost, of tiny vase-supports of the Middle Neolithic were found here. In 1866 a farmer told Lukis 'he had carted away the contents of two of the three chambers, and spread them over his fields'. Both the tombs were paved with big slabs. It is reasonable to

suppose that they once both lay under a single great mound.

185b   Alexander Thom said that 24 m to the W of the passage-graves there was a small menhir, leaning at an angle of 45° which might have been a backsight to the GRAND MENHIR BRISÉ (175a), 4 km to the SSE, aligned on the major southern moonrise. Inspection of this miserable stone, lying on a hummock and completely engulfed in gorse, suggests that it is far from being a menhir and much more likely to have been a casual lump of granite cleared off the adjacent field and dumped here.

185c   ¾ km N is a ruined passage-grave on the lane from Braden at the bend towards Kergleverit. It is on private land.

185d   There is a tradition that near Kerran there was a rock with two large concentric circles carved on it. At their centre there was a cupmark. The rock is no longer there.

186   Kerveresse, Locmariaquer. *Passage-grave*
5 km E of La Trinité-sur-Mer, 2 km N of Locmariaquer on the E (R) of the D781 in a field 130 m S of the crossroads to Kerouarch.
This is a rather untidy, half-buried monument with its surviving chamber facing NE. The two capstones cover a squarish chamber in

Kerveresse (186), passage-grave from the E.

which there are carved stones. On one orthostat there is a group of seven shepherds' crooks with a possible axe to their right and what looks like a boat at the bottom of the stone. On the underside of the larger capstone there is a myriad of cupmarks, some of them carved before the stone was set in position. It is possible, therefore, that this is yet another example of a decorated menhir being re-used for the capstone of a passage-grave as at the TABLE DES MARCHANDS (175c), and GAVR'INIS, M (132a).

187a   Kerzerho, Erdeven. *Stone rows*
13 km WSW of Auray, 8 km NW of Carnac-Ville. From Erdeven take the D781 S, and the rows are on the E (L) of the road after 900 m.
The impressive remains of ten much disturbed

Kerzerho (187a), the N row from the W.

rows can be seen alongside the road between Erdeven and Plouharnel. The gigantic blocks are the western end of a complex aligned variably ESE–WNW that was once over 2 km in length. The rows apparently started near the passage-grave of MANÉ GROH (196), led 1 km north-westwards towards the low hill of MANÉ BRAS (193a), with its two chambered tombs, before changing direction westwards through the present-day woods up to the D781. Here the rows have a width of 64 m. On the opposite side of the road there was probably a cromlech of which no trace survives.

At right-angles to the fine rows and 100 m to their N is a shorter line of twenty-three truly massive blocks up to 6 m high. Others lie broken near them. The farther end of this row is also known as the Table de Sacrifice. 'That's where the blood used to flow down.'

187b 1 km W of Erdeven the collapsed line of eight stones at **Kerascouet** can be found by taking the road W from Erdeven, turning N (R) at the Croix de Milan. There is a sign directing the visitor to these gorse-encompassed menhirs.

187c 500 m N of the Table de Sacrifice, on the W (L) of a lane between Kerzerho hamlet and Erdeven, are the remains of the **Ty-er-Mané** passage-grave, a tomb with big flagstones for the flooring of its chamber.

188 Klud-er-Yer, Plouharnel. *Passage-grave*
4 km N of Carnac-Ville, 3 km NE of Plouharnel, just to the W of the D768.
This is a transepted passage-grave, about 10 m long, facing E. It is very overgrown. The capstones are missing. There is a side chamber to the S, a larger rectangular end-chamber, and two conjoined rectangular chambers to the N. All measure about 3 × 2 m and they stood in a circular mound. Excavations in 1866 found a clay spindle-whorl, a flint knife, sherds of Middle Neolithic ware, a rough quartzite axe and some polished axes. The stone in the NE corner of the end-chamber may have some cupmarks on it.

The design of this monument is similar to that of MANÉ GROH (196) and MANÉ BRAS (193a) nearby to the W. *Klud-er-Yer* means 'the Perch of the Fowl'.

Lann Mané Kermario. *Passage-grave (see* 183a KERMARIO)

189a Lizo, Le, Penhoët. *Settlement*
5¾ km NE of Carnac-Ville, 6 km SW of Auray.
From Carnac take the D119 N for 4 km to Crucuny crossroads. Turn E (R) for 1 km and turn N (L). In 1¼ km turn E (R) to Penhoët hamlet. 300 m to its S a lane on the E (L) leads to the hill 400 m E of Penhoët.
The Neolithic settlement of Le Lizo was established on a steep-sided, rocky crest 30 m above the W bank of the River Crach. It was defended by 3-m-high stone walls, double on the N and W, enclosing an area about 200 × 155 m. Within the fortifications excavations by le Rouzic in 1926–9 discovered many floors of round- and square-compartmented huts, especially at the N, with hammerstones, querns, flint tools and arrowheads. There were some semi-circular ovens in the embankments. Visitors must be warned that in summer gorse, bracken and brambles obscure many of these features.

The occupants of Le Lizo grew barley, wheat, millet and flax, and herded cattle, pigs and sheep. Some of their burials, in cists under small mounds, were discovered. The abundant evidence of Chassey, Colpo footed bowls, Kerugou, Upper Conguel and even beaker sherds showed that this settlement was inhabited from Middle to Late Neolithic times. It was reoccupied in the Iron Age.

189b At the centre of the site, near the dividing earthen bank, there is a classic V-shaped passage-grave with an unusual south-western entrance.

1 km S of Le Lizo is the hamlet of Castellic. In 1891 many decorated pots were discovered in a cavity at Lann Vras nearby and the series of Middle Neolithic local ceramics have since been named after Castellic. At Lann Vras a tertre tumulaire excavated in 1922 yielded a C-14 assay of 3075 ± 300 bc, about 3870 BC.

190 Locmariaquer. *Megalithic centre*
11 km SSE of Auray and 10 km E of Carnac-Ville.
This pleasant fishing village with its oyster beds is a delightful and also amazing centre for the exploration of the megalithic sites in its immediate vicinity. These are some of the finest prehistoric monuments in Brittany and all of them can be seen within a day by the hurried visitor.

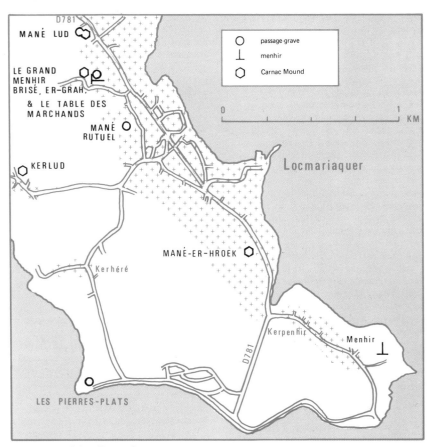

Sites in the vicinity of Locmariaquer.

In the environs of the town itself, on its NW outskirts, are the Carnac Mound and passage-grave of MANÉ LUD (199); LE GRAND MENHIR BRISÉ, against the devastated Carnac Mound of ER-GRÀH (175a, b), and the passage-grave of the TABLE DES MARCHANDS (175c). MANÉ RUTUEL passage-grave (201) is not far away. Just S of the town are the quarried ruins of the MANÉ-ER-HROEK Carnac Mound (195). 1 km to the W is the surviving chambered tomb of KERLUD Carnac Mound (182a), and a similar distance to the S there is the surprising angled passage-grave of LES PIERŘES-PLATS (208), with imposing architecture and tantalizing art. These monuments are so close together that no itinerary is necessary.

Travelling northwards along the D781 one can also go, after 2 km, to the decorated passage-grave of KERVERESSE (186), and after another 1½ km see KERCADORET dolmen (177a), and end at the crossroads of Chat Noir only 4½ km from Locmariaquer with a visit to the two passage-graves in the bushes and undergrowth of KERRAN (185a).

The excellently detailed 1:25,000 Carte Topographique map, no. 0821 Est, *Auray–Quiberon*, provides an easy means of locating the sites. The 1:50,000, no. 501, is also good, but is overlain with heavy symbols that sometimes obscure the exact position of the stones and tombs.

191 Locqueltas, Locoal-Mendon. *Passage-grave*
10 km NNW of Carnac-Ville, 9 km W of Auray, 4½ km S of Locoal-Mendon from which take the D16 SSW and in 2 km turn S (L) through Kerdelan to Locqueltas. In centre of village take road W past the chapel for 500 m. Tomb is 200 m S of the road on E side of a wood.
Here there are the good remains of a transepted passage-grave with a passage facing SE. The passage is 3.7 m long with one capstone in place. There is a large end-chamber 2.6 m long and 2 m wide with a side-cell to the NE and another to the SW still possessing a capstone. Both have narrow entrances. From excavations and restoration in 1924 came some flint flakes, beaker sherds and a tiny stone grindstone.

192 Luffang, Crach. *Passage-grave*
5 km NE of Carnac-Ville, 4 km N of La Trinité-sur-Mer. From Crach take W road for 3½ km through Luffang hamlet. 200 m W of village tomb is on S (L) side of road opposite entrance to camping site. Signposted, 'allée-couverte', which it is not.

Luffang (192), 'figurine' from the passage-grave. Cast in Carnac museum (166).

20 m into an open pine wood, half-sunken, lacking all its capstones and with many of its sidestones missing, this is still a remarkable monument. It is one of the angled passage-graves or allées-coudées of which there are several good examples in the S of Morbihan such as GOËREM, M (133), LE ROCHER (211a) and LES PIERRES-PLATS (208). These sites also contain distinctive 'figurine' carvings sometimes called cephalopods because of their superficial resemblance to the head of an octopus.

At Luffang the passage-grave was erected on a slight rise to the S. What is left of its circular mound is hard to make out in the bracken, but its short passage, facing SSE, has four sideslabs and a low septal slab from which the passage angles sharply towards the NW, curving gently northwards to a large rectangular terminal slab.

On the S side of this long chamber the sixth stone has faint carvings of concentric arcs and the seventh bears a hafted axe at its centre with a vertical 'boat' to its right. A stone, 1.9 m high and 90 cm wide, is missing from the W corner where the chamber joins the passage. On it there was a metre-high carving of an anthropomorphic figure with two small breasts which are sometimes mistaken for eyes. A cast of the stone is now in CARNAC museum (166). Standing as it did at the junction of passage and chamber it possibly had the same function as the 'guardian' stones known in other passage-graves like CRECH-QUILLÉ, CN (9) and ÎLE GUENNOC, F (52). Similar carvings occur in the other Morbihan allées-coudées.

Excavations at Luffang in 1898 and 1937 recovered Middle Neolithic material including a polished axe, a short blade of Grand Pressigny flint and a spiral of copper.

193a Mané Bras, Erdeven. *Chambered tombs*
7 km NW of Carnac-Ville, 4¼ km NNW of Plouharnel. From Erdeven take the D781 SE for 1¾ km and turn E (L) for 500 m to Kerbénés, turning NE (L) at Le Liz. At turn to Kerbénés hamlet take the footpath to the ENE and in 300 m turn N. In 250 m turn E (R) up wooded hill. Tombs are 100 m away at the summit.
There is a group of damaged megaliths here along the southern half of the low hill.

Exploration of an oval mound, arranged NW–SE and about 54 × 24 m in extent, revealed that it covered two smaller, sub-circular mounds. In the south-eastern mound was a small, transepted passage-grave facing SE. Its short passage led to a large rectangular chamber subdivided by orthostats into four small compartments in an arrangement very similar to that at MANÉ GROH (196), 1 km to the SE. From the Mané Bras chambers came beaker sherds, six flint scrapers, a diorite axe and later Middle Neolithic Souch sherds and Carn ware.

The north-western mound covered two T-shaped passage-graves unusually oriented to the SW. The north-western tomb had a short passage and a sub-circular chamber. Its partner, just to the SE, had an 8-m-long passage leading to a long chamber with a small side-cell, 1 m square, on its NW side. These monuments were restored, with some of their capstones, in 1922.

193b There is a wrecked dolmen just to the SW of the long mound. Farther down the hill's southern slope is a fallen menhir.

At the foot of the hill are several prostrate stones, once a section of the great KERZERHO rows (187a).

194 Mané Bras, Kervilor. *Passage-graves*
3½ km ENE of Carnac-Ville, 2½ km N of La Trinité-sur-Mer. From La Trinité take the D186 N and after 2 km turn NE (R) onto a side lane. In 2 km turn W (L) towards Kervilor. After 200 m, just before a wood on the S (L) a footpath alongside the wood leads S for 200 m. Site is 50 m SW of the wood's SE corner, in heathland.
Mané Bras is interesting first because it is a rare example in southern Brittany of a long mound with several passage-graves in it, and, secondly, because of the finds from it.

Excavations in 1866, 1868 and 1898 recovered material from each of the three tombs in this long oval tumulus which was restored in 1927. Some of the artefacts are now in VANNES museum, M (164), and others are in CARNAC (166).

From the passage and chamber of the most northerly tomb came footed bowls, entire vases, six arrowheads and sixteen callais beads of a necklace. The tomb next to it yielded Chassey objects, two dolerite axes, a Grand Pressigny blade and sherds of Souch and later Kerugou ware. The third passage-grave, to the S and with a lateral entrance, also contained Middle Neolithic sherds. During the 1927 restoration more pottery was found and also a small gold plaque.

195 Mané-er-Hroek, Locmariaquer.
Carnac Mound
12 km SSE of Auray, 10¾ km ESE of Carnac-Ville. 500 m ESE of Locmariaquer. From Locmariaquer take the ESE road towards the Pointe de Kerpenhir. The mound is 500 m along the road on the W (R). Signposted.
A short path leads to the shambles of the 'Fairy Stone' tumulus, mutilated like an exploded volcano. The mound is elliptical, 100 × 60 m, arranged ESE–WNW, but horribly defaced and now only 5–6 m high. It was devastatingly excavated in 1863.

There may originally have been a drystone wall around the cairn but, if so, today it has gone. Now a bleak flight of modern steps leads down to a dark chamber in the middle of these tree-ringed ruins. Take a torch.

The chamber, which never had a passage, was a drystone-walled, rock-cut pit, 3.8 × 2.9 m and 1.5 m high. It was roofed with two huge capstones. Outside, in the rubble, the diggers came upon a broken, carved slab which has now been set up inside the new entrance to the chamber.

It is for the profusion of finds in this vault that Mané-er-Hroek is deservedly renowned. Here there were 106 axes, four of diorite, twelve of jadeite, ninety of fibrolite, the largest being 46 cm long. There were also forty-nine callais beads and nine emerald-green pendants. These lovely objects, now in VANNES museum, M (164), were buried under the paving of the pit. A single jadeite axe lay above it, partly resting on a delicate annular disc of opaquely green serpentine, 11 × 10 cm in diameter but a mere, fragile 7 mm thick. The attractive stone may have come from as far away as the Alps.

The carved stone, broken in three pieces and reassembled, has carvings of hafted axes, a central 'figurine', and two crooks, a composition that suggests that where the presumably anthropomorphic 'goddess' of the figurine is missing on other carved stones the crook or the axe may be assumed to be symbols of her presence.

By the footpath, lying by an overgrown wall, are two broken pillars, 9 m and 7.6 m long. These once stood by the mound like the 'indicateurs' or marker-stones known at similar sites like ER-GRAH (175b) and LE MOUSTOIR (205a).

196 Mané Groh (Mané Croch), Erdeven. *Passage-grave*
6 km NW of Carnac-Ville, 3½ km NNW of Plouharnel. From Plouharnel take the D781 NW and in 3 km turn E (R) for 1½ km through Crucuno hamlet. Tomb is on W (L) of lane and clearly visible.

On a slight knoll the tall, exposed stones of the T-shaped passage-grave reveal its plan clearly. It was excavated in 1866 and 1883 with unknown results and it was restored in 1900 and 1920, unfortunately with the capstones replaced incorrectly.

It once stood in a long, rectangular mound with rounded corners, 22 × 10 m, aligned NNW–SSE. The well-preserved chamber is 4.7 m wide and 3 m long and has been divided into four compartments, one in each corner, by means of upright slabs. Behind it, 5 m to the NNW, there was a small, cistlike structure

of seven stones which lay under the mound. In 1883 a quern, a grinder and some hammerstones were found in it.

197a Mané Keriavel, Plouharnel. *Passage-grave*
3¼ km N of Carnac-Ville, 2¾ km NE of Plouharnel. From Plouharnel take the D768 NE for 2¾ km. Just beyond the sign to Mané Kerioned (see 198) and a minor crossroads the tomb is on the E (R). It is signposted but is not visible from the road. A little footpath leads 100 m through the airy woods to it.

Although this passage-grave is in comparative ruin it is interesting because it belongs to the coastal group of transepted tombs such as LES MOUSSEAUX, LA (121a), in south-eastern Brittany.

At Keriavel there are four transepts and an end-cell. Once covered by an oval mound, about 30 × 22 m, of which there are still signs, the tomb faces almost exactly E. A short passage leads to a NE chamber still covered by its enormous capstone. Beyond it the NW chamber has one of its two capstones in place. The end-chamber is in fair condition, but the side-cell at the SW has only its entrance

Mané Groh (196), passage-grave from the S.

stones, with two broken stones near them. The capstone of the SE chamber has fallen inwards and is now tilted against the rear stones which have fallen outwards. The length of this megalithic structure is about 9 m and its width across the transepts is 6.6 m. The largest chamber, that at the NE, is almost square, 2.4 × 2.2 m. Excavations in 1866 recovered two callais beads, two clay spindle-whorls, a flint knife and decorated sherds of Kerugou type suggesting that this Middle Neolithic tomb was in use around 3500 BC.

197b 100 m to the S of the passage-grave are the dilapidated survivors of four rows of standing stones. The fragmentary lines are perhaps 68 m long from N to S and 36 m wide. All the stones are low. The Thoms planned the site in 1976. They suggested that a sightline taken diagonally across the rows would have provided an alignment towards the MANIO menhir (202a), 2425 m to the ESE. The orientation of 119° would have been in line with the rising of the minor southern moon.

There are reasons for doubting this interpretation. The E–W alignment at the Mané Keriaval passage-grave nearby, the N–S alignments in the MANÉ KERIOND tombs (198), 200 m away across the road, and the almost perfect N–S alignments in the Keriavel rows themselves surely show that the preoccupation of their Neolithic planners was with the cardinal points rather than with the ESE and a lunar orientation.

198   Mané Kerioned, Carnac-Ville.
Passage-graves
3½ km NNW of Carnac-Ville, 2¾ km NE of Plouharnel, alongside the D768 and 70 m S of the Quelvezin-Keriavel crossroads. Signposted. A torch is recommended.

This is one of the most intriguing of the Carnac sites, containing as it does not only enigmatic carvings but also some astronomical alignments. It is sometimes known as the Grottes de Grionec and La Butte aux Nains, 'the Mound of the Dwarfs'.

In a clearing surrounded by gorse bushes the megalithic galleries lie on three sides of a rectangle open to the S. Two, which are parallel to each other at the W and E, consist of long passages gradually widening to the N into undifferentiated chambers. The third site, on an E–W axis between them, has a polygonal chamber of ash-white stones at its western end. The oval mound that covered the site was almost entirely removed during the excavations of 1866. The sites were restored in 1900 and 1921.

198a   The western passage-grave is the most conspicuous, 9 m long, its coarse sideslabs capped with granite boulders that rise in steps up to the N. The smoother sides of the uprights faced into the interior of the tomb. Some stones are now missing and the backstone has gone, so that one can pass from one end to the other as though walking along a short underpass. No human bone was found here, but a polished stone axe, flint flakes, two

Mané Kerioned (198a), west passage-grave from the SE.

Mané Kerioned (198c), east passage-grave from the SW.

clay spindle-whorls and some plain and decorated Neolithic sherds were recovered and are now in VANNES museum, M (164).

198b The central passage-grave is overgrown, ruinous and unimpressive except for a huge capstone over its chamber. Only a flint knife and some bits of pottery came from it.

198c Having seen these exposed sites the visitor should go to the subterranean eastern gallery where modern steps lead down to the entrance. Only two fragments of bone were found in the 11-m-long passage. Quite remarkably, however, no fewer than eight of the stones are adorned with unusual carvings. Several of the right-hand slabs have engravings of arcs, 'figurines', formalized axes and a series of interlocking squares. On the end wall the middle stone has similar motifs and yokes, wavy lines which may be 'serpents', and rectangles. The fourth stone on the left-hand side has three faint symbols of a yoke, a 'serpent' and a motif like a reversed E. When le Rouzic was completing the second season of restoration in 1922 he found a large slab in the mound with fine hafted axes carved on it. The stone is now in CARNAC museum (166).

The art is of particular interest because, except for the axes, yokes and serpents, it is unlike the classic representational style of the Breton passage-graves. The patterns of rectangles, thought by Zacharie le Rouzic to be degraded imitations of anthropomorphic figurines, can also be seen in the strangely decorated passage-grave of PETIT-MONT, M (154).

The alignment of the three galleries at Mané Kerioned is also different from the SE-facing chambered tombs of the Morbihan coast. Mané Kerioned has passages built by people with a decided interest in the cardinal points, particularly N and S, and it is interesting that the megalithic rectangle of CRUCUNO (171b), also with sides aligned exactly E–W and N–S, is only 1½ km to the W. The remains of a similar rectangle that may once have enclosed the mound at Mané Kerioned may be seen in the line of three stones just to the W of the complex. Another stone stands to the N of the group.

Just across the road to the NE are the ruined chambers of MANÉ KERIAVEL passage-grave (197a).

199a Mané Lud, Locmariaquer. *Carnac Mound*

9½ km E of Carnac-Ville, 10½ km S of Auray. From centre of Locmariaquer take the D781 N. In ¾ km mound is on W (L).

This incredible long mound, known locally as the Mound of Ashes, is 107 × 54 m in plan and nearly 6 m high, a flattened oval set on an ENE–WSW axis. Trees grow on and alongside it. It has been quarried for material for the nearby houses and it was excavated in 1863–4 by means of a long and untidy trench down its length. It was re-examined in 1911.

Under the huge mound there was a circular cairn, 21 m across and 3.5 m high, with an extension, like half an egg, 16 m long to the ENE. Under the cairn was a small, drystone-walled and corbelled chamber containing an inhumation and a cremation. No grave-goods were recorded. At the eastern end of the mound there was a shallow, convex arc of six small standing stones and beyond them, near the edge of the tumulus, there was a further arc of contiguous pillars, five of them having horse-skulls placed on them.

199b Passage-grave. At the WSW end of the mound, which is now truncated by the adjacent farm-buildings, there is a classic passage-grave, several of whose stones bear carvings. The long passage, approached by modern steps, is now 5 m long and leads to a slightly P-shaped chamber, 3.5 × 3 m in size. The passage faces SSE and is covered with heavy granite capstones, the one over the chamber measuring 8.5 × 4.9 m. It is broken in two.

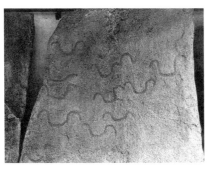

Mané Lud (199b), carvings of 'yokes' in the passage-grave.

The chamber, 1.8 m high, was paved and under the stones there was a layer of black and yellow soil and pebbles. Under it were discovered lumps of charcoal, twenty-six jasper beads, coarse sherds and a clay spindle-whorl.

The carved stones in this tomb are splendidly executed. On the E the seventh stone of the passage has what looks like a boat, a tiny rectangular 'figurine', a crook and a circle of minute cupmarks. In the chamber the NE stone has an inverted triangular axe and three yokes, one above the other. On the NW backstone there is a possible hafted axe, a shepherd's crook and a strange domed design which may be a simplified figurine. The stone to its S has a formalized axe carved on its bottom, left-hand corner. To its S the second passage stone on the left from the chamber has eleven yokes like flying birds covering its surface and the stone adjacent to it, but nearer the entrance, has a yoke and what appears to be another 'boat' below it.

Some of these symbols are difficult to make out, but the lavish decoration in the Mané Lud passage-grave, with its elusive significance, causes one to ask what connection there was between it and the dead who were to rest in the chamber.

200 Mané Roch, Kerlegad. *Menhir*
4 km N of La Trinité-sur-Mer, 5 km NE of Carnac-Ville. From La Trinité take the D186 NNW for 3 km then turn NE (R) onto lane to Kerlegad. In 1 km turn N into hamlet. Stone is in fields just N of the hamlet.
This is a magnificent menhir, 4.4 m high.

Strangely, in his survey, Alexander Thom rejected this pillar, his Stone G, and instead suggested that the unimpressive Stone A would provide an alignment to the MANIO menhir (202a), 2143 m to the WSW and to the major southern moonset.

Stone A, however, 400 m E of Mané Roch, is only 1.3 m high and its playing-card shape with sides measuring 1.3 × 0.3 m points N–S and not NE–SW as the astronomical hypothesis would require.

201 Mané Rutuel, Locmariaquer. *Passage-grave*
From the centre of Locmariaquer take the minor road W towards Kerlud and in 200 m W of the D781 turn N (R). In 250 m a narrow lane and a footpath lead W (L) past allotments to the tomb. Signposted on wall of narrow lane. A torch is helpful inside the tomb for the art.
Known variously as Mané Rethuel, Ruthuel and Bé-er-Groah, 'the Tomb of the Witch', this passage-grave is notable for its gigantic capstone and its art. Trapped between garden walls and hedges it faces ESE. Dug into in Roman times, it has suffered excavations in 1860 and 1865, was restored in 1885 and investigated again in 1923 and 1936.

From its low entrance one must bend uncomfortably along the 9.5-m-long, 1-m-wide but only 1.2-m-high passage before reaching the ease of the ovoid chamber. This is 6.7 m long and 3.4 m across at its widest and it has been subdivided by two transverse pillars into a 3-m-long antechamber and a bigger, semi-circular main chamber at the end of the monument. Beyond it is an unpleasing modern construction to hold up the incredible capstone. This is a vast slab of granite best appreciated from outside. It was broken in two when the supporting cairn was dug into. Originally this monster measured 11.3 × 4.4 × 0.6 m thick and weighed over fifty tons.

Inspection of its underside reveals a huge carving of a 'figurine', 3.3 m wide, 4 m long, with a convex 'head', inset shoulders and a little arm like a handle on its N side. Just beyond it to the N can be seen an axe-carving, its triangular tip broken showing that the capstone had probably once been a freestanding, decorated menhir that had been toppled and reduced in length for re-use as the roofing slab for the passage-grave.

Two orthostats have carvings on them. They are the stones immediately before the N transverse slab and they form the N side of the antechamber. One has two hafted axes, the other two shepherds' crooks in opposition to each other. Finds from the excavations include flint flakes, a broken diorite axe and a clay spindle-whorl, all now in VANNES museum, M (164).

202a   Manio, Géant de, Carnac-Ville.
Menhir
3 km NE of Carnac-Ville. From Kerlescan West Cromlech (180a) take main road W towards Carnac. In 200 m, immediately W of riding school on N (R) of road, take footpath to N (R). Follow for 3/4 km, veering W (L) uphill. Signposted. Menhir is in clearing near summit.
This fine stone, about 6.5 m high, stands near the crest of a ridge overlooking the Kerlescan

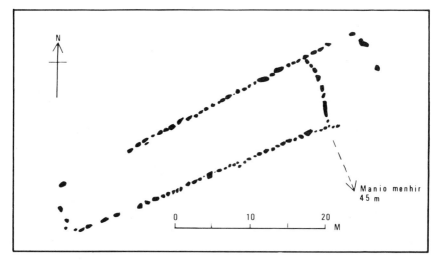

Manio III Quadrilateral (202b), plan and view from the W.

rows to the SW. It was damaged when it was re-erected at the beginning of the century.

According to Alexander Thom this stone was used as a foresight in a prehistoric megalithic observatory whose backsights were on lower ground, the celestial phenomena to be observed including the major southern moonset, midwinter sunset, midsummer sunrise, and the minor and major moonrises. Some of these hypothetical backsights are not megalithic. The remainder, described in the gazetteer, are: CRUCUNY menhir (167b); the MANÉ KERIAVEL rows (197b); KERDERFF menhir (178); a menhir to the E of MANÉ ROCH (200); KERLESCAN HAMLET menhir (181); KERLESCAN TERTRE menhir (180b); and the menhir in the KERMARIO TERTRE (183c).

202b   Manio III. 45 m to the N are the remains of a tertre tumulaire with a trapezoidal setting of low stones on it. The covering mound has gone. Known as the Manio Quadrilateral it consists of a sub-rectangular enclosure 37 m long, aligned ENE–WSW, 10 m wide at the E end and narrowing to 7 m at the W. At its broader end there is a damaged convex setting of stones very like the forecourt of a chambered tomb.

The stones stand on a huge long mound which is difficult to make out because of the trees on it. The rectangle with its convex ENE end is similar to some of the transepted chambers at LESCONIL-PLOBANNALEC, F (78).

Manio I. *Tertre tumulaire* (*see* 183c KERMARIO)

Manio Quadrilateral (Manio III). *Tertre tumulaire* (*see* 202b MANIO)

203   Ménec, Carnac-Ville. *Megaliths 600 m NNW of Carnac-Ville. From the town take the D781 NW and in 200 m turn N (R) onto the D196. In 500 m there is a car park on the E (R) of the road.*
Start at the west cromlech whose stones can be seen amongst the houses and gardens of Ménec hamlet on the lane off the D196, just W of and almost opposite to the car park.

203a   West cromlech. This damaged ring was an enormous enclosure, 91 × 71 m, of an inverted egg-shape with a perimeter, according to the Thoms, of 304.4 megalithic yards (252 m). Its long axis was oriented 142°–322°. Seventy close-set stones, standing on the natural bedrock, survive on its NNW and SW

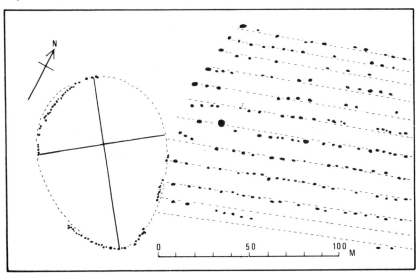

Ménec West cromlech (203a) and rows (203b). The dotted lines indicate Professor Thom's reconstruction of the original alignment of the stones. The absence of stones from the southern rows shows the extent of modern robbing for walls and roads.

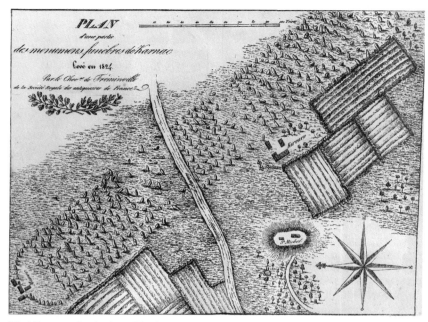

The Ménec rows (203), planned in 1824.

Ménec (203a), west arc of west cromlech.

arcs. All but five have been re-erected. The monument is easily overlooked because of the houses around it, but a good stretch is observable just to the W of the Crêperie with its cider and its postcards at the end of the rows.

The relationship of the cromlech to the rows suggests that it was put up before them where the ground levels out from the slope on which the lines stand. Like many early British stone circles, the cromlech was probably intended for a large assembly and as many as a thousand people could have stood comfortably inside it. Its long axis has no apparent astronomical significance, but its shorter SW–NE axis is in line with the midwinter sunset and midsummer sunrise, exactly the opposite orientations to those of its counterpart at the E end of the rows.

To its N are the isolated menhirs of KERDERFF (178) and CRIFOL (170).

203b   West and east stone rows.
Immediately to the E of the cromlech is the beginning of twelve rows of rough granite pillars which end in an approximately N–S line by the cromlech. From there the stones extend ENE (253°–73°) for 957 m to the remains of a second cromlech. At first sight the rows seem to be a single complex, but there are actually two groups that join near the middle at the bottom of a gentle slope where a minor road now crosses them. The rows are not parallel. They decrease in width from 116 m at the W to 63 m at the E, a fanlike layout that is repeated in all the settings near Carnac.

Of the western group the stones rise noticeably in height, from a mere 90 cm on the low ground to an average 2.5 m at the W

Ménec (203b), west end of the rows.

where the tallest, a 'Géant', 4 m high, stands in the fourth row 160 m from the end. Many of the stones were re-erected in the 1920s by le Rouzic, who put a thumbnail-sized red plug of concrete in their sides to identify them. There is a continuing debate about the accuracy of his reconstructions. The N ten rows are fairly complete but the S two have suffered from being closer to the Carnac road, conveniently placed for the waggons of stone-robbers. Although the twelve rows approach the western cromlech, those at the N are not aligned on it, and, as those at the S stop at the ring's eastern arc, it is likely that they were put up after it.

Ménec (203b), view of the rows.

The eastern section, beyond the Carnac-Cité du Runel road, has been disturbed by agriculture. Beyond the patches of heavy gorse the rows extend 500 m uphill at a slight angle (244°–64°) to the western lines. They also increase in size, the largest, beyond a 100-m-wide gap, standing against the W arc of the E cromlech. Before 1872 the Abbé Collet excavated at the foot of seven stones finding wood charcoal, sherds and flints but nothing of value for dating.

203c   East cromlech. This is extremely damaged and often passes unnoticed by the casual tourist. Twenty-five close-set stones survive, mainly along its western side where the rows converge accurately on it. The enclosure was probably egg-shaped with its wide base to the SE, the bearing of its long axis being 124°–304°. It was another vast ring measuring about 107.5 × 90 m around a space of some 7500 sq. m.

Unlike the west cromlech at Ménec, which was an inverted egg and whose shorter axis was astronomically aligned, it is the long axis here that was important, for it pointed to the midwinter sunrise and midsummer sunset suggesting that the two rings together were intended to indicate the four divisions of the solar year.

450 m to the E, along the D196, are the KERMARIO rows (183).

204a   Moulin de St Pierre Quiberon, Le. *Stone rows*
9 km SSW of Carnac-Ville, 4 km N of Quiberon. In St Pierre Quiberon follow the Rue de l'Église S to the Rue de Marthe Delpirou. The rows are 300 m down road on W (R). There is a small parking space.

In a pleasant enclosure twenty-four stones are irregularly spaced in five interrupted rows aligned ESE–WNW. The lines are slightly fan-shaped, about 55 m long and 23 m at their widest at the WNW. 75 m to their SW is the cromlech.

204b   Kerbourgnec cromlech. From the W end of the rows follow a little footpath to the W and then S for 120 m. The W arc of the cromlech is on the L opposite houses. This was once a huge enclosure of which only the western tip exists today. The forty-one stones are thin slabs about 2 m high. Alexander Thom, who planned the site, suggested the ring had been egg-shaped with a maximum

Le Moulin de St Pierre Quiberon (204a), rows from the ESE.

E–W diameter of 96 m and measuring 76 m N–S. It was possibly open to the E and may have had a similar equinoctial significance to that at KERLESCAN WEST (180a).

205a Moustoir, Le, Carnac-Ville. *Carnac Mound*
3½ km NNE of Carnac-Ville, 4 km ENE of Plouharnel. From Carnac take the D119 N for 2 km and turn NE (R) off the main road towards Le Moustoir hamlet. Mound is 1¼ km on W (L) of road 300 m before the hamlet.

This grassy and bush-thick mound, still an impressive example of the enormous, closed tumuli erected by some groups in the Middle Neolithic, has a sub-rectangular cairn aligned ENE–WSW and measuring 89 × 40 m and 8 m high. It was excavated in 1865 by the technique of driving a trench along its major axis.

Near the W end was a rectangular chamber without a passage, 4 × 2 m in size and aligned at right-angles to the main axis. Four capstones covered it. In it was a broken pot, a vase-support, beads of serpentine and jasper, three flint knives, bones and a small serpentine axe, evidence of the opulence of the society that raised these gigantic structures. The chamber can no longer be seen.

At the exact middle of the mound, instead of a cist or a chamber there was only a hearth surrounded by a circle of nine small stones. At its centre stood a round-based pot, 40 cm wide at its rim and with a tiny handle for suspension halfway up its body. The presence of any vessel is very unusual in these Carnac Mounds.

Under the E of the cairn and now accessible by a flight of modern steps from the summit were two cists 5 m apart just to the N of the mound's long axis. They contained nothing of significance. It seems likely that the original tumulus was circular, covering the western chamber, and that the cists and their mound were later additions.

205b On top of the barrow is an undramatic menhir, 2 m high but almost dwarfed by the thickets around it. To the mound's W, near the road, is a bigger standing stone, 3.3 m high, re-erected by le Rouzic in 1919. Its broad face is towards the tumulus and it perhaps acted as a marker like the GRAND MENHIR BRISÉ (175a) at the Carnac Mound of

ER-GRAH (175b). Alexander Thom suggested that the Le Moustoir mound could have been used as a backsight towards the Grand Menhir, 9½ km to the ESE, aligned on the minor southern moonrise.

206 Parc Guren I & II, Crach. *Passage-graves*
7½ km NW of Locmariaquer, 6 km SSW of Auray. From Auray take the D28 S for 6 km to Crach. Turn W (R) on lane towards Luffang. In 1½ km, at W edge of pine wood, take footpath to NE (R), not its partner to N, and in 50 m take N branch (L) for 250 m. Tombs are on W of track near end of wood.

These overgrown, small passage-graves are within 40 m of each other. Both had short passages leading to circular chambers and both faced E. The chambers were corbelled. They were excavated in 1866 and 1868 and restored in 1926, but are now almost concealed in the undergrowth. From Parc Guren II came undecorated sherds, flint flakes, sherds of bell beaker, fragments of a triangular, rivetted copper knife and a segmented blue faience bead which is now in CARNAC museum (166).

LUFFANG angled passage-grave (192) is 500 m SW.

207 Petit-Ménec, Carnac-Ville. *Stone rows*
8 km SSW of Auray, 4 km NE of Carnac-Ville. From Carnac take the D119 N and in 1¼ km turn E (R) onto the D196. Continue for 2¾ km to the T-junction with the D186. Turn N (L) and in 200 m turn E (R) onto a lane skirted with woods. After 250 m the rows are to the S (R) 120 m into the woods.

The SW and best section of these ravaged rows stands in marshy ground much disturbed by a riding school. The NE stretch, beyond a small wood, is on higher and drier ground and terminates near a country lane. The stones are taller here.

The lines have been patchily dismantled for the construction of the Belle-Île lighthouse 33 km away to the S of the Quiberon peninsula. In 1874 there were fifty-eight standing stones and 186 fallen but a few years later only 184 remained. Today there are about eight irregular lines with a hundred or so stones in them. At the WSW the group is about 50 m wide, composed of small stones, many of them re-erected. From the NW corner a ragged line or two straggles westwards for a further 130 m. The major settings run north-eastwards for 220 m and converge on what has been described as a tiny 'structure in the form of a circular sector' like that of the MOULIN DE ST PIERRE QUIBERON (204a).

208   Pierres-Plats, Les, Locmariaquer. *Passage-grave*

1½ km SSW of Locmariaquer. From the town

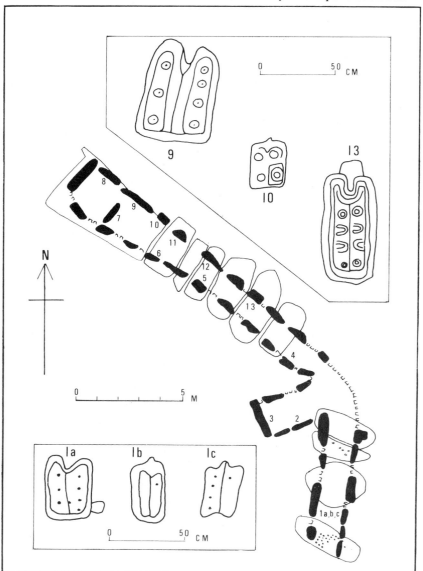

Les Pierres-Plats passage-grave (allée-coudée) (208). The numbered stones are discussed in the text.

centre take the road W towards Kerlud but in 400 m turn S (L) towards Kerhéré. In 500 m at Kerhéré turn S (L) for 600 m to coast. At T-junction tomb is 150 m to W (R). Car-parking. A torch is necessary.

This fine angled passage-grave or allée-coudée of the Middle Neolithic has no fewer than thirteen decorated uprights. Today, with its sides half-buried in the dunes, its white, rectangular and flat capstones rise in a series of steps along the passage and twisted chamber. In 1814 it was intact but two years later it was ruined after a disastrous and unrecorded excavation and it was finally restored, rather clumsily, in 1892. At the entrance, facing almost due S, there is a standing stone with cupmarks on its NE side. This, presumably, was an 'indicateur' or marker stone.

Architecturally the tomb is interesting. A shortish passage, 6 m long and 1.2 m wide but only 1.1 m high, ends with a sudden change of direction towards the NW. At the W angle there is an unexpected side-cell, 2.7 × 1.4 m wide. From this point the chamber begins, running SE–NW for 15 m, widening from a merè 80 cm to about 2 m at the far end. A small chamber has been constructed here by

the erection of a transverse slab forming a little compartment about 2 m square. This small end-cell has affinities with that in another allée-coudée at GOËREM, Gâvres, M (133), also by the sea, 35 km to the WNW.

It is the art that makes Les Pierres-Plats so important. Regrettably, many of the stones became badly weathered during their exposure and some of the motifs are hard to distinguish even with the aid of a torch held obliquely. Other stones, however, are splendidly preserved. The dominant motif, as at ÎLE LONGUE, M (140), and in many of the angled passage-graves is the anthropomorphic 'figurine' denoted by a rectangular frame, sometimes double or treble, with an incurved top and a vertical line or lines down the centre subdividing the body. In the two panels formed by this device are breasts or arcs. Such a figure seems to be the counterpart of the stelae and shaped stones in classic passage-graves such as ÎLE GUENNOC, F (52). The decorated stones, here numbered 1 to 13, are: *Short passage (1a, b, c)* The second stone on the left (W) has at least five small figurines with cupmarked breasts. The two capstones at the end of this passage may have cupmarks

Les Pierres-Plats (208), general view from the S.

and conjoined ovals carved on them.
Side-chamber (2) The first stone on the left (S)
has two arcs close together like a child's
drawing of a flying bird. *(3)* On the backstone
are cupmarks and two arcs.
Long chamber: left side (4) The second stone
has an octopus-like 'figurine' like that at
LUFFANG (192) with four breasts. *(5)* The
sixth stone has a heart-shaped motif and arcs.
(6) The ninth stone has a very eroded figurine.
End-chamber (7) The transverse slab has a
weathered figurine with two breasts. *(8)* The
N sideslab has a fine figurine, concentric in
outline, with three breasts.
Long chamber: right (N) side (9) Next to Stone
8 is another splendid figurine with three
vertical lines and eight breasts. A strange
motif has been carved on its righthand side.
(10) The adjacent stone has a figurine with an
axe carved below it. More figurines can be
seen to its left. *(11)* There are two arcs and
some cupmarks on the next stone. *(12)*
Alongside it the fifth stone on the right has a
figurine with a vertical line on either side of
which are short diagonal bars. There is an
enigmatic symbol to its right. *(13)* The next
stone is plain, but the seventh has perhaps the
best of all these magnificent carvings. Filling
almost the whole face of the slab is a great
figurine with three concentric outlines, a
vertical centre-line and four breasts in pairs
with concentric arcs between them.

The angled architecture at Les Pierres-Plats
and the highly-developed art makes it likely
that its construction belongs to the middle of
the 4th millennium BC.

209   Pors Guen, Port Blanc. *Passage-graves*
9 km SW of Carnac-Ville, 5½ km NNW of
Quiberon. From Quiberon take the D768 N for
4½ km to St Pierre Quiberon and turn W onto
the D186. In 500 m continue straight on on minor
road towards Portivy but in 250 m turn W (L)
and in ¾ km turn N (R). Road curves for ¾ km
to W towards Pors Guen on the coast. 250 m E of
ruined house known as the 'Observatory', on the
edge of the cliffs are the ruins of two tiny passage-
graves.

Les Pierres-Plats (208): (above) capstones of the
passage-grave; (far left) 'figurine' on Stone 12
and (left) 'figurine' on Stone 13.

The chamber of one and the passage of the
other are visible alongside the road which runs
from the 'Observatory' to the beach of Port
Blanc. These wrecked tombs are important
because excavations in 1883 and 1902
recovered skeletons from them, rare in the
acid soils of Brittany but preserved here by the
covering sand.

Both tombs, which faced SE, had short
passages and respectively had a rectangular
chamber, about 3 × 2.5 m, and a circular
chamber which had perhaps been corbelled.
The chambers were paved with slabs laid on
beds of rounded pebbles but the passages were
unlaid. They had been blocked when the
tombs were abandoned.

In the first passage-grave skeletons were
found on two levels with a layer of stones
between them. On the paving there were
twelve skulls arranged against the walls and
detached from their disarticulated skeletons.
Stones had been heaped over them. The upper
layer had as many skulls, of which two were
attached to their skeletons. The second
passage-grave had more complete skeletons,
one in the passage, two others placed by the
chamber walls. With them was some Upper
Conguel ware of the Late Neolithic period.

210   Roch, Dolmen du (Roh-an-Aod), St
Pierre Quiberon. *Passage-grave*
9 km S of Plouharnel, 4¾ km N of Quiberon.
From the D768 at St Pierre Quiberon take the
side road W towards Portivy into little village of
Le Roch. Rue de Dolmen, an alley, is only 200 m
from the D768 on the N (R) of the road.
Here there is a huge, sub-circular chamber of
granite stones with two capstones in position.
The chamber, about 4 m in diameter, has an
overhang of boulders laid flat on the tops of
the basal stones, suggesting that the tomb was
once corbelled. Only two stones survive of the
ESE entrance from the passage. One of them
has some cupmarks on its outer face.

211a   Rocher, Le, Bono. *Passage-grave*
7½ km N of Locmariaquer, 4¼ km SE of
Auray. From Auray take the D768 E and in
1¼ km turn S (R) onto the D101. In 4 km, 150
m after crossing bridge at Bono, turn S (R). After
250 m, leave car in square and walk 100 m to
wood on W (R) of lane. Monument is 200 m in

wood along a well-worn footpath. A torch is necessary.

Set amongst spacious pines this is an attractive angled passage-grave or allée-coudée excavated in 1844 and restored in 1904. It has a fine oval tumulus, 28 × 21 m and 4 m high, with the entrance to the tomb at the SE. A well-built passage 11.5 m long and constructed of alternate orthostats and drystone walling suddenly turns almost at right-angles to the SW for a further 7.6 m. Here it widens from a previously constant 1.3 m into a substantial sub-circular chamber 3 m across and 1.5 m high.

Several stones have strange motifs carved on them, including a snakelike meander, a 'U' alongside some geometrical patterns, a design like a hunched spider and, as usual in these allées-coudées, a 'figurine' like that at LUFFANG (192), but here with only one breast.

Articles recovered in 1844 and still for sale in 1872 comprised jade and jasper beads, flint scrapers and arrowheads, a stone axe and coarse sherds of Late Neolithic and Upper Conguel and Kerugou ware.

211b Just to the N of the tumulus is a line of small and low circular mounds. Excavated in 1868 they proved to be Iron Age barrows from one of which came a fine bronze bowl that had been placed on reed matting near a cremation.
211c Just to the S of Le Rocher is a Bronze Age barrow, 17 m in diameter with an inner retaining wall. At its NE is a little dolmen-like structure.

212 Rondossec, Plouharnel. *Passage-graves*
3½ km NW of Carnac-Ville. From Plouharnel take the D781 NW towards Erdeven. In 600 m, 300 m before the level-crossing, a small road on the W (L) leads to the passage-graves 50 m away behind the houses.
A mutilated, sandy mound about 20 m in diameter contains three passage-graves in fair condition. They were explored in 1849 and restored in 1920.

Built on a slight rise they all face SSE. That at the W is the smallest and presumably latest, having apparently been inserted between the central tomb and the western edge of the mound. Its 4.5-m-long passage leads to a sub-rectangular chamber 3 m long and 1.8 m wide. It is thought to have been corbelled.

The central tomb has a 7.5-m-long passage leading to a large chamber which simply widens from the passage like the undifferentiated passage-graves at MANÉ KERIONED (198). It is 6 m long and 2.5 m wide. Just to its E is the third tomb. Its passage, 11 m long, ends at a small sub-rectangular chamber, 3.5 × 2.5 m with a curious side-cell in the SW corner.

When the tombs were explored in 1849 bones, ashes, charcoal, sherds and a small fibrolite axe were found. Some of these finds, most of which were lost, are now in CARNAC museum (166), including a barbed-and-tanged arrowhead, a pendant and nine quartz beads. In the Musée des Antiquités Nationales, Paris, are two brilliant gold bracelets of Portuguese affinities. They were found in a large black vase under a drystone structure in the middle of the main chamber. This seems to have been an intrusive deposit or cache of about 2500 BC.

St Pierre Lopérec. *Passage-grave (see* 182b KERLUD)

213 St Barbe, Plouharnel. *Stone rows*
13 km SW of Auray, 4½ km NW of Carnac-Ville. From Plouharnel take the D781 NW for 2 km and turn W (L). The rows are 500 m along the lane on its E (L).
In 1875 Lukis reported the remains of eight rows running from ESE to WNW where the final stones were of 'prodigious size'. Near them had been a cromlech, possibly a horseshoe in shape. Today there are only thirty-seven stones standing with thirteen others concealed under sand and gravel, the relics of rows originally some 400 m long.

214 Sept-Saints, Les, Erdeven. *Passage-graves*
10 km NW of Carnac-Ville. From Erdeven take the D781 NW for 1 km and turn W (L) at Maneguen. In 600 m at Les Sept-Saints hamlet turn S (L) for 250 m to crossroads where turn W (R) for 100 m. The tombs are at the S edge of a wood on side of track on heathland.
Here there is a fine circular tumulus, about 12 m in diameter and 2 m high. In it are the tumbled remains of two passage-graves.

Table des Marchands. *Passage-grave (see* 175c GRAND MENHIR BRISÉ, LE)

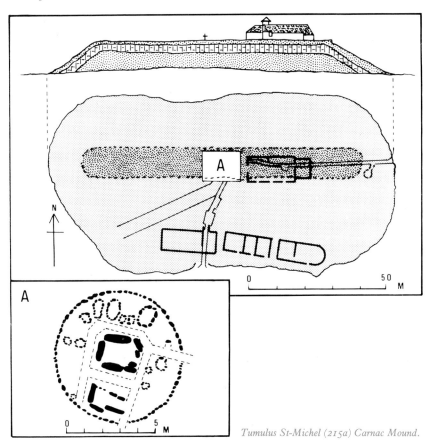

Tumulus St-Michel (215a) Carnac Mound.

215a Tumulus St-Michel, Carnac-Ville.
Carnac Mound
300 m NE of St Cornèly church in Carnac-Ville.
Take the D781 E, passing the cemetery on the N
(L). Go over the crossroads. The next road on the
left leads to the tumulus. Car park.
This is a good example of the exaggerated
Carnac Mounds built in the Middle Neolithic
period by some affluent groups in Morbihan.
The stupendous heap measures 125 × 60 m
and is 10 m high, even though it has been
somewhat lowered when it was Christianized
by having a chapel and a calvary erected on its
summit. Centuries earlier a stone-walled
building had been put up under the protection
of its southern side. The mound was excavated
by Zacharie le Rouzic between 1900 and 1907,

earlier explorations having taken place in
1862–4 by tunnelling.
  The tumulus, supported by low walls at its
E and W on its major axis, was covered with
stones under which was a thick layer of clay
covering a long, rectangular spine of stones
99 × 10 × 5.6 m high. Under this well-
constructed tumulus, at its centre, was a
trapezoidal cist, open to the E, 2.4 × 1.8 m
along its sides but only 95 cm high. The great
capstone over it had four cupmarks on its
underside. On the flat paving-stones, under
ash and scorched human bones, were 136
jasper and turquoise beads from a necklace,
nine pendants and thirty-nine stone axes,
eleven of jadeite with their blades upwards,
two deliberately broken.

Around this burial chamber were fifteen small cists with their little sidestones set, in arc-bouté fashion, leaning inwards to form ridged roofs. They contained ox-bones, perhaps to accompany the dead person on his journey to the other-world. Charcoal from le Rouzic's investigations produced, years later, some rather unhelpful determinations of 6850 ± 300 bc, 3770 ± 300 bc and 3030 ± 150 bc. The last of these would be the equivalent of about 3800 BC in the Middle Neolithic, but it must be stressed that the assay is no more significant than the other two.

It is possible to go on a guided tour of the tunnels which have been improved since the burrowing in the 19th century. Archaeologically the tour, however, is not very rewarding. The 15-minute tours are available in July and August, 0930–1930; 14 June to 30 September, 1000–1800; 29 March to 13 June, 1000–1200, 1500–1800. Price 3 Fr.

215b At the eastern end of the mound one can see the remains of a small passage-grave which had been encapsulated in the later tumulus. Its passage, facing NNE, led to an oval chamber, 2.7 × 1.8 m. It was covered by four capstones. In it were found two round-bottomed Neolithic bowls and some flint knives and flakes.

Up to the 19th century a bonfire was lit on top of the Tumulus St-Michel on the evening of the summer solstice once other fires had been kindled at Quiberon, Erdeven, Crach and Locmariaquer, all of which could clearly be seen from the vantage point of this great mound.

216 Vieux-Moulin, Le, Plouharnel. *Stone row*
12 km SW of Auray, 4 km WNW of Carnac-Ville. From Plouharnel take the D781 NW and in 1 km cross the railway line. The stones are 100 m to the E (R) of the road 250 m beyond the level crossing.
Today it is difficult to determine whether these are the stones of a row or a desecrated cromlech. According to Lukis in 1872 there were 'some large menhirs which appear to be the remains of destroyed lines' near the mill. Although they were called 'The Three Stones of the Old Mill' in his time there are, in fact, six tall granite pillars just to the SW of the mill. Standing as they do in a gradual curve, it is arguable that they are the survivors of a once-great megalithic semi-circle. To their SE are two other standing stones with a fallen pillar alongside them.

Ménec (203) in a 19th-century engraving.

Glossary

allée-coudée	A Middle Neolithic passage-grave in which the chamber was built at a sharp angle to the passage.
allée-couverte	A rectangular chambered tomb with no passage or covering mound. Such Late Neolithic sites are found mainly in the north and west of Brittany.
anthropomorph	*Anthro*, 'man', *morph*, 'shape'. A sculpting or carving in the shape of a human being.
arc-bouté	An allée-couverte with inward-leaning sideslabs making a structure like a ridge-tent.
beaker ware	Late Neolithic/Early Bronze Age central European pottery of finely-made, flat-based drinking pots and associated vessels.
callais	Or variscite. A sea-green mineral like turquoise and used for beads and pendants.
Carn ware	Early Neolithic round-based pottery associated with the primary passage-graves.
cartouche	An engraved oval or rectangular outline surrounding a carving or motif in relief.
Castellic ware	Middle Neolithic pottery of southern Brittany much influenced by Chassey ceramic traditions.
Chalcolithic	The period of transition from stone- to metal-using industries. A Copper Age in Brittany from about 2700 to 2100 BC
Chassey ware	Middle Neolithic pottery, intrusive in Brittany, with geometrically-patterned round-based bowls, flattish dishes and small, decorated vase-supports used as pedestals for round-bottomed pots.
chloromelanite	A dark-green mineral like jadeite, hard, dense and excellent for shaping into utilitarian axes.
Colpo ware	A Middle Neolithic ceramic style, found mainly in Morbihan, owing much to Chassey styles. Some Colpo vessels are like clay specimen jars, a round-based pot being attached to a flat-bottomed and concave-sided base.
Conguel ware	Late Neolithic native ware named after a passage-grave on the Quiberon peninsula. The ware is divided into an earlier Lower series with round-based bowls, and a later Upper form with flat-bottomed vessels.
corbelled	The beehive shaping of a chamber by means of instepped roofing slabs.
Creche-Quillé/ Le Mélus ware	Late Neolithic pottery, native to Brittany, influenced by SOM styles and often found in allées-couvertes.
Cypriot dagger	An Early Bronze Age metal dagger from Cyprus with a long thin blade and a hooked tang for the handle. The carvings of daggers in Brittany lack these hooks and may be representations of Breton daggers or spearheads.
dolerite	A basaltlike stone used for the manufacture of axes, many of which came from the Sélédin axe-factory.
fibrolite	Or sillimanite. A glassy brown, white or green stone found near the Gulf of Morbihan and used for the manufacture of axes.
'figurine'	A term used here to describe the rectangular carvings found in some passage-graves, particularly the allées-coudées.

Grand Pressigny	Honey-coloured, imported flint from Indre-et-Loire, used for fine knives and daggers in the Late Neolithic.
jadeite	A dense stone, green or black, suitable for the manufacture of fine, 'ceremonial' axes.
Kerugou ware	Local later Middle Neolithic pottery named after a passage-grave in southern Finistère.
menhir	*Maen*, 'stone', *hir*, 'long', a standing stone.
Neolithic	The 'New Stone Age' between about 5000 and 2500 BC in Brittany which saw the development of agriculture, pottery, polished stone axes and megalithic structures. In Brittany it is subdivided into overlapping periods of *Early, c.* 4850–4300 BC; *Middle, c.* 4400–3100 BC; and *Late, c.* 3300–2500 BC. It is followed by the Chalcolithic.
orthostat	An erect sideslab in a megalithic tomb.
peristalith	Small stones around the perimeter of a chambered tomb's mound.
petit-tranchet	A term applied to a flint arrowhead with an oblique cutting edge. Sometimes known as transverse arrowheads.
Quessoy ware	A localized form of Crech-Quillé/Le Mélus ware.
revetting	Walling set up to support the mound of a chambered tomb.
sericite	A fine-grained schist, greenish, softer than variscite and so easier to work but with less lustre. Sources are known in Loire-Atlantique.
serpentine	A green, yellow or brown igneous rock with whitish streaks, often used for personal ornaments.
SOM	The Seine-Oise-Marne culture of the Paris Basin, *c.* 3100–2000 BC, with coarse, flat-based pots, copper implements, and Grand Pressigny flints. Burials were sometimes in rectangular, semi-subterranean megalithic tombs some of which had carvings of axes and 'goddesses'. The SOM traditions affected Brittany in the Late Neolithic.
Souch ware	A Middle Neolithic native style of pottery found mainly in south-western Brittany.
steatite	A soft stone, sometimes known as soapstone, white, green, blue or brown, varying from opaque to transparent and used for the manufacture of personal ornaments.
stele	A carved standing stone.
tertre tumulaire	A long mound, possibly Early Neolithic, covering cists and deposits but with no passages.
transept	A side-cell off the passage of a chambered tomb.
transverse	*see* PETIT-TRANCHET.
tumulus	A mound of earth or stones.
variscite	*see* CALLAIS. A rare mineral. Sources in Brittany are known in Loire-Atlantique.

Place-Names of Brittany

ac	place	ker	village, house
ar	land	kerioned	of the dwarfs
Ar-goat	wooded land	kern	cairn, tumulus
Ar-mor	land by the sea	Klud-er-Yer	fowl's perch
bé	tomb	korr	dwarf
bihan	little, small	korrig	little dwarf
bossen	mound	lan, llan	church
boudig	fairy	lann	heath
bras	great, big	lech	flat stone or slab
Cado	St Cadoc, a 6th-century	lescan	burning
	contemporary of Gildas	lia ven	little, small
carn	cairn, tumulus	loc	*locus penitentiae*, hermitage
clos	field	losquet	burning
crech	height	maen, men	stone
cromlech	curved stone, 'stone circle'	mané	hill, mound
cromm	curved, bent, hooked	mario	dead
cru	rocky	Ménec	place of stones
dol	table, flat	menhir	a long stone
dolmen	table-stone, tomb with big	meur	great, large
	capstone	mor	sea
ec	place	mougau	cave
gâvre	goat	palud	marsh
goat	forest, wood	parc	field
goaz	stream	pen	head, headland
goh	old	peulvan	set stone
grah	heap, mound	plou	parish
groh, groach	witch, sorceress	pors	port, farmyard
guen	white	roch	rock, stone
guren	thunder	traon, trou	valley
hent	road	tre, tref	homestead, place
hir	long	ty	house
hroek	witch, sorceress, hag	wrach	witch, sorceress
inis	island		

Picture Credits

The photographs are by the author, except for the following:
p.16 (below) Musée Préhistorique Finistérien; p.20 Musée Archéologique James Miln-Zacharie le Rouzic; pp.43, 51, 54, 109, 125, 137 (right), 162 (below left) M. Jos Le Doaré, Châteaulin (Finistère); pp.44, 63 (above left), 88 Professor D.D.A. Simpson; p.110 (below)

Professor M.J. O'Kelly; p.121 (right) Merseyside County Museums; and p.140 (below) Dr Douglas C. Heggie.

The maps are by the author and Martin Lubikowski, the site plans and other modern drawings by the author.

Select Bibliography

Batt, M., Giot, P-R., Lecerf, Y., Lecornec, J., & le Roux, C-T. *Mégalithes au Pays de Carnac*. Le Douare, Châteaulin 1980.

Daniel, G. *The Prehistoric Chamber Tombs of France*. Thames & Hudson, London 1960.

—— *The Hungry Archaeologist in France*. Faber & Faber, London 1963.

Giot, P-R. *Brittany*. Thames & Hudson, London 1960.

—— (ed.) *Livret-Guide de l'Excursion à 3. Bretagne*. Nice 1976.

—— *Menhirs et Dolmens. Monuments Mégalithiques de Bretagne*. Le Douare, Châteaulin 1978.

—— *Les Alignements de Carnac*. Ouest France, Rennes 1983.

Giot, P-R., l'Helgouach, J., & Monnier, J.L. *La Préhistoire de la Bretagne*. Ouest France, Rennes 1979.

Green, J. *Carnac and the Megalithic Monuments of the Morbihan*. Pitkin Pictorials, London 1984.

Hadingham, E. 'The Lunar Observatory Hypothesis at Carnac: a Reconsideration', *Antiquity* 55 (1981), 35–42.

l'Helgouach, J. *Les Sépultures Mégalithiques en Armorique*. Université de Rennes, Rennes 1965.

Hibbs, J. 'The Neolithic of Brittany', in (ed. Scarre, C.) *Ancient France*. Edinburgh U.P., Edinburgh 1984, 271–323.

Lukis, W.C. *A Guide to the Principal Chambered Barrows etc. of South Brittany*. Johnson & Co., Ripon 1875.

Merritt, R.L., & Thom, A.S. 'Le Grand Menhir Brisé', *Archaeological Journal* 137 (1980), 27–39.

Miln, J. *Excavations at Carnac (Brittany)*. David Douglas, Edinburgh 1877.

—— *Excavations at Carnac. The Alignments of Kermario*. David Douglas, Edinburgh 1881.

Rollando', Y. *La Préhistoire du Morbihan*. Société Polymathique, Vannes 1971.

le Scouezec, G. *Guide de la Bretagne Mystérieuse*. Éditions Princesse, Paris 1979.

Thom, A., & A.S. *Megalithic Remains in Britain and Brittany*. Oxford U.P., Oxford 1978.

Thom, A., & A.S. & Merritt, R.L., & A.L. 'The Astronomical Significance of the Crucuno Stone Rectangle', *Current Anthropology* 14 (1973), 450–1.

Twohig-Shee, E. 'Megalithic Art in the Morbihan', in *L'Architecture Mégalithique*, Château-Gaillard, Vannes 1977, 173–86.

Index

Page numbers in bold type refer to main entries, in italics to plans and photographs.